The Winning
of
The West

The Winning

of

The West

by Theodore Roosevelt

A Modern Abridgment With Introduction

BY CHRISTOPHER LASCH

HASTINGS HOUSE • PUBLISHERS

New York 22

Contents

Editor's Introduction

THEODORE ROOSEVELT'S claim to be remembered as a scholar as well as a statesman rests on two works— *The Naval War of 1812* (1882) and *The Winning of the West*. The rest of his numerous historical works[1] were trifles, tossed off in order to supplement an income that was never more than modest, or simply (one suspects) out of a need to keep busy during seasons of political slack. Roosevelt himself was well aware of their lack of any enduring merit. But he took a good deal of pride in the other two. They were works on which he expended an enormous amount of sustained concentration and thorough, painstaking research. Not only that, but in *The Winning of the West* at least, inspired by the scope and significance of his theme, Roosevelt strove for a literary style equal to the subject. He had before him as a model the works of Francis Parkman (to whom he dedicated his own volumes)—books which treated an earlier phase of Western history with consummate literary distinction. That Parkman should have served as Roosevelt's model shows how seriously Roosevelt took the writing of *The Winning of the West*. "I realize perfectly," he wrote to his publisher, "that my chance of making a permanent literary reputation depends on how I do this big work."[2] That was in 1890, he was convinced that his days in politics were numbered, and it was this foreboding, a constant concern of his early career, that drove him on. It is not without significance that when he became governor of New York in 1898, he abandoned *The Winning*

---

1. These included biographies of Thomas Hart Benton (1887), Gouverneur Morris (1888) and Oliver Cromwell (1900); a history of New York City (1891); and a book of sketches, written jointly with Henry Cabot Lodge, *Hero Tales from American History* (1895).

2. Roosevelt to George Haven Putnam, 13 Jan. 1890, Elting E. Morison (ed.), *The Letters of Theodore Roosevelt* (Cambridge, 1951), I, 211.

of the West—for lack of incentive as much as for lack of time. He never returned to it, though he often spoke wistfully of doing so.

Roosevelt composed the first two volumes during his semi-retirement from politics in the 1880s, the last two during his years on the Civil Service Commission (1889-1895). That position left him plenty of leisure for writing; it was a position, moreover, which seemed at the time to preclude a return to active partisan politics. The first two volumes appeared in 1889, the third in 1894, the fourth in 1896. The original plan of the work dictated at least four more volumes, for it was Roosevelt's intention to deal with the whole history of American expansion from the settlement of the Trans-Alleghany West in the 18th Century down to the peopling of New Mexico and Arizona in his own day. Only the first part of this grand design was ever realized. In four volumes Roosevelt barely got out of the 18th Century; the last volume ends with an account of the Louisiana purchase and the first explorations of the Louisiana territory.

Any explanation of how Roosevelt, in his eagerness to establish himself as a scholar, came to choose the subject of westward expansion must remain a matter of conjecture. Fortunately, the known facts of Roosevelt's career make it possible to hazard an approximate explanation. First there was the example of Parkman, who demonstrated so well the literary as well as the historical possibilities of the theme. Then there was Roosevelt's own experience in the Badlands of the Dakotas, where, beginning in 1884, he spent a number of happy summers. His life on that most recent of American frontiers undoubtedly made him sensitive to the problem of the frontier in general: in *The Winning of the West* he tended to generalize from the Dakotas about other, earlier Wests; the narrative is studded with references to his own experiences. Invariably these references were meant to underline the unchanging character of frontier life, regardless of time or place.

Again, Roosevelt hoped to find out, through a study of the settlement of the West, something about the sources of American nationality—a subject that always fascinated him. A fervent nationalist, an admirer of Bismarck and other unifiers, Roosevelt never ceased to ponder on the mysterious process out of which great nations, great nationalisms, were made. But he was never able in any very precise way to relate the settling of the West to the growth of American unity and national consciousness. That was left to Frederick Jackson Turner. But there were numerous suggestions in *The Winning of the West* that the one had a great deal to do with the other. These suggestions offer another indication of the kind of interests which brought Roosevelt to the subject in the first place.

But the best clue to Roosevelt's interest in the West lies in his imperialism, as distinguished from his nationalism. *The Winning of the West* proved to be an account not so much of the shaping of American nationality as of the "race expansion" of the English-speaking peoples—a chapter not so much of American as of universal history. "Universal history" was then very much in vogue, the long view widely regarded as the proper perspective from which to study the past. The dominant school of American historians traced the origin of American institutions back to Germanic seeds planted in the distant past. American democracy was born in the "Teutonic forest." From there representative institutions spread, with modifications which in the perspective of the long view seemed less important than the underlying continuity of development, from Germany to England, and from England to America. Now, at the end of the 19th Century it was the manifest destiny of the English and still more of the Americans, their heirs in the great work, to bring the light of democracy to all those still living in darkness. So, at least, it seemed to Roosevelt. If Americans shirked the task, he thought, they would not only betray those unfortunate people in other parts of the world who remained ignorant of the advantages of civilization, they would betray themselves, betray their own heritage. Worse still, Anglo-Saxon civilization would begin to decay the moment it lost its expansive force; of that Roosevelt was convinced. Its very existence depended on those "martial virtues" which had served it so well in its prime. Conquest and civilization were inseparable.

Unfortunately there were disturbing signs, in Roosevelt's day, that the old heroic impulse was on the wane. Americans after the Civil War had grown indolent and complacent. The nation was given over to the pursuit of material gain—by definition an ignoble pursuit, in Roosevelt's eyes, for the truly creative life was a life of self-denial and self-sacrifice. His contempt for materialism drove Roosevelt to embrace an ethic of heroism (based on "pride of race")—of noble acts of courage, feats of arms. For it was only in arms, finally, that a people became a nation, all hearts beating as one. That, at bottom, was the meaning of *The Winning of the West.* It was the meaning of Roosevelt's whole career as a public prophet—the meaning, at any rate, that he attempted to convey.

The Winning of the West, then, was a sustained effort to remind Americans of their glorious past and to show them the significance of that past. In an age of affluence Roosevelt sought to fix the attention of his countrymen on an earlier epoch in which men lived in hardship in the midst of danger. He sought to remind them that the West was not, after all, merely settled, but *won*—wrested from a savage and hostile people by violence and bloodshed. He sought to remind them of the price that had been paid. Above all, he sought to remind them that the price had been worth paying—not, in the final analysis, because the United States had acquired the Western lands (that was a foregone conclusion, as Roosevelt took pains to point out), but because in paying it men had risen to heights of self-sacrifice. In dying gloriously, men had lived fully. It was to be hoped that they would learn to do so again, seeking out new adventures in which to test to the utmost their capacity to struggle and to endure. In the meantime—at the very least—men of good will might take some vicarious comfort in the memory of glorious deeds of past times.

Measured in terms of its didactic intent, *The Winning of the West,* judging from the subsequent history of the American people, was not a great success. "Materialism" continued to set the tone of American society, in spite of such temporary outbursts of heroism as the Spanish-American War and the First World War—the end of which Roosevelt did not live to see. Judged in terms of its reception as a work of history, however, *The Winning of the West* succeeded beyond Roosevelt's expectations. It won him a reputation; it established him at once as a literary man. Scholars, as well as the general public, applauded his achievement, and the scholars in recognition of its merit later elected Roosevelt president of the American Historical Association. Sweetest of all was the praise of Parkman, which Roosevelt graciously acknowledged in a letter in which he called Parkman the greatest of American historians.[3] One or two unfavorable reviews did not detract from the general acclaim.

Of special interest, in the light of later study of the West, was the opinion of Frederick Jackson Turner. Turner reviewed *The Winning of the West* on several occasions. Each time he was generous in his praise and sparing of criticism. What criticisms he made were confined to matters of detail.[4] Yet Turner's approach to the subject, in his own works, was completely different from Roosevelt's. One wonders whether in his reviews of *The Winning of the West* he did not lean over backward in order to avoid giving offense. But it is more likely that for Turner, as well as for Roosevelt, the important differences between them were curiously obscured.

The differences were obscured by a number of considerations. In the first place, there was a certain amount of agreement between them. To be sure, much of it was superficial. Thus, although Roosevelt, like Turner, stressed the connection between the frontier and the growth of democracy and nationalism, he saw the nature of the connection in a very different way. On one point, however, the agreement was real: both men emphasized the continuity of frontier experience, the essential sameness of the frontier process in different places and at different times. The point was not mentioned in the correspondence between Roosevelt and Turner, perhaps because it was taken for granted; but it could easily have led Turner to regard Roosevelt's work as in some sense complementing his own.

But if Turner did not altogether understand Roosevelt's work, still less did Roosevelt understand Turner's. The point Turner was trying to make in his essay of 1893, "The Significance of the Frontier in American History," eluded Roosevelt entirely. He read the essay, acknowledged his interest in

---

3. Roosevelt to Parkman, 13 July 1889, *Letters,* I, 172.

4. For instance, he thought Roosevelt too harsh in his treatment of Jefferson. Roosevelt admitted that Turner was right (Roosevelt to Turner, 15 Dec. 1896, *Letters,* I, 571); but his repentance, as students of Roosevelt know, was remarkably short-lived.

it, and cited it in his book; but his understanding of Western history shows very few signs of having been influenced by Turner's theory. He confessed in a letter to Turner that he was "more interested in the men themselves than in the institutions through and under which they worked."[5] (Turner in a review had confessed to a greater interest in the institutions.) But two weeks later, on further reflection, Roosevelt concluded that after all his views did not differ fundamentally from Turner's. "I really think it is more that we lay emphasis upon different points."[6]

It was, of course, not a matter of emphasis at all. The conflict between their interpretations of history was clear-cut and fundamental. Where Turner attributed American democracy to environmental influences, Roosevelt attributed it to heredity. The very first chapter of *The Winning of the West* makes that perfectly clear. It was not the environment but the innate capacity of the English people for self-government that dictated the course of American expansionism. The great virtue of the English migration, for Roosevelt, was precisely that it remained English. Unlike the Spanish, the English did not, for instance, mix racially with the natives whom they conquered. A people who *merely* conquered, Roosevelt argued—the Spanish, again, were the best example—lost their racial and ethnic identity. The Spanish conquest of Latin America led in a literal sense to the emergence of a "new man"—whose emergence in the United States, according to Turner, was associated with the breakdown of European institutions and the growth of democracy. The significance of American history, for Roosevelt, was just that American conditions had *not* bred a new race of men, even in the figurative sense. In America, on the contrary, the Englishman remained essentially an Englishman. There were differences, of course, but the differences were not as important as the persistence of racial and national characteristics. This was a far cry from the Turner thesis, which postulated the existence of a distinctive American type, the product of the frontier.

Of course there was a change in American character, Roosevelt observed, as civilization marched from the seaboard

5. Roosevelt to Turner, 10 April 1895, *Letters,* I, 440.

6. Roosevelt to Turner, 26 April 1895, *Letters,* I, 446.

into the interior of the continent. A backwoods type began to appear, democratic in manners, intolerant of social distinctions—the antithesis of the seaboard squire. On this Turner and Roosevelt agreed. But in Roosevelt's opinion—if his opinion can be inferred from a number of passages in which he raised the question indirectly—the democracy of the backwoodsman was not created by the frontier. Rather, the differences between tidewater and backcountry were to be explained by the fact that the backcountry was settled by "an entirely different stock from that which had long existed in the tidewater regions of those colonies." In the tidewater the "cavalier" type prevailed. The frontier, on the other hand, was settled by the descendants of the "roundheads"—Scotch-Irish covenanters, who were democratic before they ever got to the frontier.

If the frontier did not produce but merely heightened democracy, (if indeed it did that), neither did it produce American nationalism. Nationalism could not have been the product of the frontier, for, according to Roosevelt, "when the great westward movement began we were already a people by ourselves." So strong was his assumption that the westward movement was an expression rather than a cause of nationality that it prevented Roosevelt from seeing what was obvious to Turner—that the westward movement had been going on for 150 years before the American people even thought of becoming a nation. It led him to discount the settlement of the colonial backcountry as somehow not relevant to the winning of the "West." The West was to be thought of as the land beyond the Alleghanies, and the process of winning it, as beginning only after the birth of the American nation as a political entity.

It is for these reasons, perhaps, that *The Winning of the West* has almost dropped out of memory; for the history of the West has been written by Turnerians, not by adherents of the "germ theory."

Yet it would be a mistake to read Roosevelt's work as an expression of the germ theory and nothing more. Theory aside, *The Winning of the West* is a work of considerable literary merit, in the tradition of Parkman. Some passages— the account of the Battle of the Blue Licks (Chapter IX), the narrative of John Donelson's journey to the Cumberland

(Chapter XI), the description of the downfall of John Sevier's State of Franklin (Chapter XV)—rise to real heights. The prose throughout is clean and straightforward. The purely narrative portions develop great momentum and force; and the interpretive passages have scope and sweep. The "long view" may have led Roosevelt into what we can only regard as errors, but it freed him to speculate on a grand scale, and his errors themselves have a certain magnificence. He had hit upon a great subject, a subject that excited his sympathies and lit up his imagination, and he rose to the grandeur of his theme. His enthusiasm alone rescued the work from mediocrity.

Thus, there is every reason—quite apart from the biographical interest which attaches to the work of so prominent a public man as Theodore Roosevelt—for reviving *The Winning of the West* in a popular edition. But in order to make this edition available, it has been necessary to abridge the text to about one-third of its original length. Some explanation of how that was accomplished may help to quiet apprehensions that in the process the work has been transformed beyond all recognition.

First, the work has been stripped of its very extensive documentation. This ought to cause few regrets; Roosevelt's documentation was more often designed to display his erudition—it will be remembered that *The Winning of the West* was, among other things, a bid for scholarly acclaim—than to enlighten the reader. Sometimes, however, Roosevelt enlivened the notes by commenting on other historians or on his own experiences in the West; these comments have been preserved.

Second, the text, for all of its literary excellence, is extremely repetitive. Roosevelt wrote well, but he did not write concisely; or rather, he did not take the trouble to rewrite. (In this respect, like other fluent writers, Roosevelt was the victim of his own fluency.) Had he revised *The Winning of the West*, he himself could have reduced the text by thousands of words. Regrettably, since he did not do this himself, the task falls to his editor.

The third way in which reductions have been made in the text, and the most important way, is not so easy to defend. Even when footnotes and repetitions have been eliminated, the text remains too long for a one-volume edition. Therefore, the editor has taken the considerable liberty of confining the narrative to the settlement of the land south of the Ohio River, eliminating all of the chapters dealing with the territory to the north. This liberty can be justified, perhaps, on the grounds that the author himself was more interested in the Southwest—that is, Kentucky and Tennessee—than in the Northwest. In a chapter on the Northwest Territory—parts of which are reprinted here as an appendix—he makes it perfectly clear why. The settlement of the Southwest was a far more arduous and hazardous undertaking; it taxed the strength and courage of the settlers in a way that the migration to the Northwest did not. The settlers of the Northwest, moreover, enjoyed the protection of the federal government, whereas in the Southwest the government left the settlers to fend for themselves.

To the historian of institutions, the difference would not perhaps appear to be of much importance. To the historian of conflict, of the *winning* of the West, the difference was vital. Roosevelt aimed to show how in the work of peopling a vast continent, men had been ennobled by struggle. From this point of view, the more struggle the better. Hence the settlement of the Southwest had for Roosevelt a peculiar and personal significance. It furnished historical proof of the importance of the "strenuous life."

CHRISTOPHER LASCH

THIS BOOK
IS DEDICATED, WITH HIS PERMISSION,
TO

FRANCIS PARKMAN

TO WHOM AMERICANS WHO FEEL A PRIDE IN THE
PIONEER HISTORY OF THEIR COUNTRY
ARE SO GREATLY INDEBTED

The Winning
of
The West

"O strange New World that yit wast never young,
Whose youth from thee by gripin' need was wrung,
Brown foundlin' o' the woods, whose baby-bed
Was prowled roun' by the Injun's cracklin' tread,
And who grew'st strong thru shifts an' wants an' pains,
Nursed by stern men with empires in their brains,
Who saw in vision their young Ishmel strain
With each hard hand a vassal ocean's mane;
Thou skilled by Freedom and by gret events
To pitch new states ez Old World men pitch tents,
Thou taught by fate to know Jehovah's plan,
Thet man's devices can't unmake a man.

  .   .   .   .

"Oh, my friends, thank your God, if you have one, that he
'Twixt the Old World and you set the gulf of a sea;
Be strong-backed, brown-handed, upright as your pines,
By the scale of a hemisphere shape your designs."

—JAMES RUSSELL LOWELL

Chapter I

The Spread of the English-Speaking Peoples

D URING the past three centuries the spread of English-speaking peoples over the world's waste spaces has been not only the most striking feature in the world's history, but also the event of all others most far-reaching in its effects and its importance.

The tongue which Bacon feared to use in his writings, lest they should remain forever unknown to all but the inhabitants of a relatively unimportant insular kingdom, is now the speech of two continents. The Common Law which Coke jealously upheld in the southern half of a single European island, is now the law of the land throughout the vast regions of Australasia, and of America north of the Rio Grande. The names of the plays that Shakespeare wrote are household words in the mouths of mighty nations whose wide domains were to him more unreal than the realm of Prester John. Over half the descendants of their fellow countrymen of that day now dwell in lands which, when these three Englishmen were born, held not a single white inhabitant; the race which, when they were in their prime, was hemmed in between the North and the Irish seas, to-day holds sway over worlds whose endless coasts are washed by the waves of the three great oceans.

There have been many other races that at one time or another had their great periods of race expansion—as distinguished from mere conquest—but there has never been another whose expansion has been either so broad or so rapid.

At one time, many centuries ago, it seemed as if the Germanic peoples, like their Celtic foes and neighbors, would be absorbed into the all-conquering Roman power, and merging their identity in that of the victors, would accept their law, their speech, and their habits of thought. But this danger vanished forever on the day of the slaughter by the Teutoburger Wald, when the legions of Varus were broken by the rush of Hermann's wild warriors.

Two or three hundred years later the Germans, no longer on the defensive, themselves went forth from their marshy forests, conquering and to conquer. For century after century they swarmed out of the dark woodland east of the Rhine and north of the Danube; and as their force spent itself, the movement was taken up by their brethren who dwelt along the coasts of the Baltic and the North Atlantic. From the Volga to the Pillars of Hercules, from Sicily to Britain, every land in turn bowed to the warlike prowess of the stalwart sons of Odin. Rome and Novogorod, the imperial city of Italy as well as the squalid capital of Muscovy, acknowledged the sway of kings of Teutonic or Scandinavian blood.

In most cases, however, the victorious invaders merely intruded themselves among the original and far more numerous owners of the land, ruled over them, and were absorbed by them. This happened to both Teuton and Scandinavian—to the descendants of Alaric was well as to the children of Rurik. The Dane in Ireland became a Celt; the Goth of the Iberian peninsula became a Spaniard; Frank and Norwegian alike were merged into the mass of Romance-speaking Gauls, who themselves finally grew to be called by the names of their masters. Thus it came about that though the German tribes conquered Europe they did not extend the limits of Germany nor the sway of the German race. On the contrary, they strengthened the hands of the rivals of the people from whom they sprang. They gave rulers—kaisers, kings, barons, and knights—to all the lands they overran; here and there they imposed their own names on kingdoms and principalities— as in France, Normandy, Burgundy, and Lombardy; they grafted the feudal system on the Roman jurisprudence, and interpolated a few Teutonic words in the Latin dialects of the peoples they had conquered; but, hopelessly outnumbered, they were soon lost in the mass of their subjects, and adopted from them their laws, their culture, and their language. As a result, the mixed races of the south—the Latin nations as they are sometimes called—strengthened by the infusion of northern blood, sprang anew into vigorous life, and became for the time being the leaders of the European world.

There was but one land whereof the winning made a lasting addition to Germanic soil; but this land was destined to be of more importance in the future of the German peoples than all their continental possessions, original and acquired, put together. The day when the keels of the Low Dutch sea-thieves first grated on the British coast was big with the doom of many nations. There sprang up in conquered southern Britain, when its name had been significantly changed to England, that branch of the Germanic stock which was in the end to grasp almost literally world-wide power, and by its overshadowing growth to dwarf into comparative insignificance all its kindred folk. At the time, in the general wreck of the civilized world, the making of England attracted but little attention. Men's eyes were riveted on the empires conquered by the hosts of Alaric, Theodoric, and Clovis, not on the swarm of little kingdoms and earldoms founded by the nameless chiefs who led each his band of hard-rowing, hard-fighting henchmen across the stormy waters of the German Ocean. Yet the rule and the race of Goth, Frank, and Burgund have vanished from off the earth, while the sons of the unknown Saxon, Anglian, and Friesic warriors now hold in their hands the fate of the coming years.

After the great Teutonic wanderings were over, there came a long lull, until, with the discovery of America, a new period of even vaster race expansion began. During this lull the nations of Europe took on their present shapes. Indeed, the so-called Latin nations—the French and Spaniards, for instance—may be said to have been born after the first set of migrations ceased. Their national history, as such, does not really begin until about that time, whereas that of the Germanic peoples stretches back unbroken to the days when we first hear of their existence. It would be hard to say which one of half a dozen races that existed in Europe during the early centuries of the present era should be considered as especially the ancestor of the modern Frenchman or Spaniard. When the Romans conquered Gaul and Iberia they did not in any place drive out the ancient owners of the soil; they simply Romanized them, and left them as the base of the population. By the Frankish and Visigothic invasions another strain of blood was added, to be speedily absorbed, while the invaders took the language of the conquered people, and established themselves as the ruling class. Thus the modern nations who sprang from this mixture derive portions of their governmental system and general policy from one race, most of their blood from another, and their language, law, and culture from a third.

The English race, on the contrary, has a perfectly continuous history. When Alfred reigned, the English already had a distinct national being; when Charlemagne reigned, the French, as we use the term to-day, had no national being whatever. The Germans of the mainland merely overran the countries that lay in their path; but the sea-rovers who won England to a great extent actually displaced the native Britons. The former were absorbed by the subject-races; the latter, on the contrary, slew or drove off or assimilated the original inhabitants. Unlike all the other Germanic swarms, the English took neither creed nor custom, neither law nor speech, from their beaten foes. At the time when the dynasty of the Capets had become firmly established at Paris, France was merely part of a country where Latinized Gauls and Basques were ruled by Latinized Franks, Goths, Burgunds, and Normans; but the people across the Channel then showed little trace of Celtic or Romance influence. It would be hard to say whether Vercingetorix or Cæsar, Clovis or Syagrius, has the better right to stand as the prototype of a modern French general. There is no such doubt in the other case. The average Englishman, American, or Austrian of to-day who wishes to recall the feats of power with which his race should be credited in the shadowy dawn of its history, may go back to the half-mythical glories of Hengist and Horsa, perhaps to the deeds of Civilis the Batavian, or to those of the hero of the Teutoburger fight, but certainly to the wars neither of the Silurian chief Caractacus nor of his conqueror, the after-time Emperor Vespasian.

Nevertheless, when, in the sixteenth century, the European peoples began to extend their dominions beyond Europe, England had grown to differ profoundly from the Germanic countries of the mainland. A very large Celtic element had been introduced into the English blood, and, in addition, there had been a considerable Scandinavian admixture. More important still were the radical changes brought by the Norman conquest; chief among them the transformation of the old English tongue into the magnificent language which is now the common inheritance of so many wide-spread peoples. England's insular position, moreover, permitted it to work out its own fate comparatively unhampered by the presence of outside powers; so that it developed a type of nationality totally distinct from the types of the European mainland.

All this is not foreign to American history. The vast movement by which this continent was conquered and peopled cannot be rightly understood if considered solely by itself. It was the crowning and greatest achievement of a series of mighty movements, and it must be taken in connection with them. Its true significance will be lost unless we grasp, however roughly, the past race-history of the nations who took part therein.

When, with the voyages of Columbus and his successors, the great period of extra-European colonization began, various nations strove to share in the work. Most of them had to plant their colonies in lands across the sea; Russia, alone, was by her geographical position enabled to extend her frontiers by land, and, in consequence, her comparatively recent colonization of Siberia bears some resemblance to our own work in the Western United States. The other countries of Europe were forced to find their outlets for conquest and emigration beyond the ocean, and, until the colonists had taken firm root in their new homes, the mastery of the seas thus became a matter of vital consequence.

Among the lands beyond the ocean America was the first reached and the most important. It was conquered by different European races, and shoals of European settlers were thrust forth upon its shores. These sometimes displaced and sometimes merely overcame and lived among the natives. They also, to their own lasting harm, committed a crime whose short-sighted folly was worse than its guilt, for they brought hordes of African slaves, whose descendants now form immense populations in certain portions of the land. Throughout the continent we therefore find the white, red, and black races in every stage of purity and intermixture. One result of this great turmoil of conquest and immigration has been that, in certain parts of America, the lines of cleavage of race are so far from coinciding with the lines of cleavage of speech that they run at right angles to them—as in the four communities of Ontario, Quebec, Hayti, and Jamaica.

Each intruding European power, in winning for itself new realms beyond the seas, had to wage a twofold war, overcoming the original inhabitants with one hand, and with the other warding off the assaults of the kindred nations that were bent on the same schemes. Generally, the contests of the latter kind were much the most important. The victories by which the struggles between the European conquerors themselves were ended deserve lasting commemoration. Yet, sometimes, even the most important of them, sweeping though they were, were in parts less sweeping than they seemed. It would be impossible to overestimate the far-reaching effects of the overthrow of the French power in America; but Lower Canada, where the fatal blow was given, itself suffered nothing but a political conquest, which did not interfere in the least with the growth of a French state along both sides of the lower St. Lawrence. In a somewhat similar way Dutch communities have held their own, and indeed have sprung up, in South Africa.

All the European nations touching on the Atlantic seaboard took part in the new work, with very varying success—Germany alone, then rent by many feuds, having no share therein. Portugal founded a single state, Brazil. The Scandinavian nations did little; their chief colony fell under the control of the Dutch. The English and the Spaniards were the two nations to whom the bulk of the new lands fell, the former getting much the greater portion. The conquests of the Spaniards took place in .the sixteenth century. The West Indies and Mexico, Peru and the limitless grass plains of what is now the Argentine Confederation—all these and the lands lying between them had been conquered and colonized by the Spaniards before there was a single English settlement in the New World, and while the fleets of the Catholic king still held for him the lordship of the ocean. Then the cumbrous Spanish vessels succumbed to the attacks of the swift warships of Holland and England, and the sun of the Spanish world dominion set as quickly as it had risen. Spain at once came to a standstill; it was only here and there that she even extended her rule over a few neighboring Indian tribes, while she was utterly unable to take the offensive against the French, Dutch, and English. But it is a singular thing that these vigorous and powerful newcomers, who had so quickly put a stop to her further growth, yet wrested from her very little of what was already hers. They plundered a great many Spanish cities and captured a great many Spanish galleons, but they made no great or lasting conquest of Spanish territory. Their mutual jealousies, and the fear each felt of the others, were among the main causes of this state of things; and hence it came about that after the opening of the seventeenth century the wars they waged against one another were of far more ultimate consequence than the wars they waged against the former mistress of the western world. England in the end drove both France and Holland from the field; but it was under the banner of the American Republic, not under that of the British monarchy, that the English-speaking peoples first won vast stretches of land from the descendants of the Spanish conquerors.

The three most powerful of Spain's rivals waged many a long war with one another to decide which should grasp the sceptre that had slipped from Spanish hands. The fleets of Holland fought with stubborn obstinacy to wrest from England her naval supremacy; but they failed, and in the end the greater portion of the Dutch domains fell to their foes. The French likewise began a course of conquest and colonization at the same time the English did, and after a couple of centuries of rivalry, ending in prolonged warfare, they also succumbed. The close of the most important colonial contest ever waged left the French without a foot of soil on the North American mainland; while their victorious foes had not only obtained the lead in the race for supremacy on that continent, but had also won the command of the ocean. They thenceforth found themselves free to work their will in all sea-girt lands, unchecked by hostile European influence.

Most fortunately, when England began her career as a colonizing power in America, Spain had already taken possession of the populous tropical and subtropical regions, and the northern power was thus forced to form her settlements in the sparsely peopled temperate zone.

It is of vital importance to remember that the English and Spanish conquests in America differed from each other very much as did the original conquests which gave rise to the English and the Spanish nations. The English had exterminated or assimilated the Celts of Britain, and they substantially repeated the process with the Indians of America; although of course in America there was very little, instead of very much, assimilation. The Germanic strain is dominant in the blood of the average Englishman, exactly as the English strain is dominant in the blood of the average American. Twice a portion of the race has shifted its home, in each case undergoing a marked change, due both to outside influence and to internal development; but in the main retaining, especially in the last instance, the general race characteristics.

It was quite otherwise in the countries conquered by Cortes, Pizarro, and their successors. Instead of killing or driving off the natives as the English did, the Spaniards simply sat down in the midst of a much more numerous aboriginal population. The process by which Central and South America became Spanish bore very close resemblance to the process by which the lands of southeastern Europe were turned into Romance-speaking countries. The bulk of the original inhabitants remained unchanged in each case. There was little displacement of population. Roman soldiers and magistrates, Roman merchants and handicraftsmen were thrust in among the Celtic and Iberian peoples, exactly as the Spanish military and civil rulers, priests, traders, land-owners, and mine-owners settled down among the Indians of Peru and Mexico. By degrees, in each case, the many learnt the language and adopted the laws, religion, and governmental system of the few, although keeping certain of their own customs and habits of thought. Though the ordinary Spaniard of to-day speaks a Romance dialect, he is mainly of Celto-Iberian blood; and though most Mexicans and Peruvians speak Spanish, yet the great majority of them trace their descent back to the subject of Montezuma and the Incas. Moreover, exactly as in Europe little ethnic islands of Breton and Basque stock have remained unaffected by the Romance flood, so in America there are large communities where the inhabitants keep unchanged the speech and the customs of their Indian forefathers.

The English-speaking peoples now hold more and better land

than any other American nationality or set of nationalities. They have in their veins less aboriginal American blood than any of their neighbors. Yet it is noteworthy that the latter have tacitly allowed them to arrogate to themselves the title of "Americans," whereby to designate their distinctive and individual nationality.

So much for the difference between the way in which the English and the way in which other European nations have conquered and colonized. But there have been likewise very great differences in the methods and courses of the English-speaking peoples themselves, at different times and in different places.

The settlement of the United States and Canada, throughout most of their extent, bears much resemblance to the later settlement of Australia and New Zealand. The English conquest of India and even the English conquest of South Africa come in an entirely different category. The first was a mere political conquest, like the Dutch conquest of Java or the extension of the Roman Empire over parts of Asia. South Africa in some respects stands by itself, because there the English are confronted by another white race which it is as yet uncertain whether they can assimilate, and, what is infinitely more important, because they are there confronted by a very large native population with which they cannot mingle, and which neither dies out nor recedes before their advance. It is not likely, but it is at least within the bounds of possibility, that in the course of centuries the whites of South Africa will suffer a fate akin to that which befell the Greek colonists in the Tauric Chersonese, and be swallowed up in the overwhelming mass of black barbarism.

On the other hand, it may fairly be said that in America and Australia the English race has already entered into and begun the enjoyment of its great inheritance. When these continents were settled they contained the largest tracts of fertile, temperate, thinly peopled country on the face of the globe. We cannot rate too highly the importance of their acquisition. Their successful settlement was a feat which by comparison utterly dwarfs all the European wars of the last two centuries; just as the importance of the issues at stake in the wars of Rome and Carthage completely overshadowed

the interests for which the various contemporary Greek kingdoms were at the same time striving.

Australia, which was much less important than America,
was also won and settled with far less difficulty. The natives
were so few in number and of such a low type, that they practically offered no resistance at all, being but little more hindrance than an equal number of ferocious beasts. There was
no rivalry whatever by any European power, because the actual
settlement—not the mere expatriation of convicts—only began
when England, as a result of her struggle with Republican
and Imperial France, had won the absolute control of the seas.
Unknown to themselves, Nelson and his fellow admirals settled the fate of Australia, upon which they probably never
wasted a thought. Trafalgar decided much more than the
mere question whether Great Britain should temporarily share
the fate that so soon befell Prussia; for in all probability it
decided the destiny of the island-continent that lay in the South
Seas.

The history of the English-speaking race in America has
been widely different. In Australia there was no fighting
whatever, whether with natives or with other foreigners. In
America for the past two centuries and a half there has been
a constant succession of contests with powerful and warlike
native tribes, with rival European nations, and with American
nations of European origin. But even in America there have
been wide differences in the way the work has had to be done
in different parts of the country, since the close of the great
colonial contests between England, France, and Spain.

The extension of the English, westward through Canada,
since the War of the Revolution has been in its essential features merely a less important repetition of what has gone on
in the northern United States. The gold-miner, the trans-
continental railway, and the soldier have been the pioneers of
civilization. The chief point of difference, which was but small,
arose from the fact that the whole of western Canada was for
a long time under the control of the most powerful of all the
fur companies, in whose employ were very many French
voyageurs and coureurs de bois. From these there sprang up in
the valleys of the Red River and the Saskatchewan a singular
race of half-breeds, with a unique semicivilization of their own.
It was with these half-breeds, and not, as in the United States,

with the Indians, that the settlers of northwestern Canada had their main difficulties.

In what now forms the United States, taking the country as a whole, the foes who had to be met and overcome were very much more formidable. The ground had to be not only settled but conquered, sometimes at the expense of the natives, often at the expense of rival European races. As already pointed out, the Indians themselves formed one of the main factors in deciding the fate of the continent. They were never able in the end to avert the white conquest, but they could often delay its advance for a long spell of years. The Iroquois, for instance, held their own against all comers for two centuries. Many other tribes stayed for a time the oncoming white flood, or even drove it back; in Maine, the settlers were for a hundred years confined to a narrow strip of seacoast. Against the Spaniards, there were even here and there Indian nations who definitely recovered the ground they had lost.

When the whites first landed, the superiority and, above all, the novelty of their arms gave them a very great advantage. But the Indians soon became accustomed to the newcomers' weapons and style of warfare. By the time the English had consolidated the Atlantic colonies under their rule, the Indians had become what they have remained ever since, the most formidable savage foes ever encountered by colonists of European stock. Relatively to their numbers, they have shown themselves far more to be dreaded than the Zulus or even the Maoris.

Their presence has caused the process of settlement to go on at unequal rates of speed in different places; the flood has been hemmed in at one point, or has been forced to flow round an island of native population at another. Had the Indians been as helpless as the native Australians were, the continent of North America would have had an altogether different history. It would not only have been settled far more rapidly, but also on very different lines. Not only have the red men themselves kept back the settlements, but they have also had a very great effect upon the outcome of the struggles between the different intrusive European peoples. Had the originial inhabitants of the Mississippi valley been as numerous and unwarlike as the Aztecs, De Soto would have repeated the work of Cortes, and we would very possibly have been barred out of the greater portion of our present domain. Had it not been for their Indian allies, it would have been impossible for the French to prolong, as they did, their struggle with their much more numerous English neighbors.

The Indians have shrunk back before our advance only after fierce and dogged resistance. They were never numerous in the land, but exactly what their numbers were when the whites first appeared is impossible to tell. Probably an estimate of half a million for those within the limits of the present United States is not far wrong; but in any such calculation there is of necessity a large element of mere rough guesswork. Formerly writers greatly overestimated their original numbers, counting them by millions. Now it is the fashion to go to the other extreme, and even to maintain they have not decreased at all. This last is a theory that can only be upheld on the supposition that the whole does not consist of the sum of the parts; for whereas we can check off on our fingers the tribes that have slightly increased, we can enumerate scores that have died out almost before our eyes. Speaking broadly, they have mixed but little with the English (as distinguished from the French and Spanish) invaders. They are driven back, or die out, or retire to their own reservations; but they are not often assimilated. Still, on every frontier, there is always a certain amount of assimilation going on, much more than is commonly admitted;* and whenever a French or Spanish community has been absorbed by the energetic Americans, a certain amount of Indian blood has been absorbed also. There seems to be a chance that in one part of our country, the Indian Territory, the Indians, who are continually advancing in civilization, will remain as the ground element of the population, like the Creoles in Louisiana, or the Mexicans in New Mexico.

The Americans, when they became a nation, continued even more successfully the work which they had begun as citizens of the several English colonies. At the outbreak of the Revo-

---

* To this I can testify of my own knowledge as regards Montana, Dakota, and Minnesota. The mixture usually takes place in the ranks of the population where individuals lose all trace of their ancestry after two or three generations; so it is often honestly ignored, and sometimes mention of it is suppressed, the man regarding it as a taint. But I also know many very wealthy old frontiersmen whose half-breed children are now being educated, generally at convent schools, while in the northwestern cities I could point out some very charming men and women, in the best society, with a strain of Indian blood in their veins.

lution they still all dwelt on the seaboard, either on the coast itself or along the banks of the streams flowing into the Atlantic. When the fight at Lexington took place they had no settlements beyond the mountain chain on our western border. It had taken them over a century and a half to spread from the Atlantic to the Alleghanies. In the next three-quarters of a century they spread from the Alleghanies to the Pacific. In doing this they not only dispossessed the Indian tribes, but they also won the land from its European owners. Britain had to yield the territory between the Ohio and the Great Lakes. By a purchase, of which we frankly announced that the alternative would be war, we acquired from France the vast, ill-defined region known as Louisiana. From the Spaniards, or from their descendants, we won the lands of Florida, Texas, New Mexico, and California.

All these lands were conquered after we had become a power, independent of every other, and one within our own borders —when we were no longer a loose assemblage of petty seaboard communities, each with only such relationship to its neighbor as was implied in their common subjection to a foreign king and a foreign people. Moreover, it is well always to remember that at the day when we began our career as a nation we already differed from our kinsmen of Britain in blood as well as in name; the word American already had more than a merely geographical signification. Americans belong to the English race only in the sense in which Englishmen belong to the German. The fact that no change of language has accompanied the second wandering of our people, from Britain to America, as it accompanied their first, from Germany to Britain, is due to the further fact that when the second wandering took place the race possessed a fixed literary language, and, thanks to the ease of communication, was kept in touch with the parent stock. The change of blood was probably as great in one case as in the other. The modern Englishman is descended from a Low-Dutch stock, which, when it went to Britain, received into itself an enormous infusion of Celtic, a much smaller infusion of Norse and Danish, and also a certain infusion of Norman-French blood. When this new English stock came to America it mingled with and absorbed into itself immigrants from many European lands, and the process has gone on ever since. It is to be noted that, of

the new blood thus acquired, the greatest proportion has come
from the Dutch and German sources, and the next greatest
from Irish, while the Scandinavian element comes third, and
the only other of much consequence is French Huguenot.
Thus it appears that no new element of importance has been
added to the blood. Additions have been made to the elemental
race-strains in much the same proportion as these were
originally combined.

Some latter-day writers deplore the enormous immigration
to our shores as making us a heterogeneous instead of a
homogeneous people; but as a matter of fact we are less
heterogeneous at the present day than we were at the outbreak
of the Revolution. Our blood was as much mixed a century
ago as it is now. No State now has a smaller proportion of
English blood than New York or Pennsylvania had in 1775.
Even in New England, where the English stock is the purest,
there was a certain French and Irish mixture; in Virginia there
were Germans in addition. In the other colonies, taken as a
whole, it is not probable that much over half of the blood
was English; Dutch, French, German, and Gaelic communities
abounded.

But all were being rapidly fused into one people. As the
Celt of Cornwall and the Saxon of Wessex are now alike Englishmen, so in 1775 Hollander and Huguenot, whether in New
York or South Carolina, had become Americans, undistinguish-
able from the New Englanders and Virginians, the descendants
of the men who followed Cromwell or charged behind Rupert.
When the great Western movement began we were already
a people by ourselves. Moreover, the immense immigration
from Europe that has taken place since had little or no effect
on the way in which we extended our boundaries; it only
began to be important about the time when we acquired our
present limits. These limits would in all probability be what
they are now even if we had not received a single European
colonist since the Revolution.

Thus the Americans began their work of Western conquest
as a separate and individual people, at the moment when they
sprang into national life. It has been their great work ever
since. All other questions, save those of the preservation of
the Union itself and of the emancipation of the blacks, have
been of subordinate importance when compared with the great

question of how rapidly and how completely they were to sub-
jugate that part of their continent lying between the eastern
mountains and the Pacific. Yet the statesmen of the Atlantic
seaboard were often unable to perceive this, and indeed frequently showed the same narrow jealousy of the communities
beyond the Alleghanies that England felt for all America. Even
if they were too broad-minded and far-seeing to feel thus,
they yet were unable to fully appreciate the magnitude of
the interests at stake in the West. They thought more of our
right to the North Atlantic fisheries than of our ownership of
the Mississippi valley; they were more interested in the fate
of a bank or a tariff than in the settlement of the Oregon
boundary. Most contemporary writers showed similar short-
comings in their sense of historic perspective. The names of
Ethan Allen and Marion are probably better known than is
that of George Rogers Clark; yet their deeds, as regards their
effects, could no more be compared to his, than his could be
compared to Washington's. So it was with Houston. During
his lifetime there were probably fifty men who, east of the
Mississippi, were deemed far greater than he was. Yet in most
cases their names have already almost faded from remembrance, while his fame will grow steadily brighter as the importance of his deeds is more thoroughly realized. Fortunately,
in the long run, the mass of Easterners always backed up their
Western brethren.

The kind of colonizing conquest, whereby the people of the
United States have extended their borders, has much in common with the similar movements in Canada and Australia, all
of them standing in sharp contrast to what has gone on in
Spanish-American lands. But, of course, each is marked out
in addition by certain peculiarities of its own. Moreover, even
in the United States, the movement falls naturally into two
divisions, which on several points differ widely from each
other.

The way in which the southern part of our Western country
—that is, all the land south of the Ohio, and from thence on
to the Rio Grande and the Pacific—was won and settled,
stands quite alone. The region north of it was filled up in a
very different manner.* The Southwest, including therein what

---

* [For a fuller examination of the differences between Northwest and
Southwest, see Appendix.]

was once called simply the West, and afterward the Middle West, was won by the people themselves, acting as individuals, or as groups of individuals, who hewed out their own fortunes in advance of any governmental action. On the other hand, the Northwest, speaking broadly, was acquired by the government, the settlers merely taking possession of what the whole country guaranteed them. The Northwest is essentially a national domain; it is fitting that it should be, as it is, not only by position but also by feeling, the heart of the nation.

North of the Ohio the regular army went first. The settlements grew up behind the shelter of the federal troops of Hamar, St. Claire, and Wayne, and of their successors even to our own day. The wars in which the borderers themselves bore any part were few and trifling compared to the contests waged by the adventurers who won Kentucky, Tennessee, and Texas.

In the Southwest the early settlers acted as their own army, and supplied both leaders and men. Sevier, Robertson, Clark, and Boone led their fellow pioneers to battle, as Jackson did afterward, and as Houston did later still. Indeed the southwesterners not only won their own soil for themselves, but they were the chief instruments in the original acquisition of the Northwest also. Had it not been for the conquest of the Illinois towns in 1779 we would probably never have had any Northwest to settle; and the huge tract between the upper Mississippi and the Columbia, then called Upper Louisiana, fell into our hands only because the Kentuckians and Tennesseeans were resolutely bent on taking possession of New Orleans, either by bargain or battle. All of our territory lying beyond the Alleghanies, north and south, was first won for us by the southwesterners, fighting for their own land. The northern part was afterward filled up by the thrifty, vigorous men of the Northeast, whose sons became the real rulers as well as the preservers of the Union; but these settlements of Northerners were rendered possible only by the deeds of the nation as a whole. They entered on land that the Southerners had won, and they were kept there by the strong arm of the federal government; whereas the Southerners owed most of their victories only to themselves.

The first comers around Marietta did, it is true, share to a certain extent in the dangers of the existing Indian wars; but their trials are not to be mentioned beside those endured by the early settlers of Tennessee and Kentucky, and whereas these latter themselves subdued and drove out their foes, the former took but an insignificant part in the contest by which the possession of their land was secured. Besides, the strongest and most numerous Indian tribes were in the Southwest.

The Southwest developed its civilization on its own lines, for good and for ill; the Northwest was settled under the national ordinance of 1787, which absolutely determined its destiny, and thereby in the end also determined the destiny of the whole nation. Moreover, the Gulf coast, as well as the interior, from the Mississippi to the Pacific, was held by foreign powers; while in the North this was only true of the country between the Ohio and the Great Lakes during the first years of the Revolution, until the Kentucky backwoodsmen conquered it. Our rivals of European race had dwelt for generations along the lower Mississippi and the Rio Grande, in Florida, and in California, when we made them ours. Detroit, Vincennes, St. Louis, and New Orleans, St. Augustine, San Antonio, Santa Fé, and San Francisco are cities that were built by Frenchmen or Spaniards; we did not found them, but conquered them. All but the first two are in the Southwest, and of these two, one was first taken and governed by southwesterners. On the other hand, the northwestern cities, from Cincinnati and Chicago to Helena and Portland, were founded by our own people, by the people who now have possession of them.

The Southwest was conquered only after years of hard fighting with the original owners. The way in which this was done bears much less resemblance to the sudden filling up of Australia and California by the practically unopposed overflow from a teeming and civilized mother country, than it does to the original English conquest of Britain itself. The warlike borderers who thronged across the Alleghanies, the restless and reckless hunters, the hard, dogged, frontier farmers, by dint of grim tenacity, overcame and displaced Indians, French, and Spaniards alike, exactly as, fourteen hundred years before, Saxon and Angle had overcome and displaced the Cymric and Gaelic Celts. They were led by no one commander; they acted under orders from neither king nor congress; they were not carrying out the plans of any far-sighted leader. In obedience to the instincts working half blindly within their breasts, spurred ever onward by the fierce desires of their eager hearts, they made in the wilderness homes for their children, and by so doing wrought out the destinies of a continental nation. They warred and settled from the high hill valleys of the French Broad and the upper Cumberland to the half-tropical basin of the Rio Grande, and to where the Golden Gate lets through the long-heaving waters of the Pacific. The story of how this was done forms a compact and continuous whole. The fathers followed Boone or fought at Kings Mountain; the sons marched south with Jackson to overcome the Creeks and beat back the British; the grandsons died at the Alamo or charged to victory at San Jacinto. They were doing their share of a work that began with the conquest of Britain, that entered on its second and wider period after the defeat of the Spanish Armada, that culminated in the marvelous growth of the United States. The winning of the West and Southwest is a stage in the conquest of a continent.

Chapter II

The Appalachian Confederacies

WHEN we declared ourselves an independent nation there were on our borders three groups of Indian peoples. The northernmost were the Iroquois or Six Nations, who dwelt in New York, and stretched down into Pennsylvania. They had been for two centuries the terror of every other Indian tribe east of the Mississippi, as well as of the whites; but their strength had already departed. They numbered only some ten or twelve thousand, all told, and though they played a bloody part in the Revolutionary struggle, it was merely as subordinate allies of the British. It did not lie in their power to strike a really decisive blow. Their chastisement did not result in our gaining new territory; nor would a failure to chastise them have affected the outcome of the war nor the terms of peace. Their fate was bound up with that of the king's cause in America and was decided wholly by events unconnected with their own success or defeat.

The very reverse was the case with the Indians, tenfold more numerous, who lived along our western frontier. There they were themselves our main opponents, the British simply acting as their supporters; and instead of their fate being settled by the treaty of peace with Britain, they continued an active warfare for twelve years after it had been signed. Had they defeated us in the early years of the contest, it is more than probable that the Alleghanies would have been made our western boundary at the peace. We won from them vast stretches of territory because we had beaten their warriors, and we could not have won it otherwise, whereas the territory of the Iroquois was lost, not because of their defeat, but because of the defeat of the British.

There were two great groups of these Indians, the ethnic

39

corresponding roughly with the geographic division. In the Northwest, between the Ohio and the Lakes, were the Algonquin tribes, generally banded loosely together; in the Southwest, between the Tennessee—then called the Cherokee—and the Gulf, the so-called Appalachians lived. Between them lay a vast and beautiful region where no tribe dared dwell, but into which all ventured now and then for war and hunting.

The southwestern Indians were called Appalachians by the older writers, because this was the name then given to the southern Alleghanies. It is doubtful if the term has any exact racial significance; but it serves very well to indicate a number of Indian nations whose system of government, ways of life, customs, and general culture were much alike, and whose civilization was much higher than was that of most other American tribes.

The Appalachians were in the barbarous, rather than in the merely savage state. They were divided into five lax confederacies: the Cherokees, Chickasaws, Choctaws, Creeks, and Seminoles. The latter were merely a southern offshoot of the Creeks or Muscogees. They were far more numerous than the northwestern Indians, were less nomadic, and, in consequence, had more definite possession of particular localities; so that their lands were more densely peopled.

In all they amounted to perhaps seventy thousand souls. It is more difficult to tell the numbers of the different tribes; for the division lines between them were very ill defined, and were subject to wide fluctuations. Thus the Creeks, the most formidable of all, were made up of many bands, differing from each other both in race and speech. The language of the Chickasaws and Choctaws did not differ more from the tongue of the Cherokees than the two divisions of the latter did from each other. The Cherokees of the hills, the Otari, spoke a dialect that could not be understood by the Cherokees of the lowlands, or Erati. Towns or bands continually broke up and split off from their former associations, while ambitious and warlike chiefs kept forming new settlements, and, if successful, drew large numbers of young warriors from the older communities. Thus the boundary-lines between the confederacies were ever shifting. Judging from a careful comparison of the different authorities, the following estimate of the numbers of the Southern tribes at the outbreak of the Revolution may be considered as probably approximately correct.

The Cherokees, some twelve thousand strong, were the mountaineers of their race. They dwelt among the blue-topped ridges and lofty peaks of the southern Alleghanies, in the wild and picturesque region where the present States of Tennessee, Alabama, Georgia, and the Carolinas join one another.

To the west of the Cherokees, on the banks of the Mississippi, were the Chickasaws, the smallest of the Southern nations, numbering at the outside but four thousand souls; but they were also the bravest and most warlike, and of all these tribal confederacies theirs was the only one which was at all closely knit together. The whole tribe acted in unison. In consequence, though engaged in incessant warfare with the far more numerous Choctaws, Creeks, and Cherokees, they more than held their own against them all; besides having inflicted on the French two of the bloodiest defeats they ever suffered from Indians. Most of the remnants of the Natchez, the strange sun-worshippers, had taken refuge with the Chickasaws and become completely identified with them, when their own nationality was destroyed by the arms of New Orleans.

The Choctaws, the rudest and, historically, the least important of these Indians, lived south of the Chickasaws. They were probably rather less numerous than the Creeks. Though accounted brave, they were treacherous and thievish, and were not as well armed as the others. They rarely made war or peace as a unit, parties frequently acting in conjunction with some of the rival European powers, or else joining in the plundering inroads made by the other Indians upon the white settlements. Beyond thus furnishing auxiliaries to our other Indian foes, they had little to do with our history.

The Muscogees or Creeks were the strongest of all. Their Southern bands, living in Florida, were generally considered as a separate confederacy, under the name of Seminoles. They numbered between twenty-five and thirty thousand souls, three-fourths of them being the Muscogees proper, and the remainder Seminoles. They dwelt south of the Cherokees and east of the Choctaws, adjoining the Georgians.

The Creeks and Cherokees were thus by their position the barrier tribes of the South, who had to stand the brunt of our advance, and who acted as a buffer between us and the

French and Spaniards of the Gulf and the lower Mississippi. Their fate once decided, that of the Chickasaws and Choctaws inevitably followed.

The customs and the political and social systems of these two tribes were very similar; and those of their two western neighbors were merely ruder copies thereof. They were very much further advanced than were the Algonquin nations of the North.

The Cherokees were a bright, intelligent race, better fitted to follow the "white man's road" than any other Indians. Like their neighbors, they were exceedingly fond of games of chance and skill, as well as of athletic sports. One of the most striking of their national amusements was the kind of ballplay from which we derive the game of lacrosse. The contests excited the most intense interest, were waged with desperate resolution, and were preceded by solemn dances and religious ceremonies; they were tests of tremendous physical endurance, and were often very rough, legs and arms being occasionally broken. The Choctaws were considered to be the best ball-players.

The Cherokees were likewise fond of dances. Sometimes these were comic or lascivious, sometimes they were religious in their nature, or were undertaken prior to starting on the war trail. Often the dances of the young men and maidens were very picturesque. The girls, dressed in white, with silver bracelets and gorgets, and a profusion of gay ribbons, danced in a circle in two ranks; the young warriors, clad in their battle finery, danced in a ring around them; all moving in rhythmic step, as they kept time to the antiphonal chanting and singing, the young men and girls responding alternately to each other.

The great confederacy of the Muscogees or Creeks, consisting of numerous tribes, speaking at least five distinct languages, lay in a well-watered land of small timber. The Creeks had developed a very curious semicivilization of their own. They lived in many towns, of which the larger, or old towns, bore rule over the smaller, and alone sent representatives to the general councils. Many of these were as large as any in the back counties of the colonies; but they were shifted from time to time, as the game was totally killed off, and the land exhausted by the crops. The soil then became covered by a growth of pines, and a so-called "old field" was formed. This method of cultivation was, after all, much like that of the Southern whites, and the "old fields," or abandoned plantations grown up with pines, were common in the colonies.

Many of the chiefs owned droves of horses and horned cattle, sometimes as many as five hundred head, besides hogs and poultry; and some of them in addition had negro slaves. But the tillage of the land was accomplished by communal labor; and, indeed, the government, as well as the system of life, was in many respects a singular compound of communism and extreme individualism. The fields of rice, corn, tobacco, beans, and potatoes were sometimes rudely fenced in with split hickory poles, and were sometimes left unfenced, with huts or high scaffolds, where watchers kept guard. They were planted when the wild fruit was so ripe as to draw off the birds, and, while ripening, the swine were kept penned up and the horses were tethered with tough bark ropes. Pumpkins, melons, marshmallows, and sunflowers were often grown between the rows of corn. The planting was done on a given day, the whole town being summoned; no man was expected or was allowed to go out hunting. The under head man supervised the work.

For food they used all these vegetables, as well as beef and pork, and venison stewed in bear's oil; they had hominy and corn cakes, and a cool drink made from honey and water, besides another made from fermented corn, which tasted much like cider. They sifted their flour in wickerwork sieves, and baked the bread in kettles or on broad thin stones. Moreover, they gathered the wild fruits, strawberries, grapes, and plums, in their season, and out of the hickory-nuts they made a thick, oily paste, called hickory milk.

Although in tillage they used only the hoe, they had made much progress in some useful arts. They spun the coarse wool of the buffalo into blankets, which they trimmed with beads. They wove the wild hemp in frames and shuttles. They made their own saddles. They made beautiful baskets of fine cane splints, and very handsome blankets of turkey feathers; while out of glazed clay they manufactured bowls, pitchers, platters, and other pottery.

In summer they wore buckskin shirts and breech-clouts; in winter they were clad in the fur of the bear and wolf, or of the shaggy buffalo. They had moccasins of elk or buffalo hide, and high thigh-boots of thin deerskin, ornamented with fawns' trotters, or turkey spurs that tinkled as they walked. In their hair they braided eagle-plumes, hawk-wings, or the brilliant plumage of the tanager and redbird. Trousers or breeches of any sort they despised as marks of effeminacy.

Vermilion was their war emblem; white was only worn at the time of the Green-Corn Dance. In each town stood the war-pole or painted post, a small peeled tree trunk colored red. Some of their villages were called white or peace towns; others red or bloody towns. The white towns were sacred to peace; no blood could be spilled within their borders. They were towns of refuge, where not even an enemy taken in war could be slain; and a murderer who fled thither was safe from vengeance. The captives were tortured to death in the red towns, and it was in these that the chiefs and warriors gathered when they were planning or preparing for war.

They held great marriage feasts; the dead were burned with the goods they had owned in their lifetime.

Every night all the people of a town gathered in the council-house to dance and sing and talk. Besides this, they held there on stated occasions the ceremonial dances; such were the dances of war and of triumph, when the warriors, painted red and black, returned, carrying the scalps of their slain foes on branches of evergreen pine, while they chanted the sonorous song of victory; and such was the Dance of the Serpent, the dance of lawless love, where the women and young girls were allowed to do whatsoever they listed.

Once a year, when the fruits ripened, they held the Green-Corn Dance, a religious festival that lasted eight days in the larger towns and four in the smaller. Then they fasted and feasted alternately. They drank out of conch-shells the Black Drink, a bitter beverage brewed from the crushed leaves of a small shrub. On the third day the high priest or firemaker, the man who sat in the white seat, clad in snowy tunic and moccasins, kindled the holy fire, fanning it into flames with the unsullied wing of a swan, and burning therein offerings of the first-fruits of the year. Dance followed dance. The beloved men and beloved women, the priest and priestess, danced in three rings, singing the solemn song of which the words were never uttered at any other time; and at the end the warriors, in their wild war-gear, with white-plume headdresses, took part, and also the women and girls, decked in their best, with earrings and armlets, and terrapin shells filled with pebbles fastened to the outside of their legs. They kept time with foot and voice, the men in deep tones, with short accents, the women in a shrill falsetto; while the clay drums, with heads of taut deer-hide, were beaten, the whistles blown, and the gourds and calabashes rattled, until the air resounded with the deafening noise.

Though they sometimes burnt their prisoners and violated captive women, they generally were more merciful than the Northern tribes.

But their political and military systems could not compare with those of the Algonquins, still less with those of the Iroquois. Their confederacy was of the loosest kind. There was no central authority. Every town acted just as it pleased, making war or peace with the other towns, or with whites, Choctaws, or Cherokees. In each there was a nominal head for peace and war, the high chief and the head warrior; the former was supposed to be supreme, and was elected for life from some one powerful family—as, for instance, the families having for their totems the wind or the eagle. But these chiefs had little control, and could not do much more than influence or advise their subjects; they were dependent on the will of the majority. Each town was a little hotbed of party spirit; the inhabitants divided on almost every question. If the head chief was for peace, but the war-chief nevertheless went on the war-path, there was no way of restraining him. It was said that never, in the memory of the oldest inhabitant, had half the nation "taken the war talk" at the same time. As a consequence, war-parties of Creeks were generally merely small bands of marauders in search of scalps and plunder. In proportion to its numbers, the nation never, until 1813, undertook such formidable military enterprises as were undertaken by the Wyandots, Shawnees, and Delawares; and, though very formidable individual fighters, even in this respect it may be questioned if the Creeks equalled the prowess of their Northern kinsmen.

Yet when the Revolutionary War broke out, the Creeks were under a chieftain whose consummate craft and utterly selfish but cool and masterly diplomacy enabled them for a generation to hold their own better than any other native race against the restless Americans. This was the half-breed Alexander

McGillivray, perhaps the most gifted man who was ever born on the soil of Alabama.

His father was a Scotch trader, Lachlan McGillivray by name, who came when a boy to Charleston, then the head-quarters of the commerce carried on by the British with the Southern Indians. On visiting the traders' quarter of the town, the young Scot was strongly attracted by the sight of the weather-beaten packers, with their gaudy, half-Indian finery, their hundreds of pack-horses, their curious pack-saddles, and their bales of merchandise. Taking service with them, he was soon helping to drive a pack-train along one of the narrow trails that crossed the lonely pine wilderness. To strong, coarse spirits, that were both shrewd and daring, and willing to balance the great risks incident to their mode of life against its great gains, the business was most alluring. Young Lachlan rose rapidly, and soon became one of the richest and most influential traders in the Creek country.

Like most traders, he married into the tribe, wooing and wedding, at the Hickory Ground, beside the Coosa River, a beautiful half-breed girl, Sehoy Marchand, whose father had been a French officer, and whose mother belonged to the powerful Creek family of the Wind. There were born to them two daughters and one son, Alexander. All the traders, though facing danger at every moment, from the fickle and jealous temper of the savages, wielded immense influence over them, and none more than the elder McGillivray, a far-sighted, unscrupulous Scotchman, who sided alternately with the French and English interests, as best suited his own policy and fortunes.

His son was felt by the Creeks to be one of themselves. He was born about 1746, at Litttle Tallasee, on the banks of the clear-flowing Coosa, where he lived till he was fourteen years old, playing, fishing, hunting, and bathing with the other Indian boys, and listening to the tales of the old chiefs and warriors. He was then taken to Charleston, where he was well educated, being taught Greek and Latin, as well as English history and literature. Tall, dark, slender, with commanding figure and immovable face, of cool, crafty temper, with great ambition and a keen intellect, he felt himself called to play no common part. He disliked trade, and at the first opportunity returned to his Indian home. He had neither the moral nor

the physical gifts requisite for a warrior; but he was a consummate diplomat, a born leader, and perhaps the only man
who could have used aright such a rope of sand as was the
Creek confederacy.

The Creeks claimed him as of their own blood, and instinc-
tively felt that he was their only possible ruler. He was forthwith chosen to be their head chief. From that time on he
remained among them, at one or the other of his plantations,
his largest and his real home being at Little Tallasee, where
he lived in barbaric comfort, in a great roomy log house with
a stone chimney, surrounded by the cabins of his sixty negro
slaves.

The record of our dealings with the Cherokees and the
Creeks must in many places be unpleasant reading to us, for it
shows grave wrong-doing on our part; yet the Indians themselves lacked only the power, but not the will, to treat us worse
than we treated them, and the darkest pages of their history
recite the wrongs that we ourselves suffered at their hands.

Not only were the Indians very terrible in battle, but they
were cruel beyond all belief in victory; and the gloomy annals
of border warfare are stained with their darkest hues because
it was a war in which helpless women and children suffered
the same hideous fate that so often befell their husbands and
fathers. It was a war waged by savages against armed settlers,
whose families followed them into the wilderness. Such a war
is inevitably bloody and cruel; but the inhuman love of cruelty
for cruelty's sake, which marks the red Indian above all other
savages, rendered these wars more terrible than any others.
For the hideous, unnamable, unthinkable tortures practised by
the red men on their captured foes, and on their foes' tender
women and helpless children, were such as we read of in no
other struggle, hardly even in the revolting pages that tell the
deeds of the Holy Inquisition. It was inevitable—indeed it was
in many instances proper—that such deeds should awake in
the breasts of the whites the grimmest, wildest spirit of revenge
and hatred.

The history of the border wars, both in the ways they were
begun and in the ways they were waged, makes a long tale of
injuries inflicted, suffered, and mercilessly revenged. It could
not be otherwise when brutal, reckless, lawless borderers, de-
spising all men not of their own color, were thrown in contact

with savages who esteemed cruelty and treachery as the highest of virtues, and rapine and murder as the worthiest of
pursuits. Moreover, it was sadly inevitable that the law-abiding
borderer as well as the white ruffian, the peaceful Indian as
well as the painted marauder, should be plunged into the
struggle to suffer the punishment that should only have fallen
on their evil-minded fellows.

Looking back, it is easy to say that much of the wrong-
doing could have been prevented; but if we examine the facts
to find out the truth, not to establish a theory, we are bound
to admit that the struggle was really one that could not possibly have been avoided. The sentimental historians speak as
if the blame had been all ours, and the wrong all done to our
foes, and as if it would have been possible by any exercise
of wisdom to reconcile claims that were in their very essence
conflicting; but their utterances are as shallow as they are
untruthful. Unless we were willing that the whole continent
west of the Alleghanies should remain an unpeopled waste, the
hunting-ground of savages, war was inevitable; and even had
we been willing, and had we refrained from encroaching on
the Indians' lands, the war would have come nevertheless, for
then the Indians themselves would have encroached on ours.
Undoubtedly we have wronged many tribes; but equally undoubtedly our first definite knowledge of many others has been
derived from their unprovoked outrages upon our people. The
Chippewas, Ottawas, and Pottawatomies furnished hundreds
of young warriors to the parties that devastated our frontiers
generations before we in any way encroached upon or wronged
them.

Mere outrages could be atoned for or settled; the question
which lay at the root of our difficulties was that of the occupation of the land itself, and to this there could be no solution
save war. The Indians had no ownership of the land in the
way in which we understand the term. The tribes lived far
apart; each had for its hunting-ground all the territory from
which it was not barred by rivals. Each looked with jealousy
upon all interlopers, but each was prompt to act as an inter-
loper when occasion offered. Every good hunting-ground was
claimed by many nations. It was rare, indeed, that any tribe
had an uncontested title to a large tract of land; where such

title existed, it rested not on actual occupancy and cultivation, but on the recent butchery of weaker rivals. For instance, there were a dozen tribes, all of whom hunted in Kentucky, and fought each other there, all of whom had equally good titles to the soil, and not one of whom acknowledged the right of any other; as a matter of fact, they had therein no right, save the right of the strongest. The land no more belonged to them than it belonged to Boone and the white hunters who first visited it.

On the borders there are perpetual complaints of the encroachments of whites upon Indian lands; and naturally the central government at Washington, and before it was at Washington, has usually been inclined to sympathize with the feeling that considers the whites the aggressors, for the government does not wish a war, does not itself feel any land hunger, hears of not a tenth of the Indian outrages, and knows by experience that the white borderers are not easy to rule. As a consequence, the official reports of the people who are not on the ground are apt to paint the Indian side in its most favorable light, and are often completely untrustworthy, this being particularly the case if the author of the report is an Eastern man, utterly unacquainted with the actual condition of affairs on the frontier.

Such a man, though both honest and intelligent, when he hears that the whites have settled on Indian lands, cannot realize that the act has no resemblance whatever to the forcible occupation of land already cultivated. The white settler has merely moved into an uninhabited waste; he does not feel that he is committing a wrong, for he knows perfectly well that the land is really owned by no one. It is never even visited, except perhaps for a week or two every year, and then the visitors are likely at any moment to be driven off by a rival hunting-party of greater strength. The settler ousts no one from the land; if he did not chop down the trees, hew out the logs for a building, and clear the ground for tillage, no one else would do so. He drives out the game, however, and of course the Indians who live thereon sink their mutual animosities and turn against the intruder. The truth is, the Indians never had any real title to the soil; they had not half as good a claim to it, for instance, as the cattlemen now have

to all eastern Montana, yet no one would assert that the cattlemen have a right to keep immigrants off their vast unfenced
ranges. The settler and pioneer have at bottom had justice on
their side; this great continent could not have been kept as
nothing but a game-preserve for squalid savages. Moreover,
to the most oppressed Indian nations the whites often acted as
a protection, or, at least, they deferred instead of hastening
their fate. But for the interposition of the whites it is probable
that the Iroquois would have exterminated every Algonquin
tribe before the end of the eighteenth century; exactly as in
recent time the Crows and Pawnees would have been destroyed by the Sioux, had it not been for the wars we have
waged against the latter.

Again, the loose governmental system of the Indians made
it as difficult to secure a permanent peace with them as it was
to negotiate the purchase of the lands. The sachem, or heredi-
tary peace chief, and the elective war-chief, who wielded only
the influence that he could secure by his personal prowess and
his tact, were equally unable to control all of their tribesmen,
and were powerless with their confederated nations. If peace
was made with the Shawnees, the war was continued by the
Miamis; if peace was made with the latter, nevertheless perhaps one small band was dissatisfied, and continued the contest
on its own account; and even if all the recognized bands were
dealt with, the parties of renegades or outlaws had to be considered; and in the last resort the full recognition accorded
by the Indians to the right of private warfare made it possible
for any individual warrior who possessed any influence to go
on raiding and murdering unchecked. Every tribe, every sub-
tribe, every band of a dozen souls ruled over by a petty chief,
almost every individual warrior of the least importance, had to
be met and pacified. Even if peace were declared, the Indians
could not exist long without breaking it. There was to them
no temptation to trespass on the white man's ground for the
purpose of settling; but every young brave was brought up
to regard scalps taken and horses stolen, in war or peace, as
the highest proofs and tokens of skill and courage, the sure
means of attaining glory and honor, the admiration of men
and the love of women. Where the young men thought thus,
and the chiefs had so little real control, it was inevitable that

there should be many unprovoked forays for scalps, slaves, and horses made upon the white borderers.

As for the whites themselves, they too have many and grievous sins against their red neighbors for which to answer. They cannot be severely blamed for trespassing upon what was called the Indian's land; for, let sentimentalists say what they will, the man who puts the soil to use must of right dispossess the man who does not, or the world will come to a standstill; but for many of their other deeds there can be no pardon. On the border each man was a law unto himself, and good and bad alike were left in perfect freedom to follow out to the uttermost limits their own desires; for the spirit of individualism so characteristic of American life reached its extreme of development in the backwoods. The whites who wished peace, the magistrates and leaders, had little more power over their evil and unruly fellows than the Indian sachems had over the turbulent young braves. Each man did what seemed best in his own eyes, almost without let or hindrance; unless, indeed, he trespassed upon the rights of his neighbors, who were ready enough to band together in their own defense, though slow to interfere in the affairs of others.

Thus the men of lawless, brutal spirit who are found in every community, and who flock to places where the reign of order is lax, were able to follow the bent of their inclinations unchecked. They utterly despised the red man; they held it no crime whatever to cheat him in trading, to rob him of his peltries or horses, to murder him if the fit seized them. Criminals who generally preyed on their own neighbors found it easier, and perhaps hardly as dangerous, to pursue their calling at the expense of the redskins, for the latter, when they discovered that they had been wronged, were quite as apt to vent their wrath on some outsider as on the original offender. If they injured a white, all the whites might make common cause against them; but if they injured a red man, though there were sure to be plenty of whites who disapproved of it, there were apt to be very few indeed whose disapproval took any active shape.

Each race stood by its own members, and each held all of the other race responsible for the misdeeds of a few uncontrollable spirits; and this clannishness among those of one color, and the refusal or the inability to discriminate between the good and the bad of the other color, were the two most fruitful causes of border strife.* When, even if he sought to prevent them, the innocent man was sure to suffer for the misdeeds of the guilty, unless both joined together for defense, the former had no alternative save to make common cause with the latter. Moreover, in a sparse backwoods settlement, where the presence of a strong, vigorous fighter was a source of safety to the whole community, it was impossible to expect that he would be punished with severity for offenses which, in their hearts, his fellow townsmen could not help regarding as in some sort a revenge for the injuries they had themselves suffered. Every quiet, peaceable settler had either himself been grievously wronged, or had been an eye-witness to wrongs done to his friends; and while these were vivid in his mind, the corresponding wrongs done the Indians were never brought home to him at all. If his son was scalped or his cattle driven off, he could not be expected to remember that perhaps the Indians who did the deed had themselves been cheated by a white trader, or had lost a relative at the hands of some border ruffian, or felt aggrieved because a hundred miles off some settler had built a cabin on lands they considered their own. When he joined with other exasperated and injured men to make a retaliatory inroad, his vengeance might or might not fall on the heads of the real offenders; and, in any case, he was often not in the frame of mind to put a stop to the outrages sure to be committed by the brutal spirits among his allies—though these brutal spirits were probably in a small minority.

The excesses so often committed by the whites, when, after many checks and failures, they at last grasped victory, are causes for shame and regret; yet it is only fair to keep in mind

* It is precisely the same at the present day. I have known a party of Sioux to steal the horses of a buffalo-hunting outfit, whereupon the latter retaliated by stealing the horses of a party of harmless Grosventres: and I knew a party of Cheyennes, whose horses had been taken by white thieves, to, in revenge, assail a camp of perfectly orderly cowboys. Most of the ranchmen along the Little Missouri in 1884 were pretty good fellows, who would not wrong Indians, yet they tolerated for a long time the presence of men who did not scruple to boast that they stole horses from the latter; while our peaceful neighbors, the Grosventres, likewise permitted two notorious red-skinned horse thieves to use their reservation as a harbor of refuge, and a starting-point from which to make forays against the cattlemen.

the terrible provocations they had endured. Mercy, pity, mag-
nanimity to the fallen, could not be expected from the frontiersmen gathered together to war against an Indian tribe. Almost
every man of such a band had bitter personal wrongs to
avenge. He was not taking part in a war against a civilized foe;
he was fighting in a contest where women and children suffered
the fate of the strong men, and instead of enthusiasm for his
country's flag and a general national animosity toward its
enemies, he was actuated by a furious flame of hot anger, and
was goaded on by memories of which merely to think was
madness. His friends had been treacherously slain while on
messages of peace; his house had been burned, his cattle driven
off, and all he had in the world destroyed before he knew that
war existed and when he felt quite guiltless of all offense; his
sweetheart or wife had been carried off, ravished, and was at
the moment the slave and concubine of some dirty and brutal
Indian warrior; his son, the stay of his house, had been burned
at the stake with torments too horrible to mention;* his sister,
when ransomed and returned to him, had told of the weary
journey through the woods, when she carried around her neck
as a horrible necklace the bloody scalps of her husband and
children; seared into his eyeballs, into his very brain, he bore
ever with him, waking or sleeping, the sight of the skinned,
mutilated, hideous body of the baby who had just grown old
enough to recognize him and to crow and laugh when taken in
his arms. Such incidents as these were not exceptional; one or
more, and often all of them, were the invariable attendants of
every one of the countless Indian inroads that took place during the long generations of forest warfare. It was small wonder
that men who had thus lost everything should sometimes be
fairly crazed by their wrongs. Again and again on the frontier
we hear of some such unfortunate who has devoted all the
remainder of his wretched life to the one object of taking

---

* The expression "too horrible to mention" is to be taken literally, not
figuratively. It applies equally to the fate that has befallen every white
man or woman who has fallen into the power of hostile plains Indians
during the last ten or fifteen years. The nature of the wild Indian has
not changed. Not one man in a hundred, and not a single woman, escapes
torments which a civilized man cannot look another in the face and so
much as speak of. Impalement on charred sticks, finger-nails split off
backward, finger-joints chewed off, eyes burnt out—these tortures can be
mentioned, but there are others equally normal and customary which cannot even be hinted at, especially when women are the victims.

vengeance on the whole race of the men who had darkened his days forever. Too often the squaws and papooses fell victims of the vengeance that should have come only on the warriors; for the whites regarded their foes as beasts rather than men, and knew that the squaws were more cruel than others in torturing the prisoner, and that the very children took their full part therein, being held up by their fathers to tomahawk the dying victims at the stake.

Thus it is that there are so many dark and bloody pages in the book of border warfare, that grim and iron-bound volume, wherein we read how our forefathers won the wide lands that we inherit. It contains many a tale of fierce heroism and adventurous ambition, of the daring and resolute courage of men and the patient endurance of women; it shows us a stern race of freemen who toiled hard, endured greatly, and fronted adversity bravely, who prized strength and courage and good faith, whose wives were chaste, who were generous and loyal to their friends. But it shows us also how they spurned at restraint, and fretted under it, how they would brook no wrong to themselves, and yet too often inflicted wrongs on others; their feats of terrible prowess are interspersed with deeds of the foulest and most wanton aggression, the darkest treachery, the most revolting cruelty; and though we meet with plenty of the rough, strong, coarse virtues, we see but little of such qualities as mercy for the fallen, the weak, and the helpless, or pity for a gallant and vanquished foe.

Chapter III

The Backwoodsmen of
the Alleghanies

A LONG the western frontier of the colonies that were so
soon to be the United States, among the foot-hills of
the Alleghanies, on the slopes of the wooded mountains,
and in the long trough-like valleys that lay between the ranges,
dwelt a peculiar and characteristically American people.

These frontier folk, the people of the up-country, or backcountry, who lived near and among the forest-clad mountains,
far away from the long-settled districts of flat coast plain and
sluggish tidal river, were known to themselves and to others
as backwoodsmen. They all bore a strong likeness to one
another in their habits of thought and ways of living, and
differed markedly from the people of the older and more civilized communities to the eastward. The western border of
our country was then formed by the great barrier-chains of
the Alleghanies, which ran north and south from Pennsylvania
through Maryland, Virginia, and the Carolinas, the trend of
the valleys being parallel to the seacoast, and the mountains
rising highest to the southward. It was difficult to cross the
ranges from east to west, but it was both easy and natural to
follow the valleys between. From Fort Pitt to the high hill-
homes of the Cherokees this great tract of wooded and mountainous country possessed nearly the same features and characteristics, differing utterly in physical aspect from the alluvial
plains bordering the ocean.

So, likewise, the backwoods mountaineers who dwelt near
the great watershed that separates the Atlantic streams from
the springs of the Watauga, the Kanawha, and the Mononga-
hela, were all cast in the same mould, and resembled each other
much more than any of them did their immediate neighbors
of the plains. The backwoodsmen of Pennsylvania had little in

55

common with the peaceful population of Quakers and Germans who lived between the Delaware and the Susquehanna; and their near kinsmen of the Blue Ridge and the Great Smoky Mountains were separated by an equally wide gulf from the aristocratic planter communities that flourished in the tide-water regions of Virginia and the Carolinas. Near the coast the lines of division between the colonies corresponded fairly well with the differences between the populations; but after striking the foot-hills, though the political boundaries continued to go east and west, those both of ethnic and of physical significance began to run north and south.

The backwoodsmen were Americans by birth and parentage, and of mixed race; but the dominant strain in their blood was that of the Presbyterian Irish—the Scotch-Irish, as they were often called. Full credit has been awarded the Roundhead and the Cavalier for their leadership in our history; nor have we been altogether blind to the deeds of the Hollander and the Huguenot; but it is doubtful if we have wholly realized the importance of the part played by that stern and virile people, the Irish whose preachers taught the creed of Knox and Calvin. These Irish representatives of the Covenanters were in the West almost what the Puritans were in the Northeast, and more than the Cavaliers were in the South. Mingled with the descendants of many other races, they nevertheless formed the kernel of the distinctively and intensely American stock who were the pioneers of our people in their march westward, the vanguard of the army of fighting settlers, who, with axe and rifle, won their way from the Alleghanies to the Rio Grande and the Pacific.

The Presbyterian Irish were themselves already a mixed people. Though mainly descended from Scotch ancestors— who came originally from both lowlands and highlands, from among both the Scotch Saxons and the Scotch Celts—many of them were of English, a few of French Huguenot, and quite a number of true old Milesian Irish extraction. They were the Protestants of the Protestants; they detested and despised the Catholics, whom their ancestors had conquered, and regarded the Episcopalians, by whom they themselves had been oppressed, with a more sullen, but scarcely less intense, hatred. They were a truculent and obstinate people, and gloried in the warlike renown of their forefathers, the men who had followed Cromwell, and who had shared in the defense of Derry and in the victories of the Boyne and Aughrim.

They did not begin to come to America in any numbers till after the opening of the eighteenth century; by 1730 they were fairly swarming across the ocean, for the most part in two streams, the larger going to the port of Philadelphia, the smaller to the port of Charleston. Pushing through the long-settled lowlands of the seacoast, they at once made their abode at the foot of the mountains, and became the outposts of civilization. From Pennsylvania, whither the great majority had come, they drifted south along the foot-hills, and down the long valleys, till they met their brethren from Charleston who had pushed up into the Carolina back-country. In this land of hills, covered by unbroken forest, they took root and flourished, stretching in a broad belt from north to south, a shield of sinewy men thrust in between the people of the sea-board and the red warriors of the wilderness. All through this region they were alike; they had as little kinship with the Cavalier as with the Quaker; the West was won by those who have been rightly called the Roundheads of the South, the same men who, before any others, declared for American independence.

The two facts of most importance to remember in dealing with our pioneer history are, first, that the western portions of Virginia and the Carolinas were peopled by an entirely different stock from that which had long existed in the tide-water regions of those colonies; and, secondly, that, except for those in the Carolinas who came from Charleston, the immigrants of this stock were mostly from the North, from their great breeding-ground and nursery in western Pennsylvania.*

---

* In the "History of the People of the United States," by Professor [John Bach] McMaster (New York, 1887), p. 70, there is a mistake so glaring that it would not need notice, were it not for the many excellences and wide repute of Professor McMaster's book. He says that of the immigrants to Kentucky, most had come "from the neighboring States of Carolina and Georgia," and shows that this is not a mere slip of the pen, by elaborating the statement in the following paragraphs, again speaking of North and South Carolina and Georgia as furnishing the colonists to Kentucky. This shows a complete misapprehension not only of the feeding-grounds of the Western emigration, but of the routes it followed, and of the conditions of the Southern States. South Carolina furnished very few emigrants to Kentucky, and Georgia practically none; combined, they probably did not furnish as many as New Jersey or Maryland. Georgia was herself a frontier community; she received instead of sending out immigrants. The bulk of the South Carolina emigration went to Georgia.

That these Irish Presbyterians were a bold and hardy race is proved by their at once pushing past the settled regions, and plunging into the wilderness as the leaders of the white advance. They were the first and last set of immigrants to do this; all others have merely followed in the wake of their predecessors. But, indeed, they were fitted to be Americans from the very start; they were kinsfolk of the Covenanters; they deemed it a religious duty to interpret their own Bible, and held for a divine right the election of their own clergy. For generations their whole ecclesiastic and scholastic systems had been fundamentally democratic. In the hard life of the frontier they lost much of their religion, and they had but scant opportunity to give their children the schooling in which they believed; but what few meeting-houses and school-houses there were on the border were theirs. The numerous families of colonial English who came among them adopted their religion if they adopted any. The creed of the backwoodsman who had a creed at all was Presbyterianism; for the Episcopacy of the tide-water lands obtained no foothold in the mountains, and the Methodists and Baptists had but just begun to appear in the West when the Revolution broke out.

These Presbyterian Irish were, however, far from being the only settlers on the border, although more than any others they impressed the stamp of their peculiar character on the pioneer civilization of the West and Southwest. Great numbers of immigrants of English descent came among them from the settled districts on the east; and though these later arrivals soon became indistinguishable from the people among whom they settled, yet they certainly sometimes added a tone of their own to backwoods society, giving it here and there a slight dash of what we are accustomed to consider the distinctively Southern or cavalier spirit.* There was likewise a large German admixture, not only from the Germans of Pennsylvania, but also from those of the Carolinas. A good many Huguenots likewise came, and a few Hollanders, and even Swedes, from the banks of the Delaware, or perhaps from farther off still.

---

* Boone, though of English descent, had no Virginia blood in his veins; he was an exact type of the regular backwoodsman; but in Clark, and still more in Blount, we see strong traces of the "cavalier spirit." Of course, the Cavaliers no more formed the bulk of the Virginia people than they did of Rupert's armies; but the squires and yeomen who went to make up the mass took their tone from their leaders.

A single generation, passed under the hard conditions of life in the wilderness, was enough to weld together into one people the representatives of these numerous and widely different races; and the children of the next generation became indistinguishable from one another. Long before the first Continental Congress assembled, the backwoodsmen, whatever their blood, had become Americans, one in speech, thought, and character, clutching firmly the land in which their fathers and grandfathers had lived before them. They had lost all remembrance of Europe and all sympathy with things European; they had become as emphatically products native to the soil as were the tough and supple hickories out of which they fashioned the handles of their long, light axes. Their grim, harsh, narrow lives were yet strangely fascinating, and full of adventurous toil and danger; none but natures as strong, as freedom-loving, and as full of bold defiance as theirs could have endured existence on the terms which these men found pleasurable. Their iron surroundings made a mould which turned out all alike in the same shape. They resembled one another, and they differed from the rest of the world—even the world of America, and infinitely more, the world of Europe—in dress, in customs, and in mode of life.

Where their lands abutted on the more settled districts to the eastward, the population was of course thickest, and their peculiarities least. Here and there at such points they built small backwoods burgs or towns, rude, straggling, unkempt villages, with a store or two, a tavern—sometimes good, often a "scandalous hog-sty," where travellers were devoured by fleas, and every one slept and ate in one room—a small log schoolhouse, and a little church, presided over by a hard-featured Presbyterian preacher, gloomy, earnest, and zealous, probably bigoted and narrow-minded, but nevertheless a great power for good in the community.

However, the backwoodsmen as a class neither built towns nor loved to dwell therein. They were to be seen at their best in the vast, interminable forests that formed their chosen home. They won and kept their lands by force, and ever lived either at war or in dread of war. Hence, they settled always in groups of several families each, all banded together for mutual protection. Their red foes were strong and terrible, cunning in council, dreadful in battle, merciless beyond belief

in victory. The men of the border did not overcome and dispossess cowards and weaklings; they marched forth to spoil the
stout-hearted and to take for a prey the possessions of the men
of might. Every acre, every rood of ground which they claimed
had to be cleared by the axe and held with the rifle. Not only
was the chopping down of the forests the first preliminary to
cultivation, but it was also the surest means of subduing the
Indians, to whom the unending stretches of choked woodland
were an impenetrable cover behind which to move unseen, a
shield in making assaults, and a strong tower of defense in
repelling counter-attacks. In the conquest of the West the
backwoods axe, shapely, well-poised, with long haft and light
head, was a servant hardly standing second even to the rifle;
the two were the national weapons of the American backwoodsman, and in their use he has never been excelled.

When a group of families moved out into the wilderness
they built themselves a station or stockade fort: a square
palisade of upright logs, loopholed, with strong blockhouses
as bastions at the corners. One side at least was generally
formed by the backs of the cabins themselves, all standing in
a row; and there was a great door or gate, that could be
strongly barred in case of need. Often no iron whatever was
employed in any of the buildings. The square inside contained
the provision sheds and frequently a strong central blockhouse
as well. These forts, of course, could not stand against cannon,
and they were always in danger when attacked with fire; but
save for this risk of burning they were very effectual defenses
against men without artillery, and were rarely taken, whether
by whites or Indians, except by surprise. Few other buildings
have played so important a part in our history as the rough
stockade of the backwoods.

The families only lived in the fort when there was war with
the Indians, and even then not in the winter. At other times
they all separated out to their own farms, universally called
clearings, as they were always made by first cutting off the
timber. The stumps were left to dot the fields of grain and
Indian corn. The corn in especial was the standby and invariable resource of the Western settler; it was the crop on
which he relied to feed his family, and when hunting or on a
war trail the parched grains were carried in his leather wallet
to serve often as his only food. But he planted orchards and

raised melons, potatoes, and many other fruits and vegetables as well; and he had usually a horse or two, cows, and perhaps hogs and sheep, if the wolves and bears did not interfere. If he was poor his cabin was made of unhewn logs, and held but a single room; if well-to-do, the logs were neatly hewed, and besides the large living and eating room with its huge stone fireplace, there was also a small bedroom and a kitchen, while a ladder led to the loft above, in which the boys slept. The floor was made of puncheons, great slabs of wood hewed carefully out, and the roof of clapboards. Pegs of wood were thrust into the sides of the house, to serve instead of a wardrobe; and buck antlers, thrust into joists, held the ever-ready rifles. The table was a great clapboard set on four wooden legs; there were three-legged stools, and in the better sort of houses old-fashioned rocking-chairs. The couch or bed was warmly covered with blankets, bearskins, and deer-hides.

These clearings lay far apart from one another in the wilderness. Up to the door-sills of the log huts stretched the solemn and mysterious forest. There were no openings to break its continuity; nothing but endless leagues on leagues of shadowy, wolf-haunted woodland. The great trees towered aloft till their separate heads were lost in the mass of foliage above, and the rank underbrush choked the spaces between the trunks. On the higher peaks and ridge crests of the mountains there were straggling birches and pines, hemlocks and balsam firs; elsewhere, oaks, chestnuts, hickories, maples, beeches, walnuts, and great tulip-trees grew side by side with many other kinds. The sunlight could not penetrate the roofed archway of murmuring leaves; through the gray aisles of the forest men walked always in a kind of midday gloaming. Those who had lived in the open plains felt when they came to the backwoods as if their heads were hooded. Save on the border of a lake, from a cliff-top, or on a bald knob—that is, a bare hill-shoulder—they could not anywhere look out for any distance.

All the land was shrouded in one vast forest. It covered the mountains from crest to river-bed, filled the plains, and stretched in sombre and melancholy wastes toward the Mississippi. All that it contained, all that lay hid within it and beyond it, none could tell; men only knew that their boldest hunters, however deeply they had penetrated, had not yet gone through it, that it was the home of the game they followed and the wild beasts that preyed on their flocks, and that deep in its tangled depths lurked their red foes, hawk-eyed and wolf-hearted.

Backwoods society was simple, and the duties and rights of each member of the family were plain and clear. The man was the armed protector and provider, the bread-winner; the woman was the housewife and child-bearer. They married young and their families were large, for they were strong and healthy, and their success in life depended on their own stout arms and willing hearts. There was everywhere great equality of conditions. Land was plenty and all else scarce; so courage, thrift, and industry were sure of their reward. All had small farms, with the few stock necessary to cultivate them; the farms being generally placed in the hollows, the division lines between them, if they were close together, being the tops of the ridges and the watercourses, especially the former. The buildings of each farm were usually at its lowest point, as if in the centre of an amphitheatre. Each was on an average of about four hundred acres, but sometimes more. Tracts of low, swampy grounds, possibly some miles from the cabin, were cleared for meadows, the fodder being stacked, and hauled home in winter.

Each backwoodsman was not only a small farmer but also a hunter; for his wife and children depended for their meat upon the venison and bear's flesh procured by his rifle. The people were restless and always on the move. After being a little while in a place, some of the men would settle down permanently, while others would again drift off, farming and hunting alternately to support their families. The backwoodsman's dress was in great part borrowed from his Indian foes. He wore a fur cap or felt hat, moccasins, and either loose, thin trousers, or else simply leggings of buckskin or elk-hide, and the Indian breech-clout. He was always clad in the fringed hunting-shirt, of homespun or buckskin, the most picturesque and distinctively national dress ever worn in America. It was a loose smock or tunic, reaching nearly to the knees, and held in at the waist by a broad belt, from which hung the tomahawk and scalping-knife. His weapon was the long, small-bore, flint-lock rifle, clumsy, and ill-balanced, but exceedingly accurate. It was very heavy, and when upright, reached to the chin of a tall man; for the barrel of thick, soft iron was four feet in length, while the stock was short, and the butt scooped out. Sometimes it was plain, sometimes ornamented. It was generally bored out—or, as the expression then was, "sawed out"—to carry a ball of seventy, more rarely of thirty or forty, to the pound; and was usually of backwoods manufacture. The marksman almost always fired from a rest, and rarely at a very long range; and the shooting was marvellously accurate.

In the backwoods there was very little money; barter was the common form of exchange, and the peltries were often used as a circulating medium, a beaver, otter, fisher, dressed buckskin or large bearskin being reckoned as equal to two foxes or wildcats, four coons, or eight minks. A young man inherited nothing from his father but his strong frame and eager heart; but before him lay a whole continent wherein to pitch his farm, and he felt ready to marry as soon as he became of age, even though he had nothing but his clothes, his horses, his axe, and his rifle. If a girl was well off, and had been careful and industrious, she might herself bring a dowry, of a cow and a calf, a brood-mare, a bed well stocked with blankets, and a chest containing her clothes—the latter not very elaborate, for a woman's dress consisted of a hat or poke bonnet, a "bedgown," perhaps a jacket, and a linsey petticoat, while her feet were thrust into coarse shoepacks or moccasins. Fine clothes were rare; a suit of such cost more than two hundred acres of good land.

The first lesson the backwoodsmen learnt was the necessity of self-help; the next, that such a community could only thrive if all joined in helping one another. Log-rollings, house-raisings, house-warmings, corn-shuckings, quiltings, and the like were occasions when all the neighbors came together to do what the family itself could hardly accomplish alone. Every such meeting was the occasion of a frolic and dance for the young people, whiskey and rum being plentiful, and the host exerting his utmost power to spread the table with backwoods delicacies—bear meat and venison, vegetables from the "truck-patch," where squashes, melons, beans and the like were grown, wild fruits, bowls of milk, and apple pies, which were the acknowledged standard of luxury. At the better houses there was metheglin or small beer, cider, cheese, and biscuits. Tea was so little known that many of the backwoods people were not aware it was a beverage and at first attempted to eat the leaves with salt or butter.

The young men prided themselves on their bodily strength, and were always eager to contend against one another in athletic games, such as wrestling, racing, jumping and lifting flour-barrels; and they also sought distinction in vying with one another at their work. Sometimes they strove against one another singly, sometimes they divided into parties, each bending all its energies to be first in shucking a given heap of corn or cutting (with sickles) an allotted patch of wheat. Among the men the bravos or bullies often were dandies, also in the backwoods fashions, wearing their hair long and delighting in the rude finery of hunting-shirts embroidered with porcupine quills; they were loud, boastful, and profane, given to coarsely bantering one another. Brutally savage fights were frequent; the combatants, who were surrounded by rings of interested spectators, striking, kicking, biting, and gouging. The fall of one of them did not stop the fight, for the man who was down was maltreated without mercy until he called "enough." The victor always bragged savagely of his prowess, often leaping on a stump, crowing and flapping his arms. This last was a thoroughly American touch; but otherwise one of these contests was less a boxing-match than a kind of backwoods *pankrátion,* no less revolting than its ancient prototype of Olympic fame. Yet, if the uncouth borderers were as brutal as the highly polished Greeks, they were more manly; defeat was not necessarily considered disgrace, a man often fighting when he was certain to be beaten, while the onlookers neither hooted nor pelted the conquered. We first hear of the noted Indian fighter, Simon Kenton, as leaving a rival for dead after one of these ferocious duels, and fleeing from his home in terror of the punishment that might follow the deed. Such fights were specially frequent when the backwoodsmen went into the little frontier towns to see horse-races or fairs.

A wedding was always a time of festival. If there was a church anywhere near, the bride rode thither on horseback behind her father, and after the service her pillion was shifted to the bridegroom's steed. If, as generally happened, there was no church, the groom and his friends, all armed, rode to the house of the bride's father, plenty of whiskey being drunk, and the men racing recklessly along the narrow bridle-paths, for there were few roads or wheeled vehicles in the backwoods. At the bride's house the ceremony was performed, and then a huge dinner was eaten; after which the fiddling and dancing began, and were continued all the afternoon, and most of the night as well. A party of girls stole off the bride and put her to bed in the loft above; and a party of young men then performed the like service for the groom. The fun was hearty and coarse, and the toasts always included one to the young couple with the wish that they might have many big children; for as long as they could remember the backwoodsmen had lived at war, while looking ahead they saw no chance of its ever stopping, and so each son was regarded as a future warrior, a help to the whole community. The neighbors all joined again in chopping and rolling the logs for the young couple's future house, then in raising the house itself, and finally in feasting and dancing at the housewarming.

Funerals were simple, the dead body being carried to the grave in a coffin slung on poles and borne by four men.

There was not much schooling, and few boys or girls learnt much more than reading, writing, and ciphering up to the rule of three. Where the schoolhouses existed they were only dark, mean log huts, and, if in the Southern colonies, were generally placed in the so-called "old fields," or abandoned farms grown up with pines. The schoolmaster boarded about with the families; his learning was rarely great, nor was his discipline good, in spite of the frequency and severity of the canings. The price for such tuition was at the rate of twenty shillings a year, in Pennsylvania currency.

Each family did everything that could be done for itself. The father and sons worked with axe, hoe, and sickle. Almost every house contained a loom, and almost every woman was a weaver. Linsey-woolsey, made from flax grown near the cabin, and of wool from the backs of the few sheep, was the warmest and most substantial cloth; and when the flax-crop failed and the flocks were destroyed by wolves, the children had but scanty covering to hide their nakedness. The man tanned the buckskin, the woman was tailor and shoe-maker, and made the deerskin sifters to be used instead of bolting-cloths. There were a few pewter spoons in use; but the table furniture consisted mainly of handmade trenchers, platters, noggins, and bowls. The cradle was of peeled hickory bark. Ploughshares had to be imported, but harrows and sleds were made without difficulty; and the cooper work was well done. Chaff beds were thrown on the floor of the loft, if the house-owner was well off. Each cabin had a hand-mill and a hominy-block; the last was borrowed from the Indians, and was only a large block of wood, with a hole burned in the top, as a mortar, where the pestle was worked. If there were any sugar-maples accessible, they were tapped every year.

But some articles, especially salt and iron, could not be produced in the backwoods. In order to get them each family collected during the year all the furs possible, these being valuable and yet easily carried on pack-horses, the sole means of transport. Then, after seeding-time, in the fall, the people of a neighborhood ordinarily joined in sending down a train of peltry-laden pack-horses to some large sea-coast or tidal-river trading town, where their burdens were bartered for the needed iron and salt. The unshod horses all had bells hung round their necks; the clappers were stopped during the day, but when the train was halted for the night, and the horses were hobbled and turned loose, the bells were once more unstopped. Several men accompanied each little caravan, and sometimes they drove with them steers and hogs to sell on the seacoast. A bushel of alum salt was worth a good cow and calf, and as each of the poorly fed, undersized pack-animals could carry but two bushels, the mountaineers prized it greatly, and, instead of salting or pickling their venison, they jerked it by drying it in the sun or smoking it over a fire.

The life of the backwoodsmen was one long struggle. The forest had to be felled; droughts, deep snows, freshets, cloud-bursts, forest-fires, and all the other dangers of a wilderness life faced. Swarms of deer-flies, mosquitoes, and midges rendered life a torment in the weeks of hot weather. Rattlesnakes and copperheads were very plentiful, and, the former especially, constant sources of danger and death. Wolves and bears were incessant and inveterate foes of the live stock, and the cougar, or panther, occasionally attacked man as well. More terrible still, the wolves sometimes went mad, and the men who then encountered them were almost certain to be bitten and to die of hydrophobia.

Every true backwoodsman was a hunter. Wild turkeys were plentiful. The pigeons at times filled the woods with clouds that hid the sun and broke down the branches on their roosting-grounds as if a whirlwind had passed. The black and gray squirrels swarmed, devastating the corn-fields, and at times gathering in immense companies and migrating across mountain and river. The hunter's ordinary game was the deer, and after that the bear; the elk was already growing uncommon. No form of labor is harder than the chase, and none is so fascinating nor so excellent as a training-school for war. The successful still-hunter of necessity possessed skill in hiding and in creeping noiselessly upon the wary quarry, as well as in imitating the notes and calls of the different beasts and birds; skill in the use of the rifle and in throwing the tomahawk he already had; and he perforce acquired keenness of eye, thorough acquaintance with wood-craft, and the power of standing the severest strains of fatigue, hardship, and exposure. He lived out in the woods for many months with no food but meat, and no shelter whatever, unless he made a lean-to of brush or crawled into a hollow sycamore.

Such training stood the frontier folk in good stead when they were pitted against the Indians; without it they could not even have held their own, and the white advance would have been absolutely checked. Our frontiers were pushed westward by the warlike skill and adventurous personal prowess of the individual settlers; regular armies by themselves could have done little. For one square mile the regular armies added to our domain, the settlers added ten—a hundred would probably be nearer the truth. A race of peaceful, unwarlike farmers would have been helpless before such foes as the red Indians, and no auxiliary military force could have protected them or enabled them to move westward. Colonists fresh from the Old World, no matter how thrifty, steady-going, and industrious, could not hold their own on the frontier; they had to settle where they were protected from the Indians by a living barrier of bold and self-reliant American borderers. The West would never have been set-

tled save for the fierce courage and the eager desire to brave
danger so characteristic of the stalwart backwoodsmen.

These armed hunters, wood-choppers, and farmers were
their own soldiers. They built and manned their own forts;
they did their own fighting under their own commanders.
There were no regiments of regular troops along the frontier. In the event of an Indian inroad each borderer had
to defend himself until there was time for them all to gather
together to repel or avenge it. Every man was accustomed to
the use of arms from his childhood; when a boy was twelve
years old he was given a rifle and made a fort-soldier, with a
loophole where he was to stand if the station was attacked.
The war was never-ending, for even the times of so-called
peace were broken by forays and murders; a man might grow
from babyhood to middle age on the border, and yet never
remember a year in which some one of his neighbors did not
fall a victim to the Indians.

There was everywhere a rude military organization, which
included all the able-bodied men of the community. Every
settlement had its colonels and captains; but these officers,
both in their training and in the authority they exercised,
corresponded much more nearly to Indian chiefs than to the
regular army men whose titles they bore. They had no
means whatever of enforcing their orders, and their tumultuous and disorderly levies of sinewy riflemen were hardly as
well disciplined as the Indians themselves. The superior
officer could advise, entreat, lead, and influence his men, but
he could not command them, or, if he did, the men obeyed
him only just so far as it suited them. If an officer planned
a scout or campaign, those who thought proper accompanied
him, and the others stayed at home, and even those who
went out came back if the fit seized them, or perchance followed the lead of an insubordinate junior officer whom they
liked better than they did his superior. There was no com-
pulsion to perform military duties beyond dread of being
disgraced in the eyes of the neighbors, and there was no
pecuniary reward for performing them; nevertheless the
moral sentiment of a backwoods community was too robust
to tolerate habitual remisses in military affairs, and the coward and laggard were treated with utter scorn, and were
generally in the end either laughed out, or "hated out," of

the neighborhood, or else got rid of in a still more summary manner. Among people naturally brave and reckless, this public opinion acted fairly effectively, and there was generally but little shrinking from military service.

A backwoods levy was formidable because of the high average courage and prowess of the individuals composing it; it was on its own ground much more effective than a like force of regular soldiers, but of course it could not be trusted on a long campaign. The backwoodsmen used their rifles better than the Indians, and also stood punishment better, but they never matched them in surprises nor in skill in taking advantage of cover, and very rarely equalled their discipline in the battle itself. After all, the pioneer was primarily a husbandman; the time spent in chopping trees and tilling the soil his foe spent in preparing for or practising forest warfare, and so the former, thanks to the exercise of the very qualities which in the end gave him the possession of the soil, could not, as a rule, hope to rival his antagonist in the actual conflict itself. When large bodies of the red men and white borderers were pitted against each other, the former were if anything the more likely to have the advantage. But the whites soon copied from the Indians their system of individual and private warfare, and they probably caused their foes far more damage and loss in this way than in the large expeditions. Many noted border scouts and Indian fighters—such men as Boone, Kenton, Wetzel, Brady, McCulloch, Mansker—grew to overmatch their Indian foes at their own game, and held themselves above the most renowned warriors. But these men carried the spirit of defiant self-reliance to such an extreme that their best work was always done when they were alone or in small parties of but four or five. They made long forays after scalps and horses, going a wonderful distance, enduring extreme hardship, risking the most terrible of deaths, and harrying the hostile tribes into a madness of terror and revengeful hatred.

As it was in military matters, so it was with the administration of justice by the frontiersmen; they had few courts, and knew but little law, and yet they contrived to preserve order and morality with rough effectiveness, by combining to frown down on the grosser misdeeds, and to punish the more flagrant misdoers. Perhaps the spirit in which they acted can best be shown by the recital of an incident in the career of the three McAfee brothers, who were among the pioneer hunters of Kentucky. Previous to trying to move their families out to the new country, they made a cache of clothing, implements, and provisions, which in their absence was broken into and plundered. They caught the thief, "a little diminutive, red-headed white man," a runaway convict servant from one of the tide-water counties of Virginia. In the first impulse of anger at finding that he was the criminal, one of the McAfees rushed at him to kill him with his tomahawk; but the weapon turned, the man was only knocked down, and his assailant's gusty anger subsided as quickly as it had risen, giving way to a desire to do stern but fair justice. So the three captors formed themselves into a court, examined into the case, heard the man in his own defense, and after due consultation decided that "according to their opinion of the laws he had forfeited his life, and ought to be hung"; but none of them were willing to execute the sentence in cold blood, and they ended by taking their prisoner back to his master.

The incident was characteristic in more than one way. The prompt desire of the backwoodsman to avenge his own wrong; his momentary furious anger, speedily quelled and replaced by a dogged determination to be fair but to exact full retribution; the acting entirely without regard to legal forms or legal officials, but yet in a spirit which spoke well for the doer's determination to uphold the essentials that make honest men law-abiding; together with the good faith of the whole proceeding, and the amusing ignorance that it would have been in the least unlawful to execute their own rather harsh sentence—all these were typical frontier traits. Some of the same traits appear in the treatment commonly adopted in the backwoods to meet the case—of painfully frequent occurrence in the times of Indian wars—where a man taken prisoner by the savages, and supposed to be murdered, returned after two or three years' captivity, only to find his wife married again. In the wilderness a husband was almost a necessity to a woman; her surroundings made the loss of the protector and provider an appalling calamity; and the widow, no matter how sincere her sorrow, soon remarried— for there were many suitors where women were not over-plenty. If in such a case the one thought dead returned, the neighbors and the parties interested seem frequently to have held a sort of informal court, and to have decided that the woman should choose either of the two men she wished to be her husband, the other being pledged to submit to the decision and leave the settlement. Evidently no one had the least idea that there was any legal irregularity in such proceedings.

The McAfees themselves and the ecaped convict servant whom they captured typify the two prominent classes of the backwoods people. The frontier, in spite of the outward uniformity of means and manners, is pre-eminently the place of sharp contrasts. The two extremes of society—the strongest, best, and most adventurous, and the weakest, most shiftless, and vicious—are those which seem naturally to drift to the border. Most of the men who came to the backwoods to hew out homes and rear families were stern, manly, and honest; but there was also a large influx of people drawn from the worst immigrants that perhaps ever were brought to America—the mass of convict servants, redemptioners, and the like, who formed such an excessively undesirable substratum to the otherwise excellent population of the tidewater regions in Virginia and the Carolinas. Many of the Southern crackers or poor whites spring from this class, which also in the backwoods gave birth to generations of violent and hardened criminals, and to an even greater number of shiftless, lazy, cowardly cumberers of the earth's surface. They had in many places a permanently bad effect upon the tone of the whole community.

Moreover, the influence of heredity was no more plainly perceptible than was the extent of individual variation. If a member of a bad family wished to reform, he had every opportunity to do so; if a member of a good family had vicious propensities, there was nothing to check them. All qualities, good and bad, are intensified and accentuated in the life of the wilderness. The man who in civilization is merely sullen and bad-tempered becomes a murderous, treacherous ruffian when transplanted to the wilds; while, on the other hand, his cheery, quiet neighbor develops into a hero, ready uncomplainingly to lay down his life for his friend. One who in an Eastern city is merely a backbiter and slan-

derer, in the Western woods lies in wait for his foe with a
rifle; sharp practice in the East becomes highway robbery in
the West; but at the same time negative good-nature becomes
active self-sacrifice, and a general belief in virtue is trans-
lated into a prompt and determined war upon vice. The
ne'er-do-well of a family who in one place has his debts paid
a couple of times and is then forced to resign from his clubs
and lead a cloudy but innocuous existence on a small pension,
in the other abruptly finishes his career by being hung for
horse-stealing.

In the backwoods the lawless led lives of abandoned wickedness; they hated good for good's sake, and did their utmost to destroy it. Where the bad element was large, gangs
of horse thieves, highwaymen, and other criminals often
united with the uncontrollable young men of vicious tastes,
who were given to gambling, fighting, and the like. They
then formed half-secret organizations, often of great extent
and with wide ramifications; and if they could control a community they established a reign of terror, driving out both
ministers and magistrates, and killing without scruple those
who interfered with them. The good men in such a case
banded themselves together as regulators and put down the
wicked with ruthless severity, by the exercise of lynch-law,
shooting and hanging the worst offhand.*

Jails were scarce in the wilderness, and often were entirely wanting in a district, which, indeed, was quite likely
to lack legal officers also. If punishment was inflicted at all
it was apt to be severe, and took the form of death or whipping. An impromptu jury of neighbors decided with a rough-
and-ready sense of fair play and justice what punishment the
crime demanded, and then saw to the execution of their own
decree. Whipping was the usual reward for theft. Occasionally,
torture was resorted to, but not often; and, to their honor be
it said, the backwoodsmen were horrified at the treatment

---

* The regulators of backwoods society corresponded exactly to the
vigilantes of the Western border to-day. In many of the cases of lynch-
law which have come to my knowledge the effect has been healthy for
the community; but sometimes great injustice is done. Generally, the vigilantes, by a series of summary executions, do really good work; but I
have rarely known them fail, among the men whom they killed for good
reason, to also kill one or two either by mistake or to gratify private
malice.

accorded both to black slaves and to white convict servants in the lowlands.

They were superstitious, of course, believing in witchcraft and signs and omens; and it may be noted that their superstition showed a singular mixture of Old World survivals and of practices borrowed from the savages or evolved by the very force of their strange surroundings. At the bottom they were deeply religious in their tendencies; and although ministers and meeting-houses were rare, yet the backwoods cabins often contained Bibles, and the mothers used to instill into the minds of their children reverence for Sunday, while many even of the hunters refused to hunt on that day. Those of them who knew the right honestly tried to live up to it, in spite of the manifold temptations to backsliding offered by their lives of hard and fierce contention. But Calvinism, though more congenial to them than Episcopacy, and infinitely more so than Catholicism, was too cold for the fiery hearts of the borderers; they were not stirred to the depths of their natures till other creeds, and, above all, Methodism, worked their way into the wilderness.

Thus the backwoodsmen lived on the clearings they had hewed out of the everlasting forest; a grim, stern people, strong and simple, powerful for good and evil, swayed by gusts of stormy passion, the love of freedom rooted in their very hearts' core. Their lives were harsh and narrow, they gained their bread by their blood and sweat, in the unending struggle with the wild ruggedness of nature. They suffered terrible injuries at the hands of the red men, and on their foes they waged a terrible warfare in return. They were relentless, revengeful, suspicious, knowing neither ruth nor pity; they were also upright, resolute, and fearless, loyal to their friends, and devoted to their country. In spite of their many failings, they were of all men the best fitted to conquer the wilderness and hold it against all comers.

Chapter IV

Boone and the Long Hunters; and Their Hunting in No-Man's Land

THE AMERICAN backwoodsmen had surged up, wave upon wave, till their mass trembled in the troughs of the Alleghanies, ready to flood the continent beyond. The peoples threatened by them were dimly conscious of the danger which as yet only loomed in the distance. Far off, among their quiet adobe villages, in the sun-scorched lands by the Rio Grande, the slow Indo-Iberian peons and their monkish masters still walked in the tranquil steps of their fathers, ignorant of the growth of the power that was to overwhelm their children and successors; but nearer by, Spaniard and creole Frenchman, Algonquin, and Appalachians were all uneasy as they began to feel the first faint pressure of the American advance.

As yet they had been shielded by the forest which lay over the land like an unrent mantle. All through the mountains, and far beyond, it stretched without a break; but toward the mouth of the Kentucky and Cumberland rivers the landscape became varied with open groves of woodland, with flower-strewn glades and great barrens or prairies of long grass. This region, one of the fairest in the world, was the debatable ground between the Northern and the Southern Indians. Neither dared dwell therein, but both used it as their hunting-grounds; and it was traversed from end to end by the well-marked war traces which they followed when they invaded each other's territory. The whites, on trying to break through the barrier which hemmed them in from the Western lands, naturally succeeded best when pressing along the line of least resistance; and so their first great advance was made in this debatable land, where the uncertainly defined hunting-grounds of the Cherokee, Creek, and Chickasaw marched upon those of Northern Algonquin and Wyandot.

Unknown and unnamed hunters and Indian traders had from time to time pushed some little way into the wilderness; and they had been followed by others of whom we do indeed know the names, but little more. One explorer had found and named the Cumberland river and mountains, and the great pass called Cumberland Gap. Others had gone far beyond the utmost limits this man had reached, and had hunted in the great bend of the Cumberland and in the woodland region of Kentucky, famed amongst the Indians for the abundance of the game. But their accounts excited no more than a passing interest; they came and went without comment, as lonely stragglers had come and gone for nearly a century. The backwoods civilization crept slowly westward without being influenced in its movements by their explorations.

Finally, however, among these hunters one arose whose wanderings were to bear fruit, who was destined to lead through the wilderness the first body of settlers that ever established a community in the far West, completely cut off from the seaboard colonies. This was Daniel Boone. He was born in Pennsylvania in 1734, but when only a boy had been brought with the rest of his family to the banks of the Yadkin in North Carolina. Here he grew up, and as soon as he came of age he married, built a log hut, and made a clearing, whereon to farm like the rest of his backwoods neighbors. They all tilled their own clearings, guiding the plough among the charred stumps left when the trees were chopped down and the land burned over, and they were all, as a matter of course, hunters. With Boone, hunting and exploration were passions, and the lonely life of the wilderness, with its bold, wild freedom, the only existence for which he really cared. He was a tall, spare, sinewy man, with eyes like an eagle's, and muscles that never tired; the toil and hardship of his life made no impress on his iron frame, unhurt by intemperance of any kind, and he lived for eighty-six years, a backwoods hunter to the end of his days. His thoughtful, quiet, pleasant face, so often portrayed, is familiar to every one;

it was the face of a man who never blustered nor bullied, who would neither inflict nor suffer any wrong, and who had a limitless fund of fortitude, endurance, and indomitable resolution upon which to draw when fortune proved adverse. His self-command and patience, his daring, restless love of adventure, and, in time of danger, his absolute trust in his own powers and resources, all combined to render him peculiarly fitted to follow the career of which he was so fond.

Boone hunted on the Western waters at an early date. In the valley of Boone's Creek, a tributary of the Watauga, there is a beech-tree still standing, on which can be faintly traced an inscription setting forth that "D. Boon cilled a bar on [this] tree in the year 1760." On the expeditions of which this is the earliest record he was partly hunting on his own account, and partly exploring on behalf of another, Richard Henderson. Henderson was a prominent citizen of North Carolina, a speculative man of great ambition and energy. He stood high in the colony, was extravagant and fond of display, and his fortune being jeopardized, he hoped to more than retrieve it by going into speculation in Western lands on an unheard-of scale; for he intended to try to establish on his own account a great proprietary colony beyond the mountains. He had great confidence in Boone; and it was his backing which enabled the latter to turn his discoveries to such good account.

Boone's claim to distinction rests not so much on his wide wanderings in unknown lands, for in this respect he did little more than was done by a hundred other backwoods hunters of his generation, but on the fact that he was able to turn his daring woodcraft to the advantage of his fellows. As he himself said, he was an instrument "ordained of God to settle the wilderness." He inspired confidence in all who met him, so that the men of means and influence were willing to trust adventurous enterprises to his care; and his success as an explorer, his skill as a hunter, and his prowess as an Indian fighter, enabled him to bring these enterprises to a successful conclusion, and in some degree to control the wild spirits associated with him.

Boone's expeditions into the edges of the wilderness whetted his appetite for the unknown. He had heard of great hunting-grounds in the far interior from a stray hunter and Indian trader, who had himself seen them, and on May 1, 1769, he left his home on the Yadkin "to wander through the wilderness of America in quest of the country of Kentucky." He was accompanied by five other men, including his informant, and struck out toward the Northwest, through the tangled mass of rugged mountains and gloomy forests. During five weeks of severe toil the little band journeyed through vast solitudes, whose utter loneliness can with difficulty be understood by those who have not themselves dwelt and hunted in primeval mountain forests. Then, early in June, the adventurers broke through the interminable wastes of dim woodland, and stood on the threshold of the beautiful blue-grass region of Kentucky; a land of running waters, of groves and glades, of prairies, cane-brakes, and stretches of lofty forest. It was teeming with game. The shaggy-maned herds of unwieldy buffalo—the bison, as they should be called—had beaten out broad roads through the forests, and had furrowed the prairies with trails along which they had travelled for countless generations. The round-horned elk, with spreading, massive antlers, the lordliest of the deer tribe throughout the world, abounded, and like the buffalo travelled in bands not only through the woods but also across the reaches of waving grass-land. The deer were extraordinarily numerous, and so were bears, while wolves and panthers were plentiful. Wherever there was a salt-spring the country was fairly thronged with wild beasts of many kinds. For six months Boone and his companions enjoyed such hunting as had hardly fallen to men of their race since the Germans came out of the Hercynian forest.

In December, however, they were attacked by Indians. The attack was entirely unprovoked. The Indians had wantonly shed the first blood. The land belonged to no one tribe, but was hunted over by all, each feeling jealous of every other intruder; they attacked the whites, not because the whites had wronged them, but because their invariable policy was to kill any strangers on any grounds over which they themselves ever hunted, no matter what man had the best rights thereto. The Kentucky hunters were promptly taught that in this No-man's land, teeming with game and lacking even a solitary human habitation, every Indian must be regarded as a foe.

Boone, having been joined by his brother, Squire Boone—

himself a woodsman of but little less skill—remained on his
hunting-grounds throughout the winter, living in a little cabin.
About the 1st of May Squire set off alone to the settlements to
procure horses and ammunition. For three months Daniel
Boone remained absolutely alone in the wilderness, without
salt, sugar, or flour, and without the companionship of so
much as a horse or a dog.* But the solitude-loving hunter,
dauntless and self-reliant, enjoyed to the full his wild, lonely
life; he passed his days hunting and exploring, wandering
hither and thither over the country, while at night he lay off
in the cane-brake or thickets, without a fire, so as not to
attract the Indians. Of the latter he saw many signs, and
they sometimes came into his camp, but his sleepless wariness
enabled him to avoid capture.

Late in July his brother returned, and met him according to
appointment at the old camp. Other hunters also now came
into the Kentucky wilderness, and Boone joined a small
party of them for a short time. Such a party of hunters is
always glad to have anything wherewith to break the irksome
monotony of the long evenings passed round the camp-fire;
and a book or a greasy pack of cards was as welcome in a
camp of Kentucky riflemen in 1770 as it is to a party of
Rocky Mountain hunters in 1888. Boone has recorded in
his own quaint phraseology an incident of his life during this
summer, which shows how eagerly such a little band of frontiersmen read a book, and how real its characters became to
their minds. He was encamped with five other men on Red
River, and they had with them for their "amusement the
history of Samuel Gulliver's travels, wherein he gave an
account of his young master, Glundelick, careing [sic] him
on a market day for a show to a town called Lulbegrud." In
the party who, amid such strange surroundings, read and
listened to Dean Swift's writings was a young man named

---

* His remaining absolutely alone in the wilderness for such a length of
time is often spoken of with wonder; but here again Boone stands merely
as the backwoods type, not as an exception. To this day many hunters in
the Rockies do the same. In 1880, two men whom I knew wintered to the
west of the Bighorns, 150 miles from any human beings. They had salt
and flour, however; but they were nine months without seeing a white
face. They killed elk, buffalo, and a moose; and had a narrow escape
from a small Indian war-party. Last winter (1887-88) an old trapper,
a friend of mine in the days when he hunted buffalo, spent five months
entirely alone in the mountains north of the Flathead country.

Alexander Neely. One night he came into camp with two Indian scalps, taken from a Shawnee village he had found on a creek running into the river; and he announced to the circle of grim wilderness veterans that "he had been that day to Lulbegrud, and had killed two Brobdignags in their capital." To this day the creek by which the two luckless Shawnees lost their lives is known as Lulbegrud Creek.*

Other hunters, of whom we know even the names of only a few, had been through many parts of the wilderness before Boone, and earlier still Frenchmen had built forts and smelting-furnaces on the Cumberland, the Tennessee, and the head tributaries of the Kentucky. Boone is interesting as a leader and explorer; but he is still more interesting as a type. The West was neither discovered, won, nor settled by any single man. No keen-eyed statesman planned the movement, nor was it carried out by any great military leader; it was the work of a whole people, of whom each man was impelled mainly by sheer love of adventure; it was the outcome of the ceaseless strivings of all the dauntless, restless backwoods folk to win homes for their descendants and to each penetrate deeper than his neighbors into the remote forest hunting-grounds where the perilous pleasures of the chase and of war could be best enjoyed. We owe the conquest of the West to all the backwoodsmen, not to any solitary individual among them; where all alike were strong and daring there was no chance for any single man to rise to unquestioned pre-eminence.

In the summer of 1769 a large band of hunters crossed the mountains to make a long hunt in the Western wilderness, the men clad in hunting-shirts, moccasins, and leggings, with traps, rifles, and dogs, and each bringing with him two or three horses. They made a permanent camp in one place, and returned to it at intervals to deposit their skins and peltries. At the end of the year some of the adventurers returned home; others went north into the Kentucky country, where they hunted for several months before recrossing the moun-

---

* Frontiersmen are often content with the merest printed trash; but the better men among them appreciate really good literature quite as much as any other class of people. In the long winter evenings they study to good purpose books as varied as Dante, Josephus, Macaulay, Longfellow, Parton's "Life of Jackson," and the Rollo stories—to mention only volumes that have been especial favorites with my own cowboys and hunters.

tains; while the remainder, led by an old hunter named Kasper Mansker, built two boats and hollowed out of logs two pirogues or dugouts—clumsier but tougher craft than the light birch-bark canoes—and started down the Cumberland. They went down to Natchez, sold their furs, hides, oil, and tallow, and some returned by sea while others, including Mansker, came overland with a drove of horses that was being taken through the Indian nations to Georgia. From the length of time all these men, as well as Boone and his companions, were absent, they were known as the Long Hunters, and the fame of their hunting and exploring spread all along the border and greatly excited the young men.

The rude and fragmentary annals of the frontier are filled with the deeds of men, of whom Mansker can be taken as a type. He was a wonderful marksman and woodsman, and was afterward made a colonel of the frontier militia, though being of German descent, he spoke only broken English. Like most of the hunters he became specially proud of his rifle, calling it "Nancy"; for they were very apt to know each his favorite weapon by some homely or endearing nickname. Every forest sight or sound was familiar to him. He knew the cries of the birds and beasts so well that no imitation could deceive him. Once he was nearly taken in by an unusually perfect imitation of a wild gobbler; but he finally became suspicious, and "placed" his adversary behind a large tree. Having perfect confidence in his rifle, and knowing that the Indians rarely fired except at close range—partly because they were poor shots, partly because they loaded their guns too lightly—he made no attempt to hide. Feigning to pass to the Indian's right, the latter, as he expected, tried to follow him; reaching an opening in a glade, Mansker suddenly wheeled and killed his foe. When hunting he made his home sometimes in a hollow tree, sometimes in a hut of buffalo-hides; for the buffalo were so plenty that once when a lick was discovered by himself and a companion, the latter, though on horseback, was nearly trampled to death by the mad rush of a herd they surprised and stampeded.

The hunters were the pioneers; but close behind them came another set of explorers quite as hardy and resolute. These were the surveyors. The men of chain and compass played a part in the exploration of the West scarcely inferior to that of the heroes of axe and rifle. Often, indeed, the parts were combined; Boone himself was a surveyor. Vast tracts of Western land were continually being allotted either to actual settlers or as bounties to soldiers who had served against the French and Indians. These had to be explored and mapped, and as there was much risk as well as reward in the task it naturally proved attractive to all adventurous young men who had some education, a good deal of ambition, and not too much fortune. A great number of young men of good families, like Washington and Clark, went into the business. Soon after the return of Boone and the Long Hunters, parties of surveyors came down the Ohio, mapping out its course and exploring the Kentucky lands that lay beside it.

Among the hunters, surveyors, and explorers who came into the wilderness in 1773 was a band led by three young men named McAfee—typical backwoodsmen, hardy, adventurous, their frontier recklessness and license tempered by the Calvinism they had learned in their rough log home. They were fond of hunting, but they came to spy out the land and see if it could be made into homes for their children; and in their party were several surveyors. They descended the Ohio in dugout canoes, with their rifles, blankets, tomahawks, and fishing-tackle. They met some Shawnees and got on well with them; but while their leader was visiting the chief, Cornstalk, and listening to his fair speeches at his town of old Chillicothe, the rest of the party were startled to see a band of young Shawnee braves returning from a successful foray on the settlements, driving before them the laden pack-horses they had stolen.

They explored part of Kentucky, and visited the different licks. One, long named Big Bone Lick, was famous because there were scattered about it in incredible quantity the gigantic remains of the extinct mastodon; the McAfees made a tent by stretching their blankets over the huge fossil ribs, and used the disjointed vertebræ as stools on which to sit. Game of many kinds thronged the spaces round the licks; herds of buffalo, elk, and deer, as well as bears and wolves, were all in sight at once. The ground roundabout some of them was trodden down so that there was not as much grass left as would feed a sheep; and the game trails were like streets, or the beaten roads round a city. A little village to this day recalls by its name the fact that it stands on a former "stamp-ing-ground" of the buffalo. At one lick the explorers met with what might have proved a serious adventure. One of the McAfees and a companion were passing round its out-skirts, when some others of the party fired at a gang of buffa-loes, which stampeded directly toward the two. While his companion scampered up a leaning mulberry-bush, McAfee, less agile, leaped behind a tree trunk, where he stood side-ways till the buffalo passed, their horns scraping off the bark on either side; then he looked round to see his friend "hang-ing in the mulberry-bush like a coon."*

In Powell's Valley, on the way home, the party met other wanderers whose toil and peril had just begun. There they encountered the company which Daniel Boone was just leading across the mountains, with the hope of making a permanent settlement in the far-distant Kentucky. Boone had sold his farm on the Yadkin and all the goods he could not carry with him, and in September, 1773, he started for Kentucky with his wife and his children; five families, and forty men besides, went with him, driving their horses and cattle. It was the first attempt that was made to settle a region separated by long stretches of wil-derness from the already inhabited districts; and it was doomed to failure. On approaching the gloomy and forbidding defiles of the Cumberland Mountains the party was attacked by In-dians. Six of the men, including Boone's eldest son, were slain, and the cattle scattered; and though the backwoodsmen rallied and repulsed their assailants, yet they had suffered such loss and damage that they returned and took up their abode temporarily on the Clinch River.

In the following year numerous parties of surveyors visited the land. One of these was headed by John Floyd, who was among the ablest of the Kentucky pioneers, and afterward played a prominent part in the young commonwealth, until his death at the hands of the savages. They started on April 9, 1774—eight men in all—from their homes in Fincastle County. They went down the Kanawha in a canoe, shooting bear and deer, and catching great pike and catfish. The first

---

* A similar adventure befell my brother Elliott and my cousin John Roosevelt while they were hunting buffalo on the staked plains of Texas in 1877.

survey they made was one of two thousand acres for "Colo. Washington"; and they made another for Patrick Henry.

At the mouth of the Kanawha the adventurers found twenty or thirty men gathered together; some had come to settle, but most wished to explore or survey the lands. All were in high spirits, and resolute to go to Kentucky, in spite of Indian hostilities. Some of them joined Floyd, and raised his party to eighteen men, who started down the Ohio in four canoes. They found "a battoe loaded with corn," apparently abandoned, and took about three bushels with them. Other parties joined them from time to time, as they paddled and drifted down the stream; and one or two of their own number, alarmed by further news of Indian hostilities, went back. Once they met a party of Delawares, by whom they were not molested; and again, two or three of their number encountered a couple of hostile savages; and though no one was hurt, the party was kept on the watch all the time. They marvelled much at the great trees—one sycamore was thirty-seven feet in circumference—and on a Sunday, which they kept as a day of rest, they examined with interest the forest-covered embankments of a fort at the mouth of the Scioto, a memorial of the mound-builders who had vanished centuries before.

When they reached the mouth of the Kentucky they found two Delawares and a squaw, to whom they gave corn and salt. Here they split up, and Floyd and his original party spent a week in the neighborhood, surveying land, going some distance up the Kentucky to a salt-lick, where they saw a herd of three hundred buffalo. They then again embarked, and drifted down the Ohio. On May 26th they met two Delawares in a canoe flying a red flag; they had been sent down the river with a pass from the commandant at Fort Pitt to gather their hunters and get them home, in view of the threatened hostilities between the Shawnees and Virginians. The actions of the two Indians were so suspicious, and the news they brought was so alarming, that some of Floyd's companions became greatly alarmed, and wished to go straight on down the Mississippi; but Floyd swore that he would finish his work unless actually forced off. Three days afterward they reached the falls.

Here Floyd spent a fortnight, making surveys in every direction, and then started off to explore the land between the

Salt River and the Kentucky. Like the others, he carried his own pack, which consisted of little but his blanket and his instruments. He sometimes had difficulties with his men. One of them refused to carry the chain one day, and went off to hunt, got lost, and was not found for thirty-six hours. Another time it was noticed that two of the hunters had become sullen, and seemed anxious to leave camp. The following morning, while on the march, the party killed an elk and halted for breakfast; but the two hunters walked on, and, says the journal, "we never saw them more"; but whether they got back to the settlements or perished in the wilderness, none could tell.

The party suffered much hardship. Floyd fell sick, and for three days could not travel. They gave him an "Indian sweat," probably building just such a little sweat-house as the Indians use to this day. Others of their number at different times fell ill; and they were ever on the watch for Indians. In the vast forests, every sign of a human being was the sign of a probable enemy. Once they heard a gun, and another time a sound as of a man calling to another; and on each occasion they redoubled their caution, keeping guard as they rested, and at night extinguishing their camp-fire and sleeping a mile or two from it.

They built a bark canoe in which to cross the Kentucky, and on the 1st of July they met another party of surveyors on the banks of that stream. Two or three days afterward, Floyd and three companions left the others, agreeing to meet them on August 1st, at a cabin built by a man named Harwood, on the south side of the Kentucky, a few miles from the mouth of the Elkhorn. For three weeks they surveyed and hunted, enchanted with the beauty of the country. They then went to the cabin, several days before the appointed time; but to their surprise found everything scattered over the ground, and two fires burning, while on a tree near the landing was written: "Alarmed by finding some people killed and we are gone down." This left the four adventurers in a bad plight, as they had but fifteen rounds of powder left, and none of them knew the way home. However, there was no help for it, and they started off. When they came to the mountains they found it such hard going that they were obliged to throw away their blankets and everything else except their rifles, hunting-shirts, leggings, and moccasins. Like the other parties of returning explorers, they found this portion of their journey extremely distressing; and they suffered much from sore feet, and also from want of food, until they came on a gang of buffaloes and killed two. At last they struck Cumberland Gap, followed a blazed trail across it to Powell's Valley, and on August 9th came to the outlying settlements on Clinch River, where they found the settlers all in their wooden forts, because of the war with the Shawnees.

The outbreak of the Indian war caused all the hunters and surveyors to leave Kentucky; and at the end of 1774 there were no whites left, either there or in what is now middle Tennessee. But on the frontier all men's eyes were turned toward these new and fertile regions. The pioneer work of the hunter was over, and that of the axe-bearing settler was about to begin.

Chapter V

Sevier, Robertson, and the Watauga Commonwealth

SOON after the successful ending of the last colonial struggle with France, and the conquest of Canada, the British king issued a proclamation forbidding the English colonists from trespassing on Indian grounds, or moving west to the mountains. But in 1768, at the treaty of Fort Stanwix, the Six Nations agreed to surrender to the English all the lands lying between the Ohio and the Tennessee; and this treaty was at once seized upon by the backwoodsmen as offering an excuse for settling beyond the mountains. However, the Iroquois had ceded lands to which they had no more right than a score or more of other Indian tribes; and these latter, not having been consulted, felt at perfect liberty to make war on the intruders. In point of fact, no one tribe or set of tribes could cede Kentucky or Tennessee, because no one tribe or set of tribes owned either. The great hunting-grounds between the Ohio and the Tennessee formed a debatable land, claimed by every tribe that could hold its own against its rivals.

The eastern part of what is now Tennessee consists of a great hill-strewn, forest-clad valley, running from northeast to southwest, bounded on one side by the Cumberland, and on the other by the Great Smoky and Unaka mountains; the latter separating it from North Carolina. In this valley arise and end the Clinch, the Holston, the Watauga, the Noli-chucky, the French Broad, and the other streams, whose combined volume makes the Tennessee River. The upper end of the valley lies in southwestern Virginia, the headwaters of some of the rivers being well within that State; and though the province was really part of North Carolina, it was separated therefrom by high mountain chains, while from Virginia it was easy to follow the watercourses down the valley. Thus, as elsewhere among the mountains forming the Western frontier, the first movements of population went parallel with, rather than across, the ranges. As in western Virginia the first settlers came, for the most part, from Pennsylvania, so, in turn, in what was then western North Carolina, and is now eastern Tennessee, the first settlers came mainly from Virginia, and, indeed, in great part, from this same Pennsylvania stock. Of course, in each case there was also a very considerable movement directly westward. They were a sturdy race, enterprising and intelligent, fond of the strong excitement inherent in the adventurous frontier life.

In 1769, the year that Boone first went to Kentucky, the first permanent settlers came to the banks of the Watauga, the settlement being merely an enlargement of the Virginia settlement, which had for a short time existed on the headwaters of the Holston, especially near Wolf Hills. At first the settlers thought they were still in the domain of Virginia, for at that time the line marking her southern boundary had not been run so far west. Indeed, had they not considered the land as belonging to Virginia, they would probably not at the moment have dared to intrude farther on territory claimed by the Indians. But while the treaty between the Crown and the Iroquois at Fort Stanwix had resulted in the cession of whatever right the Six Nations had to the southwestern territory, another treaty was concluded about the same time with the Cherokees [the Treaty of Hard Labor, 1768], by which the latter agreed to surrender their claims to a small portion of this country, though as a matter of fact before the treaty was signed white settlers had crowded beyond the limits allowed them. These two treaties, in the first of which one set of tribes surrendered a small portion of land, while in the second an entirely different confederacy surrendered a large tract, which, however, included part of the first cession, are sufficient to show the absolute confusion of the Indian land titles.

But in 1771, one of the newcomers, Anthony Bledsoe, who was a practical surveyor, ran out the Virginia boundary-line some distance to the westward, and discovered that the Watauga settlement came within the limits of North Carolina. Hitherto the settlers had supposed that they themselves were governed by the Virginia law, and that their rights as against the Indians were guaranteed by the Virginian government; but this discovery threw them back upon their own resources. They suddenly found themselves obliged to organize a civil government, under which they themselves should live, and at the same time to enter into a treaty on their own account with the neighboring Indians, to whom the land they were on apparently belonged.

The first need was even more pressing than the second. North Carolina was always a turbulent and disorderly colony, unable to enforce law and justice even in the long-settled districts; so that it was wholly out of the question to appeal to her for aid in governing a remote and outlying community. Moreover, about the time that the Watauga commonwealth was founded, the troubles in North Carolina came to a head. Open war ensued between the adherents of the royal governor, Tryon, on the one hand, and the Regulators, as the insurgents styled themselves, on the other, the struggle ending with the overthrow of the Regulators at the battle of the Alamance.

As a consequence of these troubles, many people from the back counties of North Carolina crossed the mountains, and took up their abode among the pioneers on the Watauga and upper Holston; the beautiful valley of the Nolichucky soon receiving its share of this stream of immigration. Among the first comers were many members of the class of desperate adventurers always to be found hanging round the outskirts of frontier civilization. Horse thieves, murderers, escaped bond-servants, runaway debtors—all, in fleeing from the law, sought to find a secure asylum in the wilderness. The brutal and lawless wickedness of these men, whose uncouth and raw savagery was almost more repulsive than that of city criminals, made it imperative upon the decent members of the community to unite for self-protection. The desperadoes were often mere human beasts of prey; they plundered whites and Indians impartially. They not only by their thefts and murders exasperated the Indians into retaliating on innocent whites, but, on the other hand, they also often deserted their own color and went to live among the redskins, becoming their leaders in the worst outrages.

But the bulk of the settlers were men of sterling worth, fit to be the pioneer fathers of a mighty and beautiful State. Two of their number already towered head and shoulders above the rest in importance, and merit especial mention; for they were destined for the next thirty years to play the chief parts in the history of that portion of the Southwest which largely through their own efforts became the State of Tennessee. These two men, neither of them yet thirty years of age, were John Sevier and James Robertson.

Robertson first came to the Watauga early in 1770. He had then been married for two years, and had been "learning his letters and to spell" from his well-educated wife; for he belonged to a backwoods family, even poorer than the average, and he had not so much as received the rudimentary education that could be acquired at an "old-field" school. But he was a man of remarkable natural powers, above the medium height, with wiry, robust form, light-blue eyes, fair complexion, and dark hair; his somewhat sombre face had in it a look of self-contained strength that made it impressive; and his taciturn, quiet, masterful way of dealing with men and affairs, together with his singular mixture of cool caution and most adventurous daring, gave him an immediate hold even upon such lawless spirits as those of the border. He was a mighty hunter; but, unlike Boone, hunting and exploration were to him secondary affairs, and he came to examine the lands with the eye of a pioneer settler. He intended to have a home where he could bring up his family, and, if possible, he wished to find rich lands, with good springs, whereto he might lead those of his neighbors who, like himself, eagerly desired to rise in the world, and to provide for the well-being of their children.

To find such a country, Robertson, then dwelling in North Carolina, decided to go across the mountains. He started off alone on his exploring expedition, rifle in hand, and a good horse under him. He crossed the ranges that continue northward the Great Smokies, and spent the summer in the beautiful hill-country where the springs of the Western waters flowed from the ground. He had never seen so lovely a land. The high valleys, through which the currents ran, were hemmed in by towering mountain walls, with cloud-capped peaks. The fertile loam forming the bottoms was densely covered with the growth of the primeval forest, broken here and there by glade-like openings, where herds of game grazed on the tall, thick grass.

Robertson was well treated by the few settlers, and stayed long enough to raise a crop of corn, the stand-by of the backwoods pioneer; like every other hunter, explorer, Indian fighter, and wilderness wanderer, he lived on the game he shot, and the small quantity of maize he was able to carry with him. In the late fall, however, when recrossing the mountain on his way home through the trackless forests, both game and corn failed him. He lost his way, was forced to abandon his horse among impassable precipices, and finally found his rifle useless, owing to the powder having become soaked. For fourteen days he lived almost wholly on nuts and wild berries, and was on the point of death from starvation when he met two hunters on horseback, who fed him and let him ride their horses by turns, and brought him safely to his home.

Such hardships were little more than matter-of-course incidents in a life like his; and he at once prepared to set out with his family for the new land. His accounts greatly excited his neighbors, and sixteen families made ready to accompany him. The little caravan started, under Robertson's guidance, as soon as the ground had dried after the winter rains in the spring of 1771. They travelled in the usual style of backwoods emigrants; the men on foot, rifle on shoulder, the elder children driving the lean cows, while the women, the young children, and the few household goods and implements of husbandry were carried on the backs of the pack-horses; for in settling the backwoods during the last century, the pack-horse played the same part that in the present century was taken by the canvas-covered emigrant wagon, the white-topped "prairie-schooner."

Once arrived at the Watauga, the Carolina newcomers mixed readily with the few Virginians already on the ground; and Robertson speedily became one of the leading men in the little settlement. On an island in the river he built a house of logs with the bark still on them on the outside, though hewed smooth within; tradition says that it was the largest in the settlement. Certainly it belonged to the better class of backwoods cabins, with a loft and several rooms, a roof of split saplings, held down by weighty poles, a log veranda in front, and a huge fireplace of sticks and stones laid in clay, wherein the pile of blazing logs roared loudly in cool weather. The furniture was probably precisely like that in other houses of the class; a rude bed, table, settee, and chest of drawers, a spinning-jenny, and either three-legged stools or else chairs with backs and seats of undressed deer-hides. Robertson's energy and his remarkable natural ability brought him to the front at once, in every way; although, as already said, he had much less than even the average backwoods education, for he could not read when he was married, while most of the frontiersmen could not only read but also write, or at least sign their names.

Sevier, who came to the Watauga early in 1772, nearly a year after Robertson and his little colony had arrived, differed widely from his friend in almost every respect save high-mindedness and dauntless, invincible courage. He was a gentleman by birth and breeding, the son of a Huguenot who had settled in the Shenandoah valley. He had received a fair education, and though never fond of books, he was to the end of his days an interested and intelligent observer of men and things, both in America and Europe. He corresponded on intimate and equal terms with Madison, Franklin, and others of our most polished statesmen; while Robertson's letters, when he had finally learned to write them himself, were almost as remarkable for their phenomenally bad spelling as for their shrewd common sense and homely, straightforward honesty. Sevier was a very handsome man; during his lifetime he was reputed the handsomest in Tennessee. He was tall, fair-skinned, blue-eyed, brown-haired, of slender build, with erect, military carriage and commanding bearing, his lithe, finely proportioned figure being well set off by the hunting-shirt which he almost invariably wore. From his French forefathers he inherited a gay, pleasure-loving temperament, that made him the most charming of companions. His manners were polished and easy, and he had great natural dignity. Over the backwoodsmen he exercised an almost unbounded influence, due as much to his ready tact, invariable courtesy, and lavish, generous hospitality as to the skill and dashing prowess which made him the most renowned Indian fighter of the Southwest. He had an eager, impetuous nature, and was very ambitious, being almost as fond of popularity as of Indian fighting. He was already married and the father of two children when he came to the Watauga, and, like Robertson, was seeking a new and better home for his family in the West. So far, his life had been as uneventful as that of any other spirited young borderer; his business had been that of a frontier Indian trader; he had taken part in one or two unimportant Indian skirmishes. Later, he was commissioned by Lord Dunmore as a captain in the Virginia line.

Such were Sevier and Robertson, the leaders in the little frontier outpost of civilization that was struggling to maintain itself on the Watauga; and these two men afterward proved themselves to be, with the exception of George Rogers Clark, the greatest of the first generation of Trans-Alleghany pioneers.

Their followers were worthy of them. All alike were keenly alive to the disadvantages of living in a community where there was neither law nor officer to enforce it. Accordingly, with their characteristic capacity for combination, so striking as existing together with the equally characteristic capacity for individual self-help, the settlers determined to organize a government of their own. They promptly put their resolution into effect early in the spring of 1772, Robertson being apparently the leader in the movement.

They decided to adopt written articles of agreement, by which their conduct should be governed; and these were known as the Articles of the Watauga Association. They formed a written constitution, the first ever adopted west of the mountains, or by a community composed of American-born freemen. It is this fact of the early independence and self-government of the settlers along the headwaters of the Tennessee that gives to their history its peculiar importance. They were the first men of American birth to establish a free and independent community on the continent. Even before this date, there had been straggling settlements of Pennsylvanians and Virginians along the headwaters of the Ohio; but these settlements remained mere parts of the colonies behind them, and neither grew into a separate community, nor played a distinctive part in the growth of the West.

The first step taken by the Watauga settlers, when they had determined to organize, was to meet in general convention, holding a kind of folk-thing, akin to the New England town meeting. They then elected a representative assembly, a small parliament or "witanagemot," which met at Robertson's station. Apparently the freemen of each little fort or palisaded village, each blockhouse that was the centre of a group of detached cabins and clearings, sent a member to this first frontier legislature. It consisted of thirteen representatives, who proceeded to elect from their number five—among them Sevier and Robertson—to form a committee or court, which should carry on the actual business of government, and should exercise both judicial and executive functions. This court had a clerk and a sheriff, or executive officer, who respectively recorded and enforced their decrees.

The five members of this court, who are sometimes referred to as arbitrators and sometimes as commissioners, had entire control of all matters affecting the common weal; and all affairs in controversy were settled by the decision of a majority. On behalf of the community itself, they were not only permitted to control its internal affairs, but also to secure lands by making treaties with a foreign power, the Indians—a distinct exercise of the right of sovereignty. They heard and adjudicated all cases of difference between the settlers themselves; and took measures for the common safety. In fact, the dwellers, in this little outlying frontier commonwealth, exercised the rights of full statehood for a number of years; establishing in true American style a purely democratic government with representative institutions, in which, under certain restrictions, the will of the majority was supreme, while, nevertheless, the largest individual freedom and the utmost liberty of individual initiative were retained. The framers showed the American predilection for a written constitution or civil compact; and, what was more important, they also showed the common-sense American spirit that led them to adopt the scheme of government which should in the simplest way best serve their need, without bothering their heads over mere high-sounding abstractions.

The court or committee held their sessions at stated and regular times, and took the law of Virginia as their standard for decisions. They saw to the recording of deeds and wills, settled all questions of debt, issued marriage licenses, and carried on a most vigorous warfare against law-breakers, especially horse thieves. For six years their government continued in full vigor; then, in February, 1778, North Carolina having organized Washington County, which included all of what is now Tennessee, the governor of that State appointed justices of the peace and militia officers for the new county, and the old system came to an end. But Sevier, Robertson, and their fellow committeemen were all members of the new court, and continued almost without change their former simple system of procedure and direct and expeditious methods of administering justice; as justices of the peace they merely continued to act as they acted while arbitrators of the Watauga Association, and in their summary mode of dealing with evil-doers paid a good deal more heed to the essence than to the forms of law. One record shows that a horse thief was arrested on Monday, tried on Wednesday, and hung on Friday of the same week. Another deals with a claimant who, by his attorney, moved to be sworn into his office of clerk, "but the court swore in James Sevier, well knowing that said Sevier had been elected," and being evidently unwilling to waste their time hearing a contested-election case when their minds were already made up as to the equity of the matter. They exercised the right of making suspicious individuals leave the county. They also at times became censors of morals, and interfered with straightforward effectiveness to right wrongs for which a more refined and elaborate system of jurisprudence would have provided only cumbersome and inadequate remedies. Thus one of their entries is to the effect that a certain man is ordered "to return to his family and demean himself as a good citizen, he having admitted in open court that he had left his wife and took up with another woman." From the character of the judges who made the decision, it is safe to presume that the delinquent either obeyed it or else promptly fled to the Indians for safety. This fleeing to the Indians, by the way, was a feat often performed by the worst criminals—for the renegade, the man who had "painted his face" and deserted those of his own color, was a being as well known as he was abhorred and despised on the border, where such a deed was held to be the one unpardonable crime.

Thus the Watauga folk were the first Americans who, as a separate body, moved into the wilderness to hew out dwellings for themselves and their children, trusting only to their own shrewd heads, stout hearts, and strong arms, unhelped and unhampered by the power nominally their sovereign. They built up a commonwealth which had many successors; they showed that the frontiersmen could do their work unassisted; for they not only proved that they were made of stuff stern enough to hold its own against outside pressure of any sort, but they also made it evident that having won the land they were competent to govern both it and themselves. They were the first to do what the whole nation has since done. It has often been said that we owe all our success to our surroundings; that any race with our opportunities could have done as well as we have done. Undoubtedly our opportunities have been great; undoubtedly we have often and lamentably failed in taking advantage of them. But what nation ever has done all that was possible with the chances offered it? The Spaniards, the Portuguese, and the French, not to speak of the Russians in Siberia, have all enjoyed, and yet have failed to make good use of, the same advantages which we have turned to good account. The truth is, that in starting a new nation in a new country, as we have done, while there are exceptional chances to be taken advantage of, there are also exceptional dangers and difficulties to be overcome. None but heroes can succeed wholly in the work. It is a good thing for us at times to compare what we have done with what we could have done had we been better and wiser; it may make us try in the future to raise our abilities to the level of our opportunities. Looked at absolutely, we must frankly acknowledge that we have fallen very far short indeed of the high ideal we should have reached. Looked at relatively, it must also be said that we have done better than any other nation or race working under our conditions.

The Watauga settlers outlined in advance the nation's work. They tamed the rugged and shaggy wilderness, they bid defiance to outside foes, and they successfully solved the difficult problem of self-government.

Chapter VI

Boone and the Settlement of Kentucky

ON the eve of the Revolution, in 1774, the frontiersmen had planted themselves firmly among the Alleghanies. Directly west of them lay the untenanted wilderness, traversed only by the war-parties of the red men and the hunting-parties of both reds and whites. No settlers had yet penetrated it, and until they did so there could be within its borders no chance of race warfare, unless we call by that name the unchronicled and unending contest in which, now and then, some solitary white woodsman slew, or was slain by, his painted foe. But in the Southwest and the Northwest alike, the area of settlement already touched the homelands of the tribes, and hence the horizon was never quite free from the cloud of threatening Indian war; yet for the moment the Southwest was at peace, for the Cherokees were still friendly.

It was in the Northwest that the danger of collision was most imminent; for there the whites and Indians had wronged one another for a generation, and their interests were, at the time, clashing more directly than ever. [In the spring of 1774, in retaliation for murders committed by the settlers,] the savages crossed the frontier in small bands. Soon all the back country was involved in the unspeakable horrors of a bloody Indian war, with its usual accompaniments of burning houses, tortured prisoners, and ruined families; the men being killed and the women and children driven off to a horrible captivity. [The war lasted six months, ending with the victory of the settlers at the Battle of the Great Kanawha in October, 1774.] Its results were of the utmost importance. It kept the northwestern tribes quiet for the first two years of the Revolutionary struggle; and, above all, it rendered possible the settlement of Kentucky, and therefore the winning of the West. Had it not been for Lord Dunmore's war, it is more than likely that when the colonies achieved their freedom they would have found their western boundary fixed at the Alleghany Mountains.

Lord Dunmore's war, waged by Americans for the good of America, was the opening act in the drama whereof the closing scene was played at Yorktown. It made possible the twofold character of the Revolutionary War, wherein on the one hand the Americans won by conquest and colonization new lands for their children, and on the other wrought out their national independence of the British king. Save for Lord Dunmore's war, we could not have settled beyond the mountains until after we had ended our quarrel with our kinsfolk across the sea. It so cowed the Northern Indians that for two or three years they made no further organized effort to check the white advance. Their defeat gave the opportunity for Boone to settle Kentucky, and therefore for Robertson to settle Middle Tennessee, and for Clark to conquer Illinois and the Northwest; it was the first in the chain that gave us for our Western frontier in 1783 the Mississippi and not the Alleghanies.

As already mentioned, the speculative North Carolinian Henderson had for some time been planning the establishment of a proprietary colony beyond the mountains, as a bold stroke to re-establish his ruined fortunes; and early in 1775, as the time seemed favorable, he proceeded to put his venturous scheme into execution. For years he had been in close relations with Boone; and the latter had attempted to lead a band of actual settlers to Kentucky in 1773. Naturally, when Henderson wished to fix on a place wherein to plant his colony, he chose the beautiful land which the rumor of Boone's discovery had rendered famous all along the border; and equally naturally he chose the pioneer hunter himself to act as his lieutenant and as the real leader of the expedition. The result of the joint efforts of these two men was to plant in Kentucky a colony of picked settlers, backed by such moral and material support as enabled them to maintain themselves permanently in the land. Boone had not been the first to discover

Kentucky, nor was he the first to found a settlement therein; but it was his exploration of the land that alone bore lasting fruit, and the settlement he founded was the first that contained within itself the elements of permanence and growth.

Of course, as in every other settlement of inland America, the especial point to be noticed is the individual initiative of the different settlers. Neither the royal nor the provincial governments had anything to do with the various colonies that were planted almost simultaneously on the soil of Kentucky. Each little band of pioneers had its own leaders and was stirred by its own motives. All had heard, from different sources, of the beauty and fertility of the land, and as the great danger from the Indians was temporarily past, all alike went in to take possession, not only acting without previous agreement, but for the most part being even in ignorance of one another's designs. Yet the dangers surrounding these new-formed and far-off settlements were so numerous and of such grave nature, that they could hardly have proved permanent had it not been for the comparatively well-organized settlement of Boone, and for the temporary immunity which Henderson's treaty purchased from the Southern Indians.

The settlement of Kentucky was a much more adventurous and hazardous proceeding than had been the case with any previous westward extension of population from the old colonies; because Kentucky, instead of abutting on already settled districts, was an island in the wilderness, separated by two hundred miles of unpeopled and almost impassable forest from even the extreme outposts of the seacoast commonwealths. The vast belt of mountainous woodland that lay between was as complete a barrier as if it had been a broad arm of the ocean.

Henderson, and those associated with him in his scheme of land speculation, began to open negotiations with the Cherokees as soon as the victory of the Great Kanawha for the moment lessened the danger to be apprehended from the northwestern Indians. On the 17th of March, 1774, they signed with the Indians the treaty of the Sycamore Shoals. Henderson thus obtained a grant of all the lands lying along and between the Kentucky and the Cumberland rivers. He promptly named the new colony Transylvania. The purchase money was ten thousand pounds of lawful English money; but, of course, the payment was made mainly in merchandise and not specie.

It took a number of days before the treaty was finally concluded; no rum was allowed to be sold, and there was little
drunkenness; but herds of beeves were driven in, that the
Indians might make a feast.

The chiefs undoubtedly knew that they could transfer only
a very imperfect title to the land they thus deeded away. Both
Oconostota and Dragging Canoe told the white treaty-makers
that the land beyond the mountains, whither they were going,
was a "dark ground," a "bloody ground"; and warned them
that they must go at their own risk and not hold the Cherokees responsible, for the latter could no longer hold them by
the hand. Dragging Canoe especially told Henderson that
there was a black cloud hanging over the land, for it lay in
the path of the northwestern Indians—who were already at
war with the Cherokees, and would surely show as little mercy
to the white men as to the red. Another old chief said to
Boone: "Brother, we have given you a fine land, but I believe
you will have much trouble in settling it." What he said
was true, and the whites were taught by years of long warfare
that Kentucky was indeed what the Cherokees called it, a
dark and bloody ground.

After Henderson's main treaty was concluded, the Watauga
Association entered into another, by which they secured from
the Cherokees, for two thousand pounds sterling, the lands
they had already leased

As soon as it became evident that the Indians would consent
to the treaty, Henderson sent Boone ahead with a company of
thirty men to clear a trail from the Holston to the Kentucky.
This, the first regular path opened into the wilderness, was long
called Boone's trace, and became forever famous in Kentucky history as the Wilderness Road, the track along which
so many tens of thousands travelled while journeying to their
hoped-for homes in the bountiful West. Boone started on
March 10th with his sturdy band of rifle-bearing axemen,
and chopped out a narrow bridle-path—a pony trail, as it
would now be called in the West. It led over Cumberland
Gap and crossed Cumberland, Laurel, and Rockcastle rivers
at fords that were swimming deep in the time of freshets.
Where it went through tall, open timber, it was marked by
blazes on the tree trunks, while a regular path was cut and

trodden out through the thickets of underbrush and the dense cane-brakes and reed-beds.

After a fortnight's hard work the party had almost reached the banks of the Kentucky River, and deemed that their chief trials were over. But half an hour before daybreak on the morning of the 25th, as they lay around their smouldering camp-fires, they were attacked by some Indians, who killed two of them and wounded a third; the others sprang to arms at once and stood their ground without suffering further loss or damage till it grew light, when the Indians silently drew off. Continuing his course, Boone reached the Kentucky River, and on April 1st began to build Boonesborough, on an open plain where there was a lick with two sulphur springs.

Meanwhile, other pioneers, as hardy and enterprising as Boone's companions, had likewise made up their minds that they would come in to possess the land; and in bands or small parties they had crossed the mountains or floated down the Ohio, under the leadership of such men as Harrod, Logan, and the McAfees. But hardly had they built their slight log cabins, covered with brush or bark, and broken ground for the corn-planting, when some small Indian war-parties, including that which had attacked Boone's company, appeared among them. Several men were "killed and sculped," as Boone phrased it; and the panic among the rest was very great, insomuch that many forthwith set out to return. Boone was not so easily daunted; and he at once sent a special messenger to hurry forward the main body under Henderson, writing to the latter with quiet resolution and much good sense:

"My advice to you, sir, is to come or send as soon as possible. Your company is desired greatly for the people are very uneasy, but are willing to stay and venture their lives with you, and now is the time to flusterate [frustrate?] the intentions of the Indians, and keep the country whilst we are in it. If we give way to them now, it will ever be the case."

Henderson had started off as soon as he had finished the treaty. Most fortunately, a full account of his journey has been kept; for among Henderson's followers at this time was a man named William Calk, who jotted down in his diary the events of each day. It is a short record, but as amusing as it is instructive; for the writer's mind was evidently as vigorous as his language was terse and untrammelled. The opening entry contains the information that "Abram's dog's leg got broke by Drake's dog." The owner of the latter beast, by the way, could not have been a pleasant companion on a trip of this sort, for elsewhere the writer, who, like most backwoodsmen, appreciated cleanliness in essentials, records with evident disfavor the fact that "Mr. Drake Bakes bread without washing his hands." Every man who has had the misfortune to drive a pack-train in thick timber, or along a bad trail, will appreciate keenly the following incident, which occurred soon after the party had set out for home:

"I turned my hors to drive before me and he got scard ran away threw Down the Saddel Bags and broke three of our powder goards and Abram's beast Burst open a walet of corn and lost a good Deal and made a turrabel flustration amongst the Reast of the Horses Drake's mair run against a sapling and noct it down we cacht them all again and went on and lodged at John Duncan's."

Another entry records the satisfaction of the party when at a log fort (before getting into the wilderness) they procured some good loaf-bread and good whiskey.

They carried with them seed-corn and "Irish tators" to plant, and for use on the journey had bacon, and corn-meal, which was made either into baked corn-dodgers or else into johnny-cakes, which were simply cooked on a board beside the fire, or else perhaps on a hot stone or in the ashes. The meal had to be used very sparingly; occasionally a beef was killed out of the herd of cattle that accompanied the emigrants; but generally they lived on the game they shot—deer, turkeys, and, when they got to Kentucky, buffaloes. Sometimes this was killed as they travelled; more often the hunters got it by going out in the evening after they had pitched camp.

The journey was hard and tiresome. At times it rained; and again there were heavy snow-storms, in one of which an emigrant got lost and only found his way to camp by the help of a pocket-compass. The mountains were very steep, and it was painfully laborious work to climb them while chopping out a way for the pack-train. At night a watch had to be kept for Indians. It was only here and there that the beasts got good grazing. Sometimes the horses had their saddles turned while struggling through the woods. But the great difficulty came in crossing the creeks, where the banks were rotten, the bottom bad, or the water deep; then the horses would get mired down and wet their packs, or they would have to be swum across while their loads were ferried over on logs. One day, in going along a creek, they had to cross it no less than fifty times by "very bad foards."

On the 7th of April they were met by Boone's runner, bearing tidings of the loss occasioned by the Indians; and from that time on they met parties of would-be settlers, who, panic-struck by the sudden forays, were fleeing from the country. There seems no reason to doubt that the establishment of the strong, well-backed settlement of Boonesborough was all that prevented the abandonment of Kentucky at this time; and when such was the effect of a foray by small and scattered war-parties of Indians from tribes nominally at peace with us, it can easily be imagined how hopeless it would have been to have tried to settle the land had there still been in existence a strong hostile confederacy such as that presided over by Cornstalk. Beyond doubt the restless and vigorous frontiersmen would ultimately have won their way into the coveted Western lands; yet had it not been for the battle of the Great Kanawha, Boone and Henderson could not, in 1775, have planted their colony in Kentucky; and had it not been for Boone and Henderson, it is most unlikely that the land would have been settled at all until after the Revolutionary War, when perhaps it might have been British soil. Boone was essentially a type, and possesses his greatest interest for us because he represents so well the characteristics as well as the life-work of his fellow backwoodsmen; still, it is unfair not to bear in mind also the leading part he played and the great services he rendered to the nation.

The incomers soon recovered from the fright into which they had been thrown by the totally unexpected Indian attack; but the revengeful anger it excited in their breasts did not pass away.

Henderson's company came into the beautiful Kentucky country in mid-April, when it looked its best: the trees were in leaf, the air heavy with fragrance, the snowy flowers of the dogwood whitened the woods, and the banks of the streams burned dull crimson with the wealth of red-bud blossoms. The travellers reached the fort that Boone was building on the 20th of the month, being welcomed to the protection of its wooden walls by a volley from twenty or thirty rifles. They at once set to with a will to finish it, and to make it a strong place of refuge against Indian attacks. It was a typical forted village, such as the frontiersmen built everywhere in the West and Southwest during the years that they were pushing their way across the continent in the teeth of fierce and harassing warfare; in some features it was not unlike the hamlet-like "tun" in which the forefathers of these same pioneers dwelt, long centuries before, when they still lived by the sluggish waters of the lower Rhine, or had just crossed to the eastern coast of Britain.

Henderson immediately proceeded to organize the government of his colony, and accordingly issued a call for an election of delegates to the legislature of Transylvania, each of the four stations mentioned above sending members. The delegates, seventeen in all, met at Boonesborough and organized the convention on the 23d of May. Their meetings were held without the walls of the fort, on a level plain of white clover, under a grand old elm. Beneath its mighty branches a hundred people could without crowding find refuge from the noonday sun; 'twas a fit council-house for this pioneer legislature of game-hunters and Indian fighters.

These weather-beaten backwoods warriors, who held their deliberations in the open air, showed that they had in them good stuff out of which to build a free government. They were men of genuine force of character, and they behaved with a dignity and wisdom that would have well become any legislative body. Henderson, on behalf of the proprietors of Transylvania, addressed them, much as a crown governor would have done. The portion of his address dealing with the destruction of game is worth noting. Buffalo, elk, and deer had abounded immediately round Boonesborough when the settlers first arrived, but the slaughter had been so great that even after the first six weeks the hunters began to find some difficulty in getting anything without going off some fifteen or twenty miles. However, stray buffaloes were still killed near the fort once or twice a week. Calk, in his journal, quoted above, in the midst of entries about his domestic work—such as, on April 29th "we git our house kivered with bark and move our things into it at Night and Begin housekeeping"; and, on May 2d, "went and sot in to clearing for corn"—

mentions occasionally killing deer and turkey; and once, while looking for a strayed mare, he saw four "bofelos." He wounded one, but failed to get it, with the luck that generally attended backwoods hunters when they for the first time tried their small-bore rifles against these huge, shaggy-maned wild cattle.

As Henderson pointed out, the game was the sole dependence of the first settlers, who, most of the time, lived solely on wild meat, even the parched corn having been exhausted; and without game the newcomers could not have stayed in the land a week. Accordingly, he advised the enactment of game-laws; and he was especially severe in his comments upon the "foreignors" who came into the country merely to hunt, killing off the wild beasts and taking their skins and furs away, for the benefit of persons not concerned in the settlement. This last point is curious as showing how instantly and naturally the colonists succeeded not only to the lands of the Indians, but also to their habits of thought; regarding intrusion by outsiders upon their hunting-grounds with the same jealous dislike so often shown by their red-skinned predecessors.

Henderson also outlined some of the laws he thought it advisable to enact, and the legislature followed his advice. They provided for courts of law, for regulating the militia, for punishing criminals, fixing sheriffs' and clerks' fees, and issuing writs of attachment. One of the members was a clergyman: owing to him a law was passed forbidding profane swearing or Sabbath-breaking—a puritanic touch which showed the mountain rather than the seaboard origin of the men settling Kentucky. The three remaining laws the legislature enacted were much more characteristic, and were all introduced by the two Boones—for Squire Boone was still the companion of his brother. As was fit and proper, it fell to the lot of the greatest of backwoods hunters to propose a scheme for game protection, which the legislature immediately adopted; and his was likewise the "act for preserving the breed of horses"—for from the very outset, the Kentuckians showed the love for fine horses and for horse-racing which has ever since distinguished them.

It was likewise stipulated that there should be complete religious freedom and toleration for all sects. This seems natural enough now, but in the eighteenth century the precedents were the other way. Kentucky showed its essentially American character in nothing more than the diversity of religious belief among the settlers from the very start.

When the Transylvania legislature dissolved, never to meet again, Henderson had nearly finished playing his short but important part in the founding of Kentucky. He was a man of the seacoast regions, who had little in common with the backwoodsmen by whom he was surrounded; he came from a comparatively old and sober community, and he could not grapple with his new associates; in his journal he alluded to them as a set of scoundrels who scarcely believed in God or feared the devil. A British friend of his, who at this time visited the settlement, also described the pioneers as being a lawless, narrow-minded, unpolished, and utterly insubordinate set, impatient of all restraint, and relying in every difficulty upon their individual might; though he grudgingly admitted that they were frank, hospitable, energetic, daring, and possessed of much common sense. Of course, it was hopeless to expect that such bold spirits, as they conquered the wilderness, would be content to hold it even at a small quit-rent from Henderson. But the latter's colony was toppled over by a thrust from without before it had time to be rent in sunder by violence from within.

Transylvania was between two millstones. The settlers revolted against its authority and appealed to Virginia, and meanwhile Virginia, claiming the Kentucky country, and North Carolina, as mistress of the lands round the Cumberland, proclaimed the purchase of the Transylvania proprietors null and void as regards themselves, though valid as against the Indians. The title conveyed by the latter thus enured to the benefit of the colonies; it having been our policy, both before and since the Revolution, not to permit any of our citizens to individually purchase lands from the savages.

Lord Dunmore denounced Henderson and his acts; and it was in vain that the Transylvanians appealed to the Continental Congress, asking leave to send a delegate thereto, and asserting their devotion to the American cause; for Jefferson and Patrick Henry were members of that body, and, though they agreed with Lord Dunmore in nothing else, were quite as determined as he that Kentucky should remain part of

Virginia. So Transylvania's fitful life flickered out of existence, the Virginia legislature in 1778 solemnly annulling the title of the company, but very properly recompensing the originators by the gift of two hundred thousand acres. North Carolina pursued a precisely similar course; and Henderson, after the collapse of his colony, drifts out of history.

Boone remained, to be for some years one of the Kentucky leaders. Soon after the fort at Boonesborough was built, he went back to North Carolina for his family, and in the fall returned, bringing out a band of new settlers, including twenty-seven "guns"—that is, rifle-bearing men—and four women, with their families, the first who came to Kentucky, though others shortly followed in their steps. A few roving hunters and daring pioneer settlers also came to his fort in the fall.

By the end of 1775 the Americans had gained firm foothold in Kentucky. Cabins had been built and clearings made; there were women and children in the wooden forts, cattle grazed on the range, and two or three hundred acres of corn had been sown and reaped. There were perhaps some three hundred men in Kentucky, a hardy, resolute, strenuous band. They stood shoulder to shoulder in the wilderness, far from all help, surrounded by an overwhelming number of foes. Each day's work was fraught with danger as they warred with the wild forces from which they wrung their living. Around them on every side lowered the clouds of the impending death-struggle with the savage lords of the neighboring lands.

Chapter VII

In the Current of the Revolution— the Southern Backwoodsmen Overwhelm the Cherokees

THE great Western drift of our people began almost at the moment when they became Americans, and ceased to be merely British colonists. They crossed the great divide which sundered the springs of the seaboard rivers from the sources of the Western waters about the time that American citizens first publicly acted as American freemen, knit together by common ties and with interests no longer akin to those of the mother country. The movement which was to make the future nation a continental power was begun immediately after the hitherto separate colonies had taken the first step toward solidification. While the communities of the seacoast were yet in a fever-heat from the uprising against the stamp tax, the first explorers were toiling painfully to Kentucky, and the first settlers were building their palisaded hamlets on the banks of the Watauga. The year that saw the first Continental Congress saw also the short, grim tragedy of Lord Dunmore's war. The early battles of the Revolution were fought while Boone's comrades were laying the foundations of their commonwealth.

Hitherto the two chains of events had been only remotely connected; but in 1776, the year of the Declaration of Independence, the struggle between the king and his rebellious subjects shook the whole land, and the men of the Western border were drawn headlong into the full current of Revolutionary warfare. From that moment our politics became national, and the fate of each portion of our country was

107

thenceforth in some sort dependent upon the welfare of every other. Each section had its own work to do; the East won independence while the West began to conquer the continent. Yet the deeds of each were of vital consequence to the other. Washington's Continentals gave the West its freedom; and took in return for themselves and their children a share of the land that had been conquered and held by the scanty bands of tall backwoodsmen.

The backwoodsmen, the men of the up-country, were, as a whole, ardent adherents of the patriot or American side. Yet there were among them many Loyalists or Tories; and these Tories included in their ranks much the greatest portion of the vicious and the disorderly elements. This was the direct reverse of what obtained along portions of the seaboard, where large numbers of the peaceable, well-to-do people stood loyally by the king. In the up-country, however, the Presbyterian Irish, with their fellows of Calvinistic stock and faith, formed the backbone of the moral and order-loving element; and the Presbyterian Irish were almost to a man stanch and furious upholders of the Continental Congress. Naturally, the large bands of murderers, horse thieves, and other wild outlaws, whom these grim friends of order hunted down with merciless severity, were glad to throw in their lot with any party that promised revenge upon their foes. But of course there were lawless characters on both sides; in certain localities, where the crop of jealousies, always a rank backwoods growth, had been unusually large, and had therefore produced long-standing and bitter feuds, the rival families espoused opposite sides from sheer vindictive hatred of one another. As a result, the struggle in the backwoods between Tories and Whigs, King's-men and Congress-men, did not merely turn upon the questions everywhere at stake between the American and British parties. It was also in part a fight between the law-abiding and the lawless, and in part a slaking of savage personal animosities, wherein the borderers glutted their vengeance on one another. They exercised without restraint the right of private warfare, long abandoned in more civilized regions. It was natural that such a contest should be waged with appalling ferocity.

Nevertheless this very ferocity was not only inevitable, but it was in a certain sense proper; or, at least, even if many of its manifestations were blamable, the spirit that lay behind them was right. The backwoodsmen were no sentimentalists; they were grim, hard, matter-of-fact men, engaged all their lives long in an unending struggle with hostile forces, both human and natural; men who in this struggle had acquired many unamiable qualities, but who had learned likewise to appreciate at their full value the inestimable virtues of courage and common sense. The crisis demanded that they should be both strong and good; but, above all things, it demanded that they should be strong. Weakness would have ruined them. It was needful that justice should stand before mercy; and they could no longer have held their homes, had they not put down their foes, of every kind, with an iron hand. They did not have many theories; but they were too genuinely liberty-loving not to keenly feel that their freedom was jeopardized as much by domestic disorder as by foreign aggression.

The Tories were obnoxious under two heads; they were the allies of a tyrant who lived beyond the sea, and they were the friends of anarchy at home. They were felt by the frontiersmen to be criminals rather than ordinary foes. They included in their ranks the mass of men who had been guilty of the two worst frontier crimes—horse-stealing and murder; and their own feats were in the eyes of their neighbors in no way distinguishable from those of other horse thieves and murderers. Accordingly, the backwoodsmen soon grew to regard Toryism as merely another crime; and the courts sometimes executed equally summary justice on Tory, desperado, and stock thief, holding each as having forfeited his life.

The backwoodsmen were engaged in a threefold contest. In the first place, they were occasionally, but not often, opposed to the hired British and German soldiers of a foreign king. Next, they were engaged in a fierce civil war with the Tories of their own number. Finally, they were pitted against the Indians, in the ceaseless border struggle of a rude, vigorous civilization to overcome an inevitably hostile savagery. The regular British armies, marching to and fro in the course of their long campaigns on the seaboard, rarely went far enough back to threaten the frontiersmen; the latter had to do chiefly with Tories led by British chiefs, and with Indians instigated by British agents.

Soon after the conflict with the revolted colonists became

one of arms as well as one of opinions, the British began to rouse the Indian tribes to take their part. In the Northwest they were at first unsuccessful; the memory of Lord Dunmore's war was still fresh in the minds of the tribes beyond the Ohio, and they remained for the most part neutral. The Shawnees continued even in 1776 to send in to the Americans white prisoners collected from among their outlying bands, in accordance with the terms of the treaty entered into on the Pickaway plains.

But the southwestern Indians were not held in check by memories of recent defeat, and they were alarmed by the encroachments of the whites. The Cherokees, who were the nearest neighbors of the Americans, promptly took up the tomahawk at the bidding of the British. The success of the British in rousing the war spirit among the Indians, and the consequent ravages of the latter, maddened the American frontiersmen upon whom the blow fell, and changed their resentment against the British king into a deadly and lasting hatred, which their sons and grandsons inherited. Indian warfare was of such peculiar atrocity that the employment of Indians as allies forbade any further hope of reconciliation. It is not necessary to accept the American estimate of the motives inspiring the act in order to sympathize fully with the horror and anger that it aroused among the frontiersmen. They saw their homes destroyed, their wives outraged, their children captured, their friends butchered and tortured wholesale by Indians armed with British weapons, bribed by British gold, and obeying the orders of British agents and commanders. Their stormy anger was not likely to be allayed by the consideration that Congress also had at first made some effort to enlist Indians in the patriot forces, nor were they apt to bear in mind the fact that the British, instead of being abnormally cruel, were in reality less so than our former French and Spanish opponents.

Looking back, it is easy to see that the Indians were the natural foes of the American people, and therefore the natural allies of the British Government. They had constantly to fear the advance of the Americans, while from the fur traders, Indian agents, and army officers who alone represented Britain, they had nothing but coveted treasures of every kind to expect. They seemed tools forged for the hands of the royal com-

manders, whose own people lay far beyond the reach of reprisals in kind; and it was perhaps too much to expect that
in that age such tools should not be used. We had less temptation to employ them, less means wherewith to pay them, and
more cause to be hostile to and dread them; and moreover
our skirts are not quite clear in the matter, after all, for we
more than once showed a tendency to bid for their support.

But, after all is said, the fact remains that we have to deal,
not with what, under other circumstances, the Americans
might have done, but with what the British actually *did;* and
for this there can be many apologies, but no sufficient excuse.
When the commissioners to the Southern Indians wrote to
Lord George Germain, "we have been indefatigable in our endeavors to keep up a constant succession of parties of Indians
to annoy the rebels," the writers must have well known,
what the king's ministers should also have made it their business to know, that the war-parties whom they thus boasted
of continually sending against the settlements directed their
efforts mainly, indeed almost exclusively, not against bodies
of armed men, but against the husbandmen as they unsus-
pectingly tilled the fields, and against the women and children
who cowered helplessly in the log cabins. All men knew that
the prisoners who fell into Indian hands, of whatever age or
sex, often suffered a fate hideous and revolting beyond description. Such a letter as that quoted above makes the ad-
visers of King George the Third directly responsible for the
manifold and frightful crimes of their red allies.

While the Creeks were halting and considering, and while
the Choctaws and Chickasaws were being visited by British
emissaries, the Cherokees flung themselves on the frontier
folk. The main attack was made early in July, 1776, the warriors rushing down from their upland fastnesses in fierce and
headlong haste, the different bands marching north, east, and
southeast at the same moment. From the Holston to the
Tugaloo, from southwestern Virginia to northwestern Georgia,
the back-county settlements were instantly wrapped in the
sudden horror of savage warfare.

The Watauga people, the most exposed of all, received timely
warning from a friendly squaw, to whom the whites ever
after showed respect and gratitude. They at once began to
prepare for the stroke; they took refuge in their wooden forts

or stations. Those who delayed were surprised by the savages, and were slain as they fled, or else were captured, perhaps to die by torture—men, women, and children alike. The cabins were burnt, the grain destroyed, the cattle and horses driven off, and the sheep and hogs shot down with arrows; the Indians carried bows and arrows for this express purpose, so as to avoid wasting powder and lead. The bolder war-parties, in their search for scalps, penetrated into Virginia a hundred miles beyond the frontier, wasting the country with tomahawk and brand up to the Seven-Mile Ford. The roads leading to the wooden forts were crowded with settlers, who, in their mortal need of hurry, had barely time to snatch up a few of the household goods, and, if especially lucky, to mount the women and childen on horses; as usual in such a flight, there occurred many deeds of cowardly selfishness, offset by many feats of courage and self-sacrifice. Once in the fort, the backwoodsmen often banded into parties, and sallied out to fall on the Indians. Sometimes these parties were worsted; at other times they overcame their foes either by ambush or in fair fight. One such party from the Wolf Hills fort killed eleven Indian warriors; and on their return they hung the scalps of their slain foes, as trophies of triumph, from a pole over the fort gate. They were Bible-readers in this fort, and they had their Presbyterian minister with them, having organized a special party to bring in the books he had left in his cabin; they joined in prayer and thanksgiving for their successes; but this did not hinder them from scalping the men they killed. They were too well read in the merciless wars of the Chosen People to feel the need of sparing the fallen; indeed, they would have been most foolish had they done so; for they were battling with a heathen enemy more ruthless and terrible than ever was Canaanite or Philistine.

The two largest of the invading Indian bands moved, one by way of the mountains, to fall on the Watauga fort and its neighbors, and the other, led by the great war-chief, Dragging Canoe, to lay waste the country guarded by Eaton's Station.

The white scouts—trained woodsmen, whose lives had been spent in the chase and in forest warfare—kept the commanders or head men of the forts well informed of the Indian advance. As soon as it was known what part was really threatened, runners were sent to the settlements near by, calling on the riflemen to gather at Eaton's Station; whither they accordingly came in small bodies, under their respective militia captains.

No man was really in command; the senior captain exercised a vague kind of right of advice over the others, and the latter in turn got from their men such obedience as their own personal influence was able to procure. But the levy, if disorderly, was composed of excellent marksmen and woodsmen, sinewy, hardy, full of fight, and accustomed to act together. A council was held, and it was decided not to stay cooped up in the fort, like turkeys in a pen, while the Indians ravaged the fields and burnt the homesteads, but to march out at once and break the shock by a counter-stroke.

Accordingly, on the morning of the 20th of July, they filed out of the fort, one hundred and seventy strong, and bent their steps toward the Island Flats. Well versed in woodland warfare, the frontier riflemen marched as well as fought on a system of their own, much more effective for this purpose than the discipline of European regulars. The men of this little levy walked strung out in Indian file, in two parallel lines, with scouts in front, and flankers on each side. Marching thus they could not be surprised, and were ready at any moment to do battle with the Indians, in open order and taking shelter behind the trees; while regulars, crowded together, were helpless before the savages whom the forest screened from view, and who esteemed it an easy task to overcome any number of foes if gathered in a huddle.

When near the Flats the whites, walking silently with moccasined feet, came suddenly on a party of twenty Indians, who, on being attacked, fled in the utmost haste, leaving behind ten of their bundles—for the Southern warriors carried with them, when on the warpath, small bundles containing their few necessaries.

After this trifling success a council was held, and, as the day was drawing to a close, it was decided to return to the fort. Some of the men were dissatisfied with the decision, and there followed an incident as characteristic in its way as was the bravery with which the battle was subsequently fought. The discontented soldiers expressed their feelings freely, commenting especially upon the supposed lack of courage on the part of one of the captains. The latter, after brooding over the matter until the men had begun to march off the ground toward home, suddenly halted the line in which he was walking, and proceeded to harangue the troops in defense of his own reputation. Apparently no one interfered to prevent this remarkable piece of military self-justification; the soldiers were evidently accustomed openly to criticise the conduct of their commanders, while the latter responded in any manner they saw fit. As soon as the address was over, and the lines once more straightened out, the march was renewed in the original order; and immediately afterward the scouts brought news that a considerable body of Indians, misled by their retreat, was running rapidly up to assail their rear.

The right file was promptly wheeled to the right and the left to the left, forming a line of battle a quarter of a mile long, the men taking advantage of the cover when possible. There was at first some confusion and a momentary panic, which was instantly quelled, the officers and many of the men joining to encourage and rally the few whom the suddenness of the attack rendered faint-hearted. The Otari warriors, instead of showing the usual Indian caution, came running on at headlong speed, believing that the whites were fleeing in terror; while still some three hundred yards off they raised the war-whoop and charged without halting, the foremost chiefs hallooing out that the white men were running, and to come on and scalp them. They were led by Dragging Canoe himself, and were formed very curiously, their centre being cone-shaped, while their wings were curved outward: apparently they believed the white line to be wavering, and hoped to break through its middle at the same time that they outflanked it, trusting to a single furious onset instead of to their usual tactics. The result showed their folly. The frontiersmen on the right and left scattered out still farther, so that their line could not be outflanked; and waiting coolly till the Otari were close up, the whites fired into them. The long rifles cracked like four-horse whips; they were held in skilful hands, many of the assailants fell, and the rush was checked at once. A short fight at close quarters ensued here and there along the line, Dragging Canoe was struck down and severely wounded, and then the Indians fled in the utmost confusion, every man for himself. Yet they carried off their wounded and perhaps some of their dead. The whites took

thirteen scalps, and of their own number but four were seriously hurt; they also took many guns and much plunder.

In this battle of the Island Flats the whites were slightly
superior in number to their foes; and they won without difficulty, inflicting a far heavier loss than they received. In this
respect it differs markedly from most other Indian fights of
the same time; and many of its particulars render it noteworthy. Moreover, it had a very good effect, cheering the
frontiersmen greatly, and enabling them to make head against
the discouraged Indians.

On the same day the Watauga fort was attacked by a large
force at sunrise. It was crowded with women and children,
but contained only forty or fifty men. The latter, however,
were not only resolute and well armed, but were also on the
alert to guard against surprise; the Indians were discovered
as they advanced in the gray light, and were at once beaten
back with loss from the loopholed stockade. Robertson commanded in the fort, Sevier acting as his lieutenant. Of course,
the only hope of assistance was from Virginia, North Carolina
being separated from the Watauga people by great mountain
chains; and Sevier had already notified the officers of Fincastle
that the Indians were advancing. His letter was of laconic
brevity, and contained no demand for help; it was merely
a warning that the Indians were undoubtedly about to start,
and that "they intended to drive the country up to New River
before they returned"—so that it behooved the Fincastle men
to look to their own hearthsides. Sevier was a very fearless,
self-reliant man, and doubtless felt confident that the settlers
themselves could beat back their assailants. His forecast
proved correct; for the Indians, after maintaining an irregular
siege of the fort for some three weeks, retired, almost at
the moment that parties of frontiersmen came to the rescue
from some of the neighboring forts.

While the foe was still lurking about the fort the people
within were forced to subsist solely on parched corn; and from
time to time some of them became so irritated by the irksome
monotony of their confinement, that they ventured out heedless
of the danger. Three or four of them were killed by the Indians, and one boy was carried off to one of their towns, where
he was burnt at the stake; while a woman, who was also
captured at this time, was only saved from a like fate by the

exertions of the same Cherokee squaw already mentioned as warning the settlers. Tradition relates that Sevier, now a young widower, fell in love with the woman he soon afterward married during the siege. Her name was Kate Sherrill. She was a tall girl, brown-haired, comely, lithe, and supple "as a hickory sapling." One day while without the fort she was almost surprised by some Indians. Running like a deer, she reached the stockade, sprang up so as to catch the top with her hands, and drawing herself over was caught in Sevier's arms on the other side; through a loophole he had already shot the headmost of her pursuers.

Soon after the baffled Otari retreated from Robertson's fort the other war-parties likewise left the settlements. The Watauga men, together with the immediately adjoining Virginian frontiersmen, had beaten back their foes unaided, save for some powder and lead they had received from the older settlements; and, moreover, had inflicted more loss than they suffered. They had made an exceedingly vigorous and successful fight.

The outlying settlements scattered along the western border of the Carolinas and Georgia had been attacked somewhat earlier; the Cherokees from the lower towns, accompanied by some Creeks and Tories, beginning their ravages in the last days of June. A small party of Georgians had, just previously, made a sudden march into the Cherokee country. They were trying to capture the British agent Cameron, who, being married to an Indian wife, dwelt in her town, and owned many negroes, horses, and cattle. The Cherokees, who had agreed not to interfere, broke faith and surprised the party, killing some and capturing others, who were tortured to death.

The frontiers were soon in a state of wild panic; for the Cherokee inroad was marked by the usual features. Cattle were driven off, houses burned, plantations laid waste, while the women and children were massacred indiscriminately with the men. The people fled from their homes and crowded into the stockade forts; they were greatly hampered by the scarcity of guns and ammunition, as much had been given to the troops called down to the coast by the war with Britain. All the Southern colonies were maddened by the outbreak, and prepared for immediate revenge, knowing that if they were quick they would have time to give the Cherokees a good drubbing before the British could interfere. The plan was that they should act together, the Virginians invading the Overhill country at the same time that the forces from North and South Carolina and Georgia destroyed the valley and lower towns. Thus the Cherokees would be crushed with little danger. It proved impossible, however, to get the attacks made quite simultaneously.

The back districts of North Carolina suffered heavily at the outset; however, the inhabitants showed that they were able to take care of themselves. The Cherokees came down the Catawba, murdering many people; but most of the whites took refuge in the little forts, where they easily withstood the Indian assaults. General Griffith Rutherford raised a frontier levy and soon relieved the besieged stations.

The heaviest blow fell on South Carolina, where the Cherokees were led by Cameron himself, accompanied by most of his Tories. Falling furiously on the scattered settlers, they killed them or drove them into the wooden forts, ravaging, burning, and murdering as elsewhere, and sparing neither age nor sex. Colonel Andrew Williamson was in command of the western districts, and he at once began to gather together a force, taking his station at Pickens's fort, with forty men, on July 3d. It was with the utmost difficulty that he could get troops, guns, or ammunition; but his strenuous and unceasing efforts were successful, and his force increased day by day.

By the end of July, Williamson had gathered over eleven hundred militia (including two small rifle companies), and advanced against the Indian towns, sending his spies and scouts before him. On the last day of the month he made a rapid night march, with three hundred and fifty horsemen, to surprise Cameron, who lay with a party of Tories and Indians, encamped at Oconoree Creek, beyond the Cherokee town of Eseneka, which commanded the ford of the River Keowee. The cabins and fenced gardens of the town lay on both sides of the river. Williamson had been told by his prisoners that the hither bank was deserted, and advanced heedlessly, without scouts or flankers. In consequence, he fell into an ambush, for when he reached the first houses, hidden Indians suddenly fired on him from front and flank. Many horses, including that of the commander, were shot down, and the startled troops began a disorderly retreat, firing at random. Colonel Hammond rallied about twenty of the coolest, and ordering them to reserve their fire, he charged the fence from behind into the dark figures crouching behind it, and jumping over charged home. The Indians immediately fled, leaving one dead and three wounded in the hands of the whites. The action was over; but the by-no-means-reassured victors had lost five men mortally and thirteen severely wounded, and were still rather nervous. At daybreak, Williamson destroyed the houses near by, and started to cross the ford. But his men, in true militia style, had become sulky and mutinous, and refused to cross, until Colonel Hammond swore he would go alone, and plunged into the river, followed by three volunteers, whereupon the whole army crowded after. The revulsion in their feelings was instantaneous; once across they seemed to have left all fear as well as all prudence behind. On the hither side there had been no getting them to advance; on the farther there was no keeping them together, and they scattered everywhere. Luckily the Indians were too few to retaliate; and, besides, the Cherokees were not good marksmen, using so little powder in their guns that they made very ineffective weapons. After all the houses had been burned, and some six thousand bushels of corn, besides peas and beans, destroyed, Williamson returned to his camp. Next day he renewed his advance, and sent out detachments against all the other lower towns, utterly destroying every one by the middle of August, although not without one or two smart skirmishes. His troops were very much elated, and only the lack of provisions prevented his marching against the middle towns. As it was, he retired to refit, leaving a garrison of six hundred men at Eseneka, which he christened Fort Rutledge. This ended the first stage of the retaliatory campaign, undertaken by the whites in revenge for the outbreak. The South Carolinians, assisted slightly by a small independent command of Georgians, who acted separately, had destroyed the lower Cherokee towns, at the same time that the Watauga people repulsed the attack of the Overhill warriors.

The second and most important movement was to be made by South Carolina, North Carolina, and Virginia jointly, each sending a column of two thousand men, the two former against the middle and valley, the latter against the Overhill towns. If the columns acted together the Cherokees would be overwhelmed by a force three times the number of all their warriors. The plan succeeded well, although the Virginia division was delayed, so that its action, though no less effective, was much later than that of the others, and though the latter likewise failed to act in perfect unison.

Rutherford and his North Carolinians were the first to take the field. He had an army of two thousand gunmen, besides pack-horsemen and men to tend the drove of bullocks, together with a few Catawba Indians—a total of twenty-four hundred. He passed over the Blue Ridge at Swannanoa Gap, crossed the French Broad at the Warrior's Ford, and then went through the mountains to the middle towns, a detachment of a thousand men making a forced march in advance. Rutherford had expected to meet Williamson at this place, but the latter did not appear, and so the North Carolina commander determined to proceed alone against the valley towns along the Hiawassee. Taking with him only nine hundred picked men, he attempted to cross the rugged mountain chains which separated him from his destination; but he had no guide, and missed the regular pass—a fortunate thing for him, as it afterward turned out, for he thus escaped falling into an ambush of five hundred Cherokees who were encamped along it. After in vain trying to penetrate the tangle of gloomy defiles and wooded peaks, he returned to the middle towns at Cannucca on September 18th. Here he met Williamson, who had just arrived, having been delayed so that he could not leave Fort Rutledge until the 13th. The South Carolinians, two thousand strong, had crossed the Blue Ridge near the sources of the Little Tennessee.

While Rutherford rested, Williamson, on the 19th, pushed on through Noewee pass, and fell into the ambush which had been laid for the former. The pass was a narrow, open valley, walled in by steep and lofty mountains. The Indians waited until the troops were struggling up to the outlet, and then assailed them with a close and deadly fire. The surprised soldiers recoiled and fell into confusion; and they were for the second time saved from disaster by the gallantry of Colonel Hammond, who with voice and action rallied them, endeavoring to keep them firm while a detachment was sent to clamber

up the rocks and outflank the Indians. At the same time Lieutenant Hampton got twenty men together, out of the rout, and
ran forward, calling out: "Loaded guns advance, empty guns
fall down and load." Being joined by some thirty men more
he pushed desperately upward. The Indians fled from the
shock; and the army thus owed its safety solely to two gallant
officers. Of the whites seventeen were killed and twenty-nine
wounded; they took fourteen scalps.

Although the distance was but twenty-odd miles, it took
Williamson five days of incredible toil before he reached the
valley towns. The troops showed the utmost patience, clearing
a path for the pack-train along the sheer mountainsides and
through the dense, untrodden forests in the valleys. The trail
often wound along cliffs where a single misstep of a pack-
animal resulted in its being dashed to pieces. But the work,
though fatiguing, was healthy; it was noticed that during the
whole expedition not a man was laid up for any length of
time by sickness.

Rutherford joined Williamson immediately afterward, and
together they utterly laid waste the valley towns; and then, in
the last week of September, started homeward. All the Cherokee settlements west of the Appalachians had been destroyed
from the face of the earth, neither crops nor cattle being left,
and most of the inhabitants were obliged to take refuge with
the Creeks.

Rutherford reached home in safety, never having experienced any real resistance; he had lost but three men in all. He
had killed twelve Indians, and had captured nine more, besides
seven whites and four negroes. He had also taken piles of
deerskins, a hundredweight of gunpowder, and twenty-five
hundred pounds of lead; and, moreover, had wasted and destroyed to his heart's content.

Williamson, too, reached home without suffering further
damage, entering Fort Rutledge on October 7th. In his two
expeditions he had had ninety-four men killed and wounded,
but he had done much more harm than any one else to the
Indians. It was said the South Carolinians had taken seventy-
five scalps; at any rate, the South Carolina legislature had
offered a reward of seventy-five pounds for every warrior's
scalp, as well as one hundred pounds for every Indian and
eighty pounds for every Tory or negro taken prisoner. But

the troops were forbidden to sell their prisoners as slaves—not
a needless injunction, as is shown by the fact that when it
was issued there had already been at least one case in Williamson's own army where a captured Indian was sold into bondage.

The Virginia troops had meanwhile been slowly gathering
at the Great Island of the Holston, under Colonel William
Christian, preparatory to assaulting the Overhill Cherokees.
On the 1st of October the army started, two thousand strong,
including some troops from North Carolina, and all the gunmen who could be spared from the little stockaded hamlets
scattered along the Watauga, the Holston, and the Clinch.
Except a small force of horse-riflemen, the men were on foot,
each with tomahawk, scalping-knife, and long, grooved flint-
lock; all were healthy, well equipped, and in fine spirits, driving their pack-horses and bullocks with them. Characteristically
enough, a Presbyterian clergyman, following his backwoods
flock, went along with this expedition as chaplain. The army
moved very cautiously, the night encampments being made
behind breastworks of felled timbers. There was therefore no
chance for a surprise; and their great inferiority in number
made it hopeless for the Cherokees to try a fair fight. In their
despair they asked help from the Creeks; but the latter replied
that they had plucked the thorn of warfare from their (the
Creeks') foot, and were welcome to keep it.

The Virginians came steadily on until they reached the
Big Island of the French Broad. Here the Cherokees had
gathered their warriors, and they sent a Tory trader across with
a flag of truce. Christian, well knowing that the Virginians
greatly outnumbered the Indians, let the man go through his
camp at will, and sent him back with word that the Cherokee
towns were doomed, for that he would surely march to them
and destroy them. That night he left half of his men in camp,
lying on their arms by the watch-fires, while with the others
he forded the river below and came round to surprise the Indian encampment from behind; but he found that the Indians
had fled, for their hearts had become as water, nor did they
venture at any time, during this expedition, to molest the white
forces. Following them up, Christian reached the towns early
in November, and remained two weeks, sending out parties to
burn the cabins and destroy the stores of corn and potatoes.
The Indians sent in a flag to treat for peace, surrendering

the horses and prisoners they had taken, and agreeing to fix a boundary and give up to the settlers the land they already had, as well as some additional territory. Christian made peace on these terms and ceased his ravages, but he excepted the town of Tuskega, whose people had burned alive the boy taken captive at Watauga. This town he reduced to ashes.

Nor would the chief Dragging Canoe accept peace at all; but gathering round him the fiercest and most unruly of the young men, he left the rest of the tribe and retired to the Chickamauga fastnesses.

When the preliminary truce had been made, Christian marched his forces homeward, and disbanded them a fortnight before Christmas, leaving a garrison at Holston, Great Island. During the ensuing spring and summer peace treaties were definitely concluded between the Upper Cherokees and Virginia and North Carolina at the Great Island of the Holston, and between the Lower Cherokees and South Carolina and Georgia at De Witt's Corners. The Cherokees gave up some of their lands; of the four seacoast provinces South Carolina gained most, as was proper, for she had done and suffered most.

The Watauga people and the Westerners generally were the real gainers by the war. Had the Watauga settlements been destroyed, they would no longer have covered the Wilderness Road to Kentucky; and so Kentucky must perforce have been abandoned. But the followers of Robertson and Sevier stood stoutly for their homes; not one of them fled over the mountains. The Cherokees had been so roughly handled that for several years they did not again go to war as a body; and this not only gave the settlers a breathing time, but also enabled them to make themselves so strong that when the struggle was renewed they could easily hold their own. The war was thus another and important link in the chain of events by which the West was won; and had any link in the chain snapped during these early years, the peace of 1783 would probably have seen the Trans-Alleghany country in the hands of a non-American power.

Chapter VIII

Growth and Civil
Organization of Kentucky

B Y the end of 1775 Kentucky had been occupied by
those who were permanently to hold it. Stout-hearted
men, able to keep what they had grasped, moved in, and
took with them their wives and children. There was also, of
course, a large shifting element, composing, indeed, the bulk of
the population: hunters who came out for the season; "cabin-
ners," or men who merely came out to build a cabin and partially clear a spot of ground, so as to gain a right to it under
the law; surveyors, and those adventurers always to be found
in a new country, who are too restless, or too timid, or too
irresolute to remain.

The men with families and the young men who intended
to make permanent homes formed the heart of the community,
the only part worth taking into account. There was a steady
though thin stream of such immigrants, and they rapidly
built up around them a life not very unlike that which they
had left behind with their old homes. Even in 1776 there was
marrying and giving in marriage, and children were born in
Kentucky. The newcomers had to settle in forts, where the
young men and maidens had many chances for courtship. They
married early, and were as fruitful as they were hardy. Most
of these marriages were civil contracts, but some may have
been solemnized by clergymen, for the commonwealth received
from the outset occasional visits from ministers.

These ministers belonged to different denominations, but all
were sure of a hearing. The backwoodsmen were forced by
their surroundings to exercise a grudging charity toward the
various forms of religious belief entertained among them-

123

selves—though they hated and despised French and Spanish Catholics. And after the outbreak of the Revolution, the Kentuckians, in common with other backwoodsmen, grew to thoroughly dislike one religious body which they already distrusted; this was the Church of England, the Episcopal Church. They long regarded it as merely the persecuting ecclesiastical arm of the British Government. Such of them as had been brought up in any faith at all had for the most part originally professed some form of Calvinism; they had very probably learnt their letters from a primer which, in one of its rude cuts, represented John Rogers at the stake, surrounded by his wife and seven children, and in their afterlives they were more familiar with the "Pilgrim's Progress" than with any other book, save the Bible; so that it was natural for them to distrust the successors of those who had persecuted Rogers and Bunyan. Still, the border communities were, as times then went, very tolerant in religious matters; and of course most of the men had no chance to display, or indeed to feel, sectarianism of any kind, for they had no issue to join, and rarely a church about which to rally.

By the time Kentucky was settled the Baptists had begun to make headway on the frontier, at the expense of the Presbyterians. The rough democracy of the border welcomed a sect which was itself essentially democratic. To many of the backwoodsmen's prejudices, notably their sullen and narrow hostility toward all ranks, whether or not based on merit and learning, the Baptists' creed appealed strongly. Where their preachers obtained foothold, it was made a matter of reproach to the Presbyterian clergymen that they had been educated in early life for the ministry as for a profession. The love of liberty, and the defiant assertion of equality, so universal in the backwoods, and so excellent in themselves, sometimes took very warped and twisted forms, notably when they betrayed the backwoodsmen into the belief that the true democratic spirit forbade any exclusive and special training for the professions that produce soldiers, statesmen, or ministers.

The fact that the Baptist preachers were men exactly similar to their fellows in all their habits of life not only gave them a good standing at once, but likewise enabled them very early to visit the farthest settlements, travelling precisely like other backwoodsmen; and once there, each preacher, each earnest

professor, doing bold and fearless missionary work, became
the nucleus round which a little knot of true believers gathered.
Two or three of them made short visits to Kentucky during
the first few years of its existence. One, the Rev. William
Hickman of Virginia, who went thither in the early spring of
1776, kept a journal of his trip. He travelled over the Wilderness Road with eight other men. Three of them were Baptists
like himself, who prayed every night; and their companions,
though they did not take part in the praying, did not interrupt
it. Their journey through the melancholy and silent wilderness
resembled in its incidents the countless other similar journeys
that were made at that time and later. They suffered from cold
and hunger and lack of shelter; they became footsore and
weary, and worn out with driving the pack-horses. On the top
of the lonely Cumberland Mountains they came upon the wolf-
eaten remains of a previous traveller, who had recently been
killed by Indians. At another place they met four men returning—cowards, whose hearts had failed them when in
sight of the promised land. While on the great Indian war
trail they killed a buffalo, and thenceforth lived on its jerked
meat. One night the wolves smelt the flesh, and came up to
the camp-fire; the strong hunting-dogs rushed out with clamorous barking to drive them away, and the sudden alarm for
a moment made the sleepy wayfarers think that roving Indians
had attacked them. When they reached Crab Orchard their
dangers were for the moment past; all travellers grew to regard with affection the station by this little grove of wild apple-
trees. It is worthy of note that the early settlers loved to build
their homes near these natural orchards, moved by the
fragrance and beauty of the bloom in spring.

The tired Baptist was not overpleased with Harrodstown,
though he there listened to the preaching of one of his own
sect. He remarked "a poor town it was in those days," a couple
of rows of smoky cabins, tenanted by dirty women and
ragged children, while the tall, unkempt frontiersmen lounged
about in greasy hunting-shirts, breech-clouts, leggings, and
moccasins. There was little or no corn until the crops were
gathered, and, like the rest, he had to learn to eat wild meat
without salt. The settlers—as is always the case in frontier
towns where the people are wrapped up in their own pursuits
and rivalries, and are obliged to talk of one another for lack

of outside interests—were divided by bickering, gossiping jealousies; and at this time they were quarrelling as to whether the Virginian cabin-rights or Henderson's land-grants would prove valid. As usual, the zealous Baptist preacher found that the women were the first to "get religion," as he phrased it. Sometimes their husbands likewise came in with them; at other times they remained indifferent. Often they savagely resented their wives and daughters being converted, visiting on the head of the preacher an anger that did not always find vent in mere words; for the backwoodsmen had strong, simple natures, powerfully excited for good or evil, and those who were not God-fearing usually became active and furious opponents of all religion.

It is curious to compare the description of life in a frontier fort as given by this undoubtedly prejudiced observer with the equally prejudiced, but golden, instead of sombre, hued, reminiscences of frontier life, over which the pioneers lovingly lingered in their old age. To these old men the long-vanished stockades seemed to have held a band of brothers, who were ever generous, hospitable, courteous, and fearless, always ready to help one another, never envious, never flinching from any foe. Neither account is accurate; but the last is quite as near the truth as the first. On the border, as elsewhere, but with the different qualities in even bolder contrast, there was much both of good and bad, of shiftless viciousness and resolute honesty. Many of the hunters were mere restless wanderers, who soon surrendered their clearings to small farming squatters but a degree less shiftless than themselves; the latter brought the ground a little more under cultivation, and then likewise left it and wandered onward, giving place to the third set of frontiersmen, the steady men who had come to stay. But often the first hunters themselves stayed and grew up as farmers and landed proprietors. Many of the earliest pioneers, including most of their leaders, founded families, which took root in the land and flourish to this day, the children, grandchildren, and great-grandchildren of the old-time Indian fighters becoming Congressmen and judges, and officers in the regular army and in the Federal and Confederate forces during the Civil War. In fact, the very first comers to a wild and dangerous country are apt to be men with fine qualities of heart and head; it is not until they have partly tamed the land that the scum of the frontier drifts into it.*

Though obliged to be very careful and to keep their families in forts, and in spite of a number of them being killed by the savages, the settlers in 1776 were able to wander about and explore the country thoroughly, making little clearings as the basis of "cabin claims," and now and then gathering into stations which were for the most part broken up by the Indians and abandoned. What was much more important, the permanent settlers in the well-established stations proceeded to organize a civil government.

They by this time felt little but contempt for the Henderson or Transylvania government. Having sent a petition against it to the provincial authorities, they were confident that what faint shadow of power it still retained would soon vanish; so they turned their attention to securing a representation in the Virginia Convention. All Kentucky was still considered as a part of Fincastle County, and the inhabitants were therefore unrepresented at the capital. They determined to remedy this; and, after due proclamation, gathered together at Harrodstown early in June, 1776. During five days an election was held, and two delegates, Clark, of course, being one, were chosen to go to Williamsburg, then the seat of government. They carried a petition for admission as a separate county.

Armed with this document and their credentials, Clark and his companion set off across the desolate and Indian-haunted mountains. They travelled very fast, the season was extremely wet, and they did not dare to kindle fires for fear of the Indians; in consequence, they suffered torments from cold, hunger, and especially from "scalded" feet. Yet they hurried on, and presented their petition to the governor and council—the legislature having adjourned. Clark also asked for five hundredweight of gunpowder, of which the Kentucky settlement stood in sore and pressing need. This the council at first refused to give; whereupon Clark informed them that if the country was not worth defending, it was not worth claiming, making it

---

* This is as true to-day in the far West as it was formerly in Kentucky and Tennessee; at least, to judge by my own experience in the Little Missouri region, and in portions of the Kootenai, Cœur d'Alêne, and Bighorn countries.

plain that if the request was not granted, and if Kentucky was forced to assume the burdens of independence, she would likewise assume its privileges. After this plain statement, the council yielded. Clark took the powder down the Ohio River, and got it safely through to Kentucky; though a party sent under John Todd to convey it overland from the Limestone Creek was met at the Licking and defeated by the Indians, Clark's fellow delegate being among the killed.

Before returning, Clark had attended the fall meeting of the Virginia legislature, and in spite of the opposition of Henderson, who was likewise present, he procured the admission of Kentucky as a separate county, with boundaries corresponding to those of the present State. Early in the ensuing year, 1777, the county was accordingly organized; Harrodstown, or Harrodsburg, as it was now beginning to be called, was made the county-seat, having by this time supplanted Boonesborough in importance. Two burgesses were chosen to represent the county in the General Assembly of Virginia. In later years Daniel Boone himself served as a Kentucky burgess in the Virginia legislature; a very different body from the little Transylvania parliament in which he began his career as a lawmaker. The old backwoods hero led a strange life; varying his long wanderings and explorations, his endless campaigns against savage men and savage beasts, by serving as roadmaker, town-builder, and commonwealth-founder, sometimes organizing the frontiersmen for foreign war and again doing his share in devising the laws under which they were to live and prosper.

But the pioneers were speedily drawn into a life-and-death struggle which engrossed their whole attention to the exclusion of all merely civil matters; a struggle in which their land became in truth what the Indians called it—a dark and bloody ground, a land with blood-stained rivers.

It was impossible long to keep peace on the border between the ever-encroaching whites and their fickle and bloodthirsty foes. The hard, reckless, often brutalized frontiersmen, greedy of land and embittered by the memories of untold injuries, regarded all Indians with sullen enmity, and could not be persuaded to distinguish between the good and the bad. The central government was as powerless to restrain as to protect these far-off and unruly citizens. On the other hand, the Indians were as treacherous as they were ferocious—Delawares, Shawnees, Wyandots, and all. While deceiving the commandants of the posts by peaceful protestations, they would steadily continue their ravages and murders; and while it was easy to persuade a number of the chiefs and warriors of a tribe to enter into a treaty, it was impossible to make the remainder respect it. The chiefs might be for peace, but the young braves were always for war, and could not be kept back.

Throughout the year the outlook continued to grow more and more threatening. Parties of young men kept making inroads on the settlements, especially in Kentucky; not only did the Shawnees, Wyandots, Mingos, and Iroquois act thus, but they were even joined by bands of Ottawas, Pottawatomies, and Chippewas from the lakes, who thus attacked the white settlers long ere the latter had either the will or the chance to hurt them.

Until the spring of 1777 the outbreak was not general, and it was supposed that only some three or four hundred warriors had taken up the tomahawk. Yet the outlying settlers were all the time obliged to keep as sharp a lookout as if engaged in open war. Throughout the summer of 1776 the Kentucky settlers were continually harassed. Small parties of Indians were constantly lurking round the forts, to shoot down the men as they hunted or worked in the fields, and to carry off the women. There was a constant and monotonous succession of unimportant forays and skirmishes.

One band of painted marauders carried off Boone's daughter Jemima. She was in a canoe with two other girls, Betsy and Fanny Callaway, on the river near Boonesborough when they were pounced on by five Indians. The two younger girls gave way to despair when captured; but Betsy Callaway was sure they would be followed and rescued. To mark the line of their flight she broke off twigs from the bushes, and when threatened with the tomahawk for doing this, she tore off strips from her dress. The Indians carefully covered their trail, compelling the girls to walk apart, as their captors did, in the thick cane, and to wade up and down the little brooks.

Boone started in pursuit the same evening. All next day he followed the tangled trail like a bloodhound, and early the following morning came on the Indians, camped by a buffalo calf which they had just killed and were about to cook. The rescue was managed very adroitly; for had any warning been given the Indians would have instantly killed their captives, according to their invariable custom. Boone and Floyd each shot one of the savages, and the remaining three escaped almost naked, without gun, tomahawk, or scalping-knife. The girls were unharmed; for the Indians rarely molested their captives on the journey to the home towns, unless their strength gave out, when they were tomahawked without mercy.

Thus for two years the pioneers worked in the wilderness, harassed by unending individual warfare, but not threatened by any formidable attempt to oust them from the lands that they had won. During this breathing spell they established civil government, explored the country, planted crops, and built strongholds. Then came the inevitable struggle. When in 1777 the snows began to melt before the lengthening spring days, the riflemen who guarded the forts were called on to make head against a series of resolute efforts to drive them from Kentucky.

Chapter IX

Kentucky Until the End of
The Revolution

IN the fall of 1776 it became evident that a formidable
Indian war was impending. In Virginia and Pennsylvania
the Indian outrages meant only the harassing of the borderers; in Kentucky, they threatened the complete destruction
of the vanguard of the white advance and, therefore, the
stoppage of all settlement west of the Alleghanies until after
the Revolutionary War, when very possibly the soil might not
have been ours to settle. Fortunately, the British lieutenant-
governor of the northwestern region, Henry Hamilton, did not
yet realize the importance of the Kentucky settlements, nor
the necessity of crushing them, and during 1777 the war bands
organized at his headquarters at Detroit were sent against the
country round Pittsburgh, while the feeble forts in the far
Western wilderness were only troubled by smaller war-parties
raised among the tribes on their own account. A strong expedition, led by Hamilton in person, would doubtless at this
time have crushed them.

As it was, there were still so few whites in Kentucky that
they were greatly outnumbered by the invading Indians. They
were, in consequence, unable to meet the enemy in open field,
and gathered in their stations or forted villages. Therefore
the early conflicts, for the most part, took the form of sieges
of these wooden forts. Such sieges had little in common with
the corresponding operations of civilized armies. The Indians usually tried to surprise a fort; if they failed, they occasionally tried to carry it by open assault, or by setting fire
to it, but very rarely, indeed, beleaguered it in form. For this
they lacked both the discipline and the commissariat. Accord-

131

ingly, if their first rush miscarried, they usually dispersed in the woods to hunt, or look for small parties of whites; always, however, leaving some of their number to hover round the fort and watch anything that took place. Masters in the art of hiding, and able to conceal themselves behind a bush, a stone, or a tuft of weeds, they skulked round the gate before dawn, to shoot the white sentinels; or they ambushed the springs, and killed those who came for water; they slaughtered all of the cattle that had not been driven in, and any one venturing incautiously beyond the walls was certain to be waylaid and murdered. Those who were thus hemmed in the fort were obliged to get game on which to live; the hunters accordingly were accustomed to leave before daybreak, travel eight or ten miles, hunt all day at the risk of their lives, and return after dark. Being of course the picked men of the garrison, they often eluded the Indians, or slew them if an encounter took place, but very frequently indeed they were themselves slain. Only a very few of the whites became, like Boone and Kenton, able to beat the best of the savages at their own game.

The innumerable sieges that took place during the long years of Indian warfare differed in detail, but generally closely resembled one another as regards the main points. Those that occurred in 1777 may be considered as samples of the rest; and accounts of these have been preserved by the two chief actors, Boone and Clark. Boonesborough, which was held by twenty-two riflemen, was attacked twice, once in April and again in July, on each occasion by a party of fifty or a hundred warriors. The first time the garrison was taken by surprise; one man lost his scalp, and four were wounded, including Boone himself, who had been commissioned as captain in the county militia. The Indians promptly withdrew when they found they could not carry the fort by a sudden assault. On the second occasion the whites were on their guard, and though they had one man killed and two wounded (leaving but thirteen unhurt men in the fort), they easily beat off the assailants, and slew half a dozen of them. This time the Indians stayed around two days, keeping up a heavy fire, under cover of which they several times tried to burn the fort.

Logan's Station at St. Asaphs was likewise attacked; it was held by only fifteen gunmen. When the attack was made the women, guarded by part of the men, were milking the cows outside the fort. The Indians fired at them from the thick cane that stood near by, killing one man and wounding two others, one mortally. The party, of course, fled to the fort, and on looking back they saw their mortally wounded friend weltering on the ground. His wife and family were within the walls; through the loopholes they could see him yet alive, and exposed every moment to death. So great was the danger that the men refused to go out to his rescue, whereupon Logan alone opened the gate, bounded out, and seizing the wounded man in his arms, carried him back unharmed through a shower of bullets. The Indians continued to lurk around the neighborhood, and the ammunition grew very scarce. Thereupon Logan took two companions and left the fort at night to go to the distant settlements on the Holston, where he might get powder and lead. He knew that the Indians were watching the Wilderness Road, and, trusting to his own hardiness and consummate woodcraft, he struck straight out across the cliff-broken, wood-covered mountains, sleeping wherever night overtook him, and travelling all day long with the tireless speed of a wolf. He returned with the needed stores in ten days from the time he set out. These tided the people over the warm months.

In the fall, when the hickories had turned yellow and the oaks deep red, during the weeks of still, hazy weather that mark the Indian summer, their favorite hunting-season, savages again filled the land, and Logan was obliged to repeat his perilous journey. He also continually led small bands of his followers against the Indian war and hunting parties, sometimes surprising and dispersing them, and harassing them greatly. Moreover, he hunted steadily throughout the year, for the most skilful hunters were, in those days of scarcity, obliged to spend much of their time in the chase. Once, while at a noted game-lick, waiting for deer, he was surprised by the Indians, and by their fire was wounded in the breast and had his right arm broken. Nevertheless, he sprang on his horse and escaped, though the savages were so close that one, leaping at him, for a moment grasped the tail of the horse. Every one of these pioneer leaders, from Clark and Boone to Sevier and Robertson, was required constantly to expose his life; each lost sons or brothers at the hands of the In-

dians, and each thinned the ranks of the enemy with his own
rifle. In such a primitive state of society the man who led
others was expected to show strength of body no less than
strength of mind and heart; he depended upon his physical
prowess almost as much as upon craft, courage, and head-work.
The founder and head of each little community needed not
only a shrewd brain and commanding temper, but also the
thews and training to make him excel as woodsman and hunter,
and the heart and eye to enable him to stand foremost in every
Indian battle.

Throughout these years the obscure strife, made up of the
individual contests of frontiersman and Indian, went on almost
without a break. The sieges, surprises, and skirmishes in
which large bands took part were chronicled; but there is little reference in the books to the countless conflicts wherein
only one or two men on a side were engaged. Much of the
greatest loss, however, both to Indians and whites, was caused
by this unending personal warfare. Every hunter, almost
every settler, was always in imminent danger of Indian attack, and in return was ever ready, either alone or with one
or two companions, to make excursions against the tribes
for scalps and horses. One or two of Simon Kenton's experiences during this year [1778] may be mentioned less for
their own sake than as examples of innumerable similar deeds
that were done, and woes that were suffered, in the course
of the ceaseless struggle.

Kenton was a tall, fair-haired man of wonderful strength
and agility; famous as a runner and wrestler, an unerring
shot, and a perfect woodsman. Like so many of these early
Indian fighters, he was not at all bloodthirsty. He was a
pleasant, friendly, and obliging companion; and it was hard
to rouse him to wrath. When once aroused, however, few
were so hardy as not to quail before the terrible fury of his
anger. He was so honest and unsuspecting that he was very
easily cheated by sharpers; and he died a poor man. He was
a stanch friend and follower of Boone. Once, in a fight outside the stockade of Boonesborough, he saved the life of his
leader by shooting an Indian who was on the point of toma-
hawking him. Boone was a man of few words, cold and
grave, accustomed to every kind of risk and hairbreadth
escape, and as little apt to praise the deeds of others as he

was to mention his own; but on this occasion he broke through his usual taciturnity to express his thanks for Kenton's help and his admiration for Kenton himself.

Kenton went with his captain on the expedition to the Scioto. Pushing ahead of the rest, he was attracted by the sound of laughter in a cane-brake. Hiding himself, he soon saw two Indians approach, both riding on one small pony, and chatting and laughing together in great good humor. Aiming carefully, he brought down both at once, one dead and the other severely wounded. As he rushed up to finish his work, his quick ears caught a rustle in the cane, and looking around he saw two more Indians aiming at him. A rapid spring to one side on his part made both balls miss. Other Indians came up; but, at the same time, Boone and his companions appeared, running as fast as they could while still keeping sheltered. A brisk skirmish followed, the Indians retreated, and Kenton got the coveted scalp. When Boone returned to the fort, Kenton stayed behind with another man and succeeded in stealing four good horses, which he brought back in triumph.

Much pleased with his success he shortly made another raid into the Indian country, this time with two companions. They succeeded in driving off a whole band of one hundred and sixty horses, which they brought in safety to the banks of the Ohio. But a strong wind was blowing, and the river was so rough that in spite of all their efforts they could not get the horses to cross; as soon as they were beyond their depth the beasts would turn round and swim back. The reckless adventurers could not make up their minds to leave the booty; and stayed so long, waiting for a lull in the gale, and wasting their time in trying to get the horses to take to the water in spite of the waves, that the pursuing Indians came up and surprised them. Their guns had become wet and useless, and no resistance could be made. One of them was killed, another escaped, and Kenton himself was captured.

The Indians asked him if "Captain Boone" had sent him to steal horses; and when he answered frankly that the stealing was his own idea, they forthwith proceeded to beat him lustily with their ramrods, at the same time showering on him epithets that showed they had at least learned the profanity of the traders. They staked him out at night; tied so that he could move neither hand nor foot; and during the day he was bound on an unbroken horse, with his hands tied behind him so that he could not protect his face from the trees and bushes. This was repeated every day. After three days he reached the town of Chillicothe, stiff, sore and bleeding.

Next morning he was led out to run the gantlet. A row of men, women, and boys, a quarter of a mile long, was formed, each with a tomahawk, switch, or club; at the end of the line was an Indian with a big drum, and beyond this was the council-house, which, if he reached, would for the time being protect him. The moment for starting arrived; the big drum was beaten; and Kenton sprang forward in the race. Keeping his wits about him he suddenly turned to one side and darted off with the whole tribe after him. His wonderful speed and activity enabled him to keep ahead, and to dodge those who got in his way, and by a sudden double he rushed through an opening in the crowd, and reached the council-house, having been struck but three or four blows.

He was not further molested that evening. Next morning a council was held to decide whether he should be immediately burnt at the stake, or should first be led round to the different villages. The warriors sat in a ring to pass judgment, passing the war-club from one to another; those who passed it in silence thereby voted in favor of sparing the prisoner for the moment, while those who struck it violently on the ground thus indicated their belief that he should be immediately put to death. The former prevailed, and Kenton was led from town to town. At each place he was tied to the stake, to be switched and beaten by the women and boys; or else was forced to run the gantlet, while sand was thrown in his eyes and guns loaded with powder fired against his body to burn his flesh.

Once, while on the march, he made a bold rush for liberty, all unarmed though he was; breaking out of the line and running into the forest. His speed was so great and his wind so good that he fairly outran his pursuers; but by ill luck, when almost exhausted, he came against another party of Indians. After this he abandoned himself to despair. He was often terribly abused by his captors; once one of them cut his shoulder open with an axe, breaking the bone.

His face was painted black, the death color, and he was twice sentenced to be burned alive at the Pickaway plains and at Sandusky. But each time he was saved at the last moment, once through a sudden spasm of mercy on the part of the renegade Girty, his old companion in arms at the time of Lord Dunmore's war, and again by the powerful intercession of the great Mingo chief, Logan. At last, after having run the gantlet eight times and been thrice tied to the stake, he was ransomed by some traders. They hoped to get valuable information from him about the border forts, and took him to Detroit. Here he stayed until his battered, wounded body was healed. Then he determined to escape, and formed his plan in concert with two other Kentuckians, who had been in Boone's party that was captured at the Blue Licks. They managed to secure some guns, got safely off, and came straight down through the great forests to the Ohio, reaching their homes in safety.*

Boone and Kenton have always been favorite heroes of frontier story—as much so as ever were Robin Hood and Little John in England. Both lived to a great age, and did and saw many strange things, and in the backwoods cabins

---

* McClung [John Alexander McClung, *Sketches of Western Adventure* (Maysville, Ky., 1832)] gives the exact conversations that took place between Kenton, Logan, Girty, and the Indian chiefs. They are very dramatic, and may possibly be true; the old pioneer would probably always remember even the words used on such occasions; but I hesitate to give them because McClung is so loose in his statements. In the account of this very incident he places it in '77, and says Kenton then accompanied Clark to the Illinois. But in reality—as we know from Boone—it took place in '78, and Kenton must have gone with Clark first.

During the early part of this century our more pretentious historians who really did pay some heed to facts and wrote books that—in addition to their mortal dulness—were quite accurate, felt it undignified and beneath them to notice the deeds of mere ignorant Indian fighters. They had lost all power of doing the best work; for they passed their lives in a circle of small literary men, who shrank from any departure from conventional European standards.

On the other hand, the men who wrote history for the mass of our people, not for the scholars, although they preserved much important matter, had not been educated up to the point of appreciating the value of evidence, and accepted undoubted facts and absurd traditions with equal good faith. Some of them (notably [Timothy] Flint and one or two of Boone's other biographers) evidently scarcely regarded truthfulness and accuracy of statement as being desirable qualities in a history. Others wished to tell the facts, but lacked all power of discrimination. Certain of their books had a very wide circulation. In some out-of-the-way places they formed, with the almanac, the staple of secular literature. But they did not come under the consideration of trained scholars, so their errors remained uncorrected; and at this day it is a difficult, and often an impossible task, to tell which of the statements to accept and which to reject.

the tale of their deeds has been handed down in traditional form from father to son and to son's son. They were known to be honest, fearless, adventurous, mighty men of their hands; fond of long, lonely wanderings; renowned as woodsmen and riflemen, as hunters and Indian fighters. In course of time it naturally came about that all notable incidents of the chase and woodland warfare were incorporated into their lives by the story-tellers. The facts were altered and added to by tradition year after year; so that the two old frontier warriors already stand in that misty group of heroes whose rightful title to fame has been partly overclouded by the haze of their mythical glories and achievements.

From 1778 to 1781 the Indian war dragged on much as usual. But 1782 proved to be Kentucky's year of blood. The British at Detroit had strained every nerve to drag into the war the entire Indian population of the Northwest. They had finally succeeded in arousing even the most distant tribes— not to speak of the twelve thousand savages immediately tributary to Detroit. So lavish had been the expenditure of money and presents to secure the good-will of the savages and enlist their active services against the Americans, that it had caused serious complaint at headquarters.

Early in the spring the Indians renewed their forays; horses were stolen, cabins burned, and women and children carried off captive. The people were confined closely to their stockaded forts, from which small bands of riflemen sallied to patrol the country. From time to time these encountered marauding-parties, and in the fights that followed sometimes the whites, sometimes the reds, were victorious.

These various ravages and skirmishes were but the prelude to a far more serious attack. In July, the British captains Caldwell and McKee came down from Detroit with a party of rangers, and gathered together a great army of over a thousand Indians—the largest body of either red men or white that was ever mustered west of the Alleghanies during the Revolution. They meant to strike at Wheeling; but while on their march thither were suddenly alarmed by the rumor that Clark intended to attack the Shawnee towns. They at once countermarched, but on reaching the threatened towns found that the alarm had been groundless. Most of the savages, with characteristic fickleness of temper, then declined to go farther; but a body of somewhat over three hundred Hurons and Lake Indians remained. With these and their Detroit rangers, Caldwell and McKee crossed the Ohio and marched into Kentucky, to attack the small forts of Fayette County.

Fayette lay between the Kentucky and the Ohio rivers, and was then the least populous and most exposed of the three counties into which the growing young commonwealth was divided. In 1782 it contained but five of the small stockaded towns in which all the early settlers were obliged to gather. The best defended and most central was Lexington, round which were grouped the four—Bryan's (which was the largest), McGee's, McConnell's, and Boone's. Bryan's on the south bank of the Elkhorn was the northernmost outpost of the settlers. Its stout, loopholed palisades enclosed some forty cabins, there were strong blockhouses at the corners, and it was garrisoned by fifty good riflemen. The rangers and warriors moved down through the forest with the utmost speed and stealth, hoping to take the fort by surprise.

The attack was made early on the morning of the 16th of August. Some of the settlers were in the cornfields, and the rest inside the palisade of standing logs; they were preparing to follow the band of marauders who had gone south of the Kentucky. A few outlying Indian spies were discovered, owing to their eagerness; and the whites being put on their guard, the attempt to carry the fort by the first rush was, of course, foiled. Like so many other stations— but unlike Lexington—Bryan's had no spring within its walls; and as soon as there was reason to dread an attack, it became a matter of vital importance to lay in a supply of water. It was feared that to send the men to the spring would arouse suspicion in the minds of the hiding savages; and, accordingly, the women went down with their pails and buckets, as usual. The younger girls showed some nervousness, but the old housewives marshalled them as coolly as possible, talking and laughing together, and by their unconcern completely deceived the few Indians who were lurking near by—for the main body had not yet come up. This advance-guard of the savages feared that, if they attacked the women, all chance of surprising the fort would be lost; and so the water-carriers were suffered to go back unharmed. Hardly were they within the fort, however, when some of the Indians found that they had been discovered, and the attack began so quickly that one or two of the men who had lingered in the corn-fields were killed, or else were cut off and fled to Lexington; while, at the same time, swift-footed runners were sent out to carry the alarm to the different stockades and summon their riflemen to the rescue.

At first but a few Indians appeared, on the side of the Lexington road; they whooped and danced defiance to the fort, evidently inviting an attack. Their purpose was to lure the defenders into sallying out after them, when their main body was to rush at the stockade from the other side. But they did not succeed in deceiving the veteran Indian fighters who manned the heavy gates of the fort, stood behind the loop-holed walls, or scanned the country roundabout from the high blockhouses at the corners. A dozen active young men were sent out on the Lexington road to carry on a mock skirmish with the decoy-party, while the rest of the defenders gathered behind the wall on the opposite side. As soon as a noisy but harmless skirmish had been begun by the sallying-party, the main body of warriors burst out of the woods and rushed toward the western gate. A single volley from the loopholes drove them back, while the sallying-party returned at a run and entered the Lexington gate unharmed, laughing at the success of their counter-stratagem.

The Indians surrounded the fort, each crawling up as close as he could find shelter behind some stump, tree, or fence. An irregular fire began, the whites, who were better covered, having slightly the advantage, but neither side suffering much. This lasted for several hours, until early in the afternoon a party from Lexington suddenly appeared and tried to force its way into the fort.

The runners who slipped out of the fort at the first alarm went straight to Lexington. There they found that the men had just started out to cut off the retreat of the marauding savages who were ravaging south of the Kentucky. Following their trail they speedily overtook the troops, and told of the attack on Bryan's. Instantly forty men under Major Levi Todd countermarched to the rescue. Being ignorant of the strength of the Indians they did not wait for the others, but pushed boldly forward, seventeen being mounted and the others on foot.

The road from Lexington to Bryan's for the last few hundred yards led beside a field of growing corn, taller than a man. Some of the Indians were lying in this field when they were surprised by the sudden appearance of the rescuers, and promptly fired on them. Levi Todd and the horsemen, who were marching in advance, struck spurs into their steeds, and, galloping hard through the dust and smoke, reached the fort in safety. The footmen were quickly forced to retreat toward Lexington; but the Indians were too surprised by the unlooked-for approach to follow, and they escaped with the loss of one man killed and three wounded.

That night the Indians tried to burn the fort, shooting flaming arrows onto the roofs of the cabins and rushing up to the wooden wall with lighted torches. But they were beaten off at each attempt. When day broke they realized that it was hopeless to make any further effort, though they still kept up a desultory fire on the fort's defenders; they had killed most of the cattle and pigs and some of the horses, and had driven away the rest.

The Indians knew well that the riflemen were mustering at all the neighboring forts; and, as soon as their effort to treat failed, they withdrew during the forenoon of the 17th. They were angry and sullen at their discomfiture. Five of their number had been killed and several wounded. Of the fort's defenders four had been killed and three wounded.

All this time the runners sent out from Bryan's had been speeding through the woods, summoning help from each of the little walled towns. The Fayette troops quickly gathered. As soon as Boone heard the news he marched at the head of the men of his station, among them his youngest son Israel, destined shortly to be slain before his eyes. The men from Lexington, McConnell's, and McGee's, rallied under John Todd, who was county lieutenant, and, by virtue of his commission in the Virginia line, the ranking officer of Kentucky, second only to Clark. Troops also came from south of the Kentucky River; Lieutenant-Colonel Trigg and Majors McGarry and Harlan led the men from Harrodsburg, who were soonest ready to march, and likewise brought the news that Logan, their county lieutenant, was raising the whole force of Lincoln in hot haste, and would follow in a couple of days.

These bands of rescuers reached Bryan's Station on the

afternoon of the day the Indians had left. The men thus gathered were the very pick of the Kentucky pioneers; sinewy veterans of border strife, skilled hunters and woodsmen, long wonted to every kind of hardship and danger. They were men of the most dauntless courage, but unruly and impatient of all control. Only a few of the cooler heads were willing to look before they leaped; and even their chosen and trusted leaders were forced to advise and exhort rather than to command them. All were eager for battle and vengeance, and were excited and elated by the repulse that had just been inflicted on the savages; and they feared to wait for Logan lest the foe should escape. Next morning they rode out in pursuit, one hundred and eighty-two strong, all on horseback, and all carrying long rifles. There was but one sword among them, which Todd had borrowed from Boone—a rough weapon, with short steel blade and buckhorn hilt. As with most frontier levies, the officers were in large proportion; for, owing to the system of armed settlement and half-military organization, each wooden fort, each little group of hunters or hard-fighting backwoods farmers, was forced to have its own captain, lieutenant, ensign, and sergeant.

The Indians, in their unhurried retreat, followed the great buffalo trace that led to the Blue Licks, a broad road, beaten out through the forest by the passing and repassing of the mighty herds through countless generations. They camped on the farther side of the river; some of the savages had left, but there were still nearly three hundred men in all—Hurons and Lake Indians, with the small party of rangers.

The backwoods horsemen rode swiftly on the trail of their foes, and before evening came to where they had camped the night before. A careful examination of the camp-fires convinced the leaders that they were heavily outnumbered; nevertheless they continued the pursuit, and overtook the savages early the following morning, the 19th of August.

As they reached the Blue Licks, they saw a few Indians retreating up a rocky ridge that led from the north bank of the river. The backwoodsmen halted on the south bank, and a short council was held. All turned naturally to Boone, the most experienced Indian fighter present, in whose cool courage and tranquil self-possession all confided. The wary old pioneer strongly urged that no attack be made at the moment, but that they should await the troops coming up under Logan. The Indians were certainly much superior in numbers to the whites; they were aware that they were being followed by a small force, and from the confident, leisurely way in which they had managed their retreat, were undoubtedly anxious to be overtaken and attacked. The hurried pursuit had been quite proper in the first place, for if the Indians had fled rapidly they would surely have broken up into different bands, which could have been attacked on even terms, while delay would have permitted them to go off unscathed. But, as it was, the attack would be very dangerous; while the delay of waiting for Logan would be a small matter, for the Indians could still be overtaken after he had arrived.

Well would it have been for the frontiersmen had they followed Boone's advice. Todd and Trigg both agreed with him, and so did many of the cooler riflemen—among others a man named Netherland, whose caution caused the young hotheads to jeer at him as a coward. But the decision was not suffered to rest with the three colonels who nominally commanded. Doubtless the council was hasty and tumultuous, being held by the officers in the open, closely pressed upon and surrounded by a throng of eager, unruly soldiers, who did not hesitate to offer advice or express dissatisfaction. Many of the more headlong and impatient among the bold spirits looking on desired instant action; and these found a sudden leader in Major Hugh McGarry. He was a man utterly unsuited to command of any kind; and his retention in office after repeated acts of violence and insubordination shows the inherent weakness of the frontier militia system. He not only chafed at control, but he absolutely refused to submit to it; and his courage was of a kind better fitted to lead him into a fight than to make him bear himself well after it was begun. He wished no delay, and was greatly angered at the decision of the council; nor did he hesitate to at once appeal therefrom. Turning to the crowd of backwoodsmen he suddenly raised the thrilling war-cry, and spurred his horse into the stream, waving his hat over his head and calling on all who were not cowards to follow him. The effect was electrical. In an instant all the hunter-soldiers plunged in after him with a shout, and splashed across the ford of the shallow river in huddled confusion.

Boone and Todd had nothing to do but follow. On the

other side they got the men into order, and led them on, the only thing that was possible under the circumstances. These two leaders acted excellently throughout; and they now did their best to bring the men with honor through the disaster into which they had been plunged by their own headstrong folly.

As the Indians were immediately ahead, the array of battle was at once formed.The troops spread out into a single line. The right was led by Trigg, the centre by Colonel-Commandant Todd in person, with McGarry under him, and an advance-guard of twenty-five men under Harlan in front; while the left was under Boone. The ground was equally favorable to both parties, the timber being open and good. But the Indians had the advantage in numbers, and were able to outflank the whites.

In a minute the spies brought word that the enemy were close in front. The Kentuckians galloped up at speed to within sixty yards of their foes, leaped from their horses, and instantly gave and received a heavy fire. Boone was the first to open the combat; and under his command the left wing pushed the Indians opposite them back for a hundred yards. The old hunter, of course, led in person; his men stoutly backed him up, and their resolute bearing and skilful marksmanship gave to the whites in this part of the line a momentary victory. But on the right of the Kentucky advance affairs went badly from the start. The Indians were thrown out so as to completely surround Trigg's wing. Almost as soon as the firing became heavy in front, crowds of painted warriors rose from some hollows of long grass that lay on Trigg's right and poured in a close and deadly volley. Rushing forward, they took his men in rear and flank, and rolled them up on the centre, killing Trigg himself. Harlan's advance-guard was cut down almost to a man, their commander being among the slain. The centre was then assailed from both sides by overwhelming numbers. Todd did all he could by voice and example to keep his men firm and cover Boone's successful advance, but in vain. Riding to and fro on his white horse he was shot through the body, and mortally wounded. He leaped on his horse again, but his strength failed him; the blood gushed from his mouth; he leaned forward, and fell heavily from the saddle. Some say that his horse carried him to the river, and that he fell into its current. With his death the centre gave way; and of course Boone and the men of the left wing, thrust in advance, were surrounded on three sides. A wild rout followed, every one pushing in headlong haste for the ford. "He that could re-mount a horse was well off; he that could not, had no time for delay," wrote Levi Todd. The actual fighting had only occupied five minutes.

In a mad and panic race the Kentuckians reached the ford, which was fortunately but a few hundred yards from the battle-field, the Indians being mixed in with them. Among the first to cross was Netherland, whose cautious advice had been laughed at before the battle. No sooner had he reached the south bank, than he reined up his horse and leaped off, calling on his comrades to stop and cover the flight of the others; and most of them obeyed him. The ford was choked with a strug-gling mass of horsemen and footmen, fleeing whites and fol-lowing Indians. Netherland and his companions opened a brisk fire upon the latter, forcing them to withdraw for a mo-ment and let the remainder of the fugitives cross in safety. Then the flight began again. The check that had been given the Indians allowed the whites time to recover heart and breath. Retreating in groups or singly through the forest, with their weapons reloaded, their speed of foot and woodcraft enabled such as had crossed the river to escape without further serious loss.

Boone was among the last to leave the field. His son Israel was slain, and he himself was cut off from the river; but, turning abruptly to one side, he broke through the ranks of the pursuers, outran them, swam the river, and returned un-harmed to Bryan's Station.

The loss of the defeated Kentuckians had been very great. Seventy were killed outright, including Colonel Todd and Lieutenant-Colonel Trigg, the first and third in command. Seven were captured, and twelve of those who escaped were badly wounded. The victors lost one of the Detroit rangers (a Frenchman), and six Indians killed and ten Indians wounded. Almost their whole loss was caused by the successful advance of Boone's troops, save what was due to Netherland when he rallied the flying backwoodsmen at the ford.

Of the seven white captives four were put to death with

torture, three eventually rejoining their people. One of them owed his being spared to a singular and amusing feat of strength and daring. When forced to run the gantlet he, by his activity, actually succeeded in reaching the council-house unharmed; when almost to it, he turned, seized a powerful Indian and hurled him violently to the ground, and then, thrusting his head between the legs of another pursuer, he tossed him clean over his back, after which he sprang on a log, leaped up and knocked his heels together, crowed in the fashion of backwoods victors, and rallied the Indians as a pack of cowards. One of the old chiefs immediately adopted him into the tribe as his son.

All the little forted villages north of the Kentucky, and those lying near its southern bank, were plunged into woe and mourning by the defeat. In every stockade, in almost every cabin, there was weeping for husband or father, son, brother, or lover. The best and bravest blood in the land had been shed like water. There was no one who had not lost some close and dear friend, and the heads of all the people were bowed and their hearts sore stricken.

The bodies of the dead lay where they had fallen, on the hill-slope and in the shallow river, torn by wolf, vulture, and raven, or eaten by fishes. In a day or two Logan came up with four hundred men from south of the Kentucky, tall Simon Kenton marching at the head of the troops, as captain of a company. They buried the bodies of the slain on the battlefield, in long trenches, and heaped over them stones and logs. Meanwhile, the victorious Indians, glutted with vengeance, recrossed the Ohio and vanished into the northern forests.

The Indian ravages continued throughout the early fall months; all the outlying cabins were destroyed, the settlers were harried from the clearings, and a station on Salt River was taken by surprise, thirty-seven people being captured. Stunned by the crushing disaster at the Blue Licks, and utterly disheartened and cast down by the continued ravages, many of the settlers threatened to leave the country. The county officers sent long petitions to the Virginia legislature, complaining that the troops posted at the Falls were of no assistance in checking the raids of the Indians, and asserting that the operations carried on by order of the Executive for the past eighteen months had been a detriment rather than a help. The utmost confusion and discouragement prevailed everywhere.

At last the news of repeated disaster roused Clark into his old-time energy. He sent out runners through the settlements, summoning all the able-bodied men to make ready for a blow at the Indians. The pioneers turned with eager relief toward the man who had so often led them to success. They answered his call with quick enthusiasm; beeves, pack-horses, and supplies were offered in abundance, and every man who could shoot and ride marched to the appointed meeting-places. The men from the eastern stations gathered at Bryan's, under Logan; those from the western, at the Falls, under Floyd. The two divisions met at the mouth of the Licking, where Clark took supreme command. On the 4th of November, he left the banks of the Ohio, and struck off northward through the forest, at the head of one thousand and fifty mounted riflemen. On the 10th he attacked the Miami towns. His approach was discovered just in time to prevent a surprise. The Indians hurriedly fled to the woods, those first discovered raising the alarm-cry, which could be heard an incredible distance, and thus warning their fellows. In consequence, no fight followed, though there was sharp skirmishing between the advance-guard and the hindermost Indians. Ten scalps were taken and seven prisoners, besides two whites being captured. Of Clark's men, one was killed and one wounded. The flight of the Indians was too hasty to permit them to save any of their belongings. All the cabins were burned, together with an immense quantity of corn and provisions—a severe loss at the opening of winter. McKee, the Detroit partisan, attempted to come to the rescue with what Indians he could gather, but was met and his force promptly scattered. Logan led a detachment to the head of the Miami, and burned the stores of the British traders. The loss to the savages at the beginning of cold weather was very great; they were utterly cast down and panic-stricken at such a proof of the power of the whites, coming as it did so soon after the battle of the Blue Licks. The expedition returned in triumph, and the Kentuckians completely regained their self-confidence; and though for ten years longer Kentucky suffered from the inroads of small parties of savages, it was never again threatened by a serious invasion.

At the beginning of 1783, when the news of peace was spread abroad, immigration began to flow to Kentucky down the Ohio, and over the Wilderness Road, in a flood of which the volume dwarfed all former streams into rivulets. Indian hostilities continued at intervals throughout this year, but they were not of a serious nature. Most of the tribes concluded at least a nominal peace, and liberated over two hundred white prisoners, though they retained nearly as many more.

The inrush of new settlers was enormous, and Kentucky fairly entered on its second stage of growth. The days of the first game-hunters and Indian fighters were over. By this year the herds of the buffalo, of which the flesh and hides had been so important to the early pioneers, were nearly exterminated; though bands still lingered in the remote recesses of the mountains, and they were plentiful in Illinois.

Thus the settlers could no longer always kill their own game; and there were churches, schools, mills, stores, race-tracks, and markets in Kentucky.

Chapter X

The Holston Settlements

THE history of Kentucky has now been traced from the date of the Cherokee war to the close of the Revolution. Those portions of the southwestern lands that were afterward made into the State of Tennessee had meanwhile developed with almost equal rapidity. Both Kentucky and Tennessee grew into existence and power at the same time, and were originally settled and built up by precisely the same class of American backwoodsmen. But there were one or two points of difference in their methods of growth. Kentucky sprang up afar off in the wilderness, and as a separate entity from the beginning. The present State has grown steadily from a single centre, which was the part first settled; and the popular name of the commonwealth has always been Kentucky. Tennessee, on the other hand, did not assume her present name until a quarter of a century after the first exploration and settlement had begun; and the State grew from two entirely distinct centres. The first settlements, known as the Watauga, or afterward more generally as the Holston, settlements, grew up while keeping close touch with the Virginians, who lived around the Tennessee headwaters, and also in direct communication with North Carolina, to which State they belonged. It was not until 1779 that a portion of these Holston people moved to the bend of the Cumberland River and started a new community, exactly as Kentucky had been started before. At first this new community, known as the Cumberland settlement, was connected by only the loosest tie with the Holston settlements. The people of the two places were not grouped together; they did not even have a common name. The three clusters of Holston, Cumberland, and Kentucky settlements developed independently of one

149

another, and though their founders were in each case of the same kind, they were at first only knit one to another by a lax bond of comradeship.

In 1776, the Watauga pioneers probably numbered some six hundred souls in all. Having at last found out the State in which they lived, they petitioned North Carolina to be annexed thereto as a district or county. The legislature of the State granted the prayer of the petitioners, Washington District was annexed, and four representatives therefrom, one of them Sevier, took their seats that fall in the Provincial Congress at Halifax. But no change whatever was made in the government of the Watauga people until 1777. In the spring of that year laws were passed providing for the establishment of courts of pleas and quarter sessions in the district, as well as for the appointment of justices of the peace, sheriffs, and militia officers; and in the fall the district was made a county, under the same name. The boundaries of Washington County were the same as those of the present State of Tennessee, and seem to have been outlined by Sevier, the only man who at that time had a clear idea as to what should be the logical and definite limits of the future State.

The nominal change of government worked little real alteration in the way the Holston people managed their affairs. The members of the old committee became the justices of the new court, and, with a slight difference in forms, proceeded against all offenders with their former vigor. Being eminently practical men, and not learned in legal technicalities, their decisions seem to have been governed mainly by their own ideas of justice, which, though genuine, were rough. As the war progressed and the Southern States fell into the hands of the British, the disorderly men who had streamed across the mountains became openly defiant toward the law. The Tories gathered in bands, and every man who was impatient of legal restraint, every murderer, horse thief, and highway robber in the community flocked to join them. The militia who hunted them down soon ceased to discriminate between Tories and other criminals, and the courts rendered decisions to the same effect. The caption of one indictment that has been preserved reads against the defendant "in Toryism." He was condemned to imprisonment during the war, half his goods was confiscated to the use of the State, and the other half was turned over for the support of his family. In another case the court granted a still more remarkable order, upon the motion of the State attorney, which set forth that fifteen hundred pounds, due to a certain H., should be retained in the hands of the debtor, because "there is sufficient reason to believe that the said H's estate will be confiscated to the use of the State for his misdemeanours."

There is something refreshing in the solemnity with which these decisions are recorded, and the evident lack of perception on the part of the judges that their records would, to their grandchildren, have a distinctly humorous side. To Tories and evil-doers generally, the humor was doubtless very grim; but, as a matter of fact, the decisions, though certainly of unusual character, were needful and just. The friends of order had to do their work with rough weapons, and they used them most efficiently. Under the stress of so dire an emergency as that they confronted they were quite right in attending only to the spirit of law and justice, and refusing to be hampered by the letter. They would have discredited their own energy and hard common sense had they acted otherwise, and, moreover, would have inevitably failed to accomplish their purpose.

In the summer of '78, when Indian hostilities almost entirely ceased, most of the militia were disbanded, and, in consequence the parties of Tories and horse thieves sprang into renewed strength, and threatened to overawe the courts and government officers. Immediately the leaders among the Whigs, the friends of order and liberty, gathered together and organized a vigilance committee. The committee raised two companies of mounted riflemen, who were to patrol the country and put to death all suspicious characters who resisted them or who refused to give security to appear before the committee in December. The proceedings of the committee were thus perfectly open; the members had no idea of acting secretly or against order. It was merely that in a time of general confusion they consolidated themselves into a body which was a most effective, though irregular, supporter of the cause of law. The mounted riflemen scoured the country and broke up the gangs of evil-doers, hanging six or seven of the leaders, while a number of the less prominent were brought before the committee, who fined some and condemned others

to be whipped or branded. All of doubtful loyalty were com-
pelled to take the test oath.

Such drastic measures soon brought about peace; and the
growing security, the opening of the land-office, and the increase of knowledge concerning the country, produced a
great inflow of settlers in 1779. From that time onward the
volume of immigration steadily increased.

Many of these newcomers were "poor whites," or crackers;
lank, sallow, ragged creatures, living in poverty, ignorance,
and dirt, who regarded all strangers with suspicion as "out-
landish folks." With every chance to rise, these people remained
mere squalid cumberers of the earth's surface, a rank, up-
country growth, containing within itself the seeds of vicious,
idle pauperism and semicriminality. They clustered in little
groups, scattered throughout the backwoods settlements, in
strong contrast to the vigorous and manly people around them.

By far the largest number of the newcomers were of the
true hardy backwoods stock, fitted to grapple with the wilderness and to hew out of it a prosperous commonwealth. The
leading settlers began, by thrift and industry, to acquire what
in the backwoods passed for wealth. Their horses, cattle, and
hogs throve and multiplied. The stumps were grubbed out
of the clearings, and different kinds of grains and roots were
planted. Wings were added to the houses, and sometimes they
were roofed with shingles. The little town of Jonesboro, the
first that was not a mere stockaded fort, was laid off midway
between the Watauga and the Nolichucky.

As elsewhere, the settlers were predominantly of Calvinistic
stock; for of all the then prominent faiths Calvinism was nearest to their feelings and ways of thought. Of the great recognized creeds it was the most republican in its tendencies,
and so the best suited to the backwoodsmen. They disliked
Anglicanism as much as they abhorred and despised Romanism
—theoretically at least, for practically then, as now, frontiersmen were liberal to one another's religion opinions, and the
stanch friend and good hunter might follow whatever creed
he wished, provided he did not intrude it on others. But backwoods Calvinism differed widely from the creed at first taught.
It was professed by thorough-going Americans, essentially free
and liberty-loving, who would not for a moment have tolerated
a theocracy in their midst. Their social, religious, and po-

litical systems were such as naturally flourished in a country remarkable for its temper of rough and self-asserting equality. Nevertheless, the old Calvinistic spirit left a peculiar stamp on this wild border democracy. More than anything else, it gave the backwoodsmen their code of right and wrong. Though they were a hard, narrow, dogged people, yet they intensely believed in their own standards and ideals. Often warped and twisted, mentally and morally, by the strain of their existence, they at least always retained the fundamental virtues of hardihood and manliness.

Presbyterianism was not, however, destined even here to remain the leading frontier creed. Other sects still more democratic, still more in keeping with backwoods life and thought, largely supplanted it. Methodism did not become a power until after the close of the Revolution; but the Baptists followed close on the heels of the Presbyterians. They, too, soon built log meeting-houses here and there, while their preachers cleared the forest and hunted elk and buffalo like the other pioneer settlers.

To all the churches the preacher and congregation alike went armed, the latter leaning their rifles in their pews or near their seats, while the pastor let his stand beside the pulpit. On week-days the clergymen usually worked in the fields in company with the rest of the settlers; all with their rifles close at hand and a guard stationed. In more than one instance when such a party was attacked by Indians the servant of the Lord showed himself as skilled in the use of carnal weapons as were any of his warlike parishioners.

The leaders of the frontiersmen were drawn from among several families, which, having taken firm root, were growing into the position of backwoods gentry. Of course, the use of this term does not imply any sharp social distinctions in backwoods life, for there were none such. The poorest and richest met on terms of perfect equality, slept in one another's houses and dined at one another's tables. But certain families, by dint of their thrift, the ability they showed in civil affairs, or the prowess of some of their members in time of war, had risen to acknowledged headship.

The part of Washington County northwest of the Holston was cut off and made into the county of Sullivan by the North Carolina legislature in 1779. The Virginian settlements on the

Holston, adjoining those of North Carolina, were in 1777 likewise made into a county of Washington.

The leading family among these Holston Virginians was that of the Campbells, who lived near Abingdon. The two chief members were cousins, Arthur and William. Arthur was captured by the Northern Indians when sixteen, and was kept a prisoner among them several years; when Lord Dunmore's war broke out he made his escape, and acted as scout to the earl's army. He served as militia colonel in different Indian campaigns, and was for thirty years a magistrate of the county; he was a man of fine presence, but of jealous, ambitious, overbearing temper. He combined with his fondness for Indian and hunter life a strong taste for books, and gradually collected a large library.

William Campbell stood next in rank. He was a man of giant strength, standing six feet two inches in height, and straight as a spear-shaft, with fair complexion, red hair, and piercing, light-blue eyes. A firm friend and stanch patriot, a tender and loving husband and father, gentle and courteous in ordinary intercourse with his fellows, he was, nevertheless, if angered, subject to fits of raging wrath that impelled him to any deed of violence. He was a true type of the Roundheads of the frontier, the earnest, eager men who pushed the border ever farther westward across the continent. He followed Indians and Tories with relentless and undying hatred; for the long list of backwoods virtues did not include pity for either public or private foes. The Tories threatened his life and the lives of his friends and families; they were hand in glove with the outlaws who infested the borders, the murderers, horse thieves, and passers of counterfeit money. He hunted them down with a furious zest, and did his work with merciless thoroughness, firm in the belief that he thus best served the Lord and the nation. One or two of his deeds illustrate admirably the grimness of the times, and the harsh contrast between the kindly relations of the border folks with their friends and their ferocity toward their foes. They show how the better backwoodsmen—the upright, churchgoing men, who loved their families, did justice to their neighbors, and sincerely tried to serve God—not only waged an unceasing war on the red and white foes of the State and of order, but carried it on with a certain ruthlessness that indicated less a disbelief in, than an utter lack of knowledge of, such a virtue as leniency to enemies.

One Sunday, Campbell was returning from church with his wife and some friends, carrying his baby on a pillow in front of his saddle, for they were all mounted. Suddenly a horseman crossed the road close in front of them, and was recognized by one of the party as a noted Tory. Upon being challenged, he rode off at full speed. Instantly Campbell handed the baby to a negro slave, struck spur into his horse, and galloping after the fugitive, overtook and captured him. The other men of the party came up a minute later. Several recognized the prisoner as a well-known Tory; he was riding a stolen horse; he had on him letters to the British agents among the Cherokees, arranging for an Indian rising. The party of returning churchgoers were accustomed to the quick and summary justice of lynch-law. With stern gravity they organized themselves into a court. The prisoner was adjudged guilty, and was given but a short shrift; for the horsemen hung him to a sycamore-tree before they returned to the road where they had left their families.

On another occasion, while Campbell was in command of a camp of militia, at the time of a Cherokee outbreak, he wrote a letter to his wife, a sister of Patrick Henry, that gives us a glimpse of the way in which he looked at Indians. His letter began, "My dearest Betsy;" in it he spoke of his joy at receiving her "sweet and affectionate letter;" he told how he had finally got the needles and pins she wished, and how pleased a friend had been with the apples she had sent him. He urged her to buy a saddle-horse, of which she had spoken, but to be careful that it did not start nor stumble, which were bad faults, "especially in a woman's hackney." In terms of endearment that showed he had not sunk the lover in the husband, he spoke of his delight at being again in the house where he had for the first time seen her loved face, "from which happy moment he dated the hour of all his bliss," and besought her not to trouble herself too much about him, quoting to her Solomon's account of a good wife, as reminding him always of her; and he ended by commending her to the peculiar care of Heaven. It was a letter that it was an honor to a true man to have written; such a letter as the best of women and wives might be proud to have received. Yet in the middle of it he promised to bring a strange trophy to show his tender and God-fearing spouse. He was speaking of the Indians; how they had murdered men, women, and children near by, and how they had been beaten back; and he added: "I have now the scalp of one who was killed eight or nine miles from my house about three weeks ago. The first time I go up I shall take it along to let you see it." Evidently, it was as natural for him to bring home to his wife and children the scalp of a slain Indian as the skin of a slain deer.

The times were hard, and they called for men of flinty fibre. Those of softer, gentler mould would have failed in the midst of such surroundings. The iron men of the border had a harsh and terrible task allotted them; and though they did it roughly, they did it thoroughly and on the whole well. They may have failed to learn that it is good to be merciful, but at least they knew that it is still better to be just and strong and brave; to see clearly one's rights, and to guard them with a ready hand.

Chapter XI

Robertson Founds the Cumberland Settlement

R OBERTSON had been for ten years a leader among the Holston and Watauga people. He had at different times played the foremost part in organizing the civil government and in repelling outside attack. He had been particularly successful in his dealings with the Indians, and by his missions to them had managed to keep the peace unbroken on more than one occasion when a war would have been disastrous to the whites. He was prosperous and successful in his private affairs; nevertheless, in 1779, the restless cravings for change and adventure surged so strongly in his breast that it once more drove him forth to wander in the forest. In the true border temper, he determined to abandon the home he had made, and to seek out a new one hundreds of miles farther in the heart of the hunting-grounds of the red warriors.

The point pitched upon was the beautiful country lying along the great bend of the Cumberland. Many adventurous settlers were anxious to accompany Robertson, and, like him, to take their wives and children with them into the new land. It was agreed that a small party of explorers should go first in the early spring to plant corn, that the families might have it to eat when they followed in the fall.

As soon as the corn was planted and cabins put up, most of the intending settlers returned to their old homes to bring out their families, leaving three of their number "to keep the buffaloes out of the corn." Robertson himself first went north through the wilderness to see George Rogers Clark in Illinois, to purchase cabin rights from him. This act gives an insight into at least some of the motives that influenced the ad-

157

venturers. Doubtless, they were impelled largely by sheer restlessness and love of change and excitement, and these motives would probably have induced them to act as they did, even had there been no others. But another and most powerful spring of action was the desire to gain land—not merely land for settlement, but land for speculative purposes. Wild land was then so abundant that the quantity literally seemed inexhaustible; and it was absolutely valueless until settled. Our forefathers may well be pardoned for failing to see that it was of more importance to have it owned in small lots by actual settlers than to have it filled up quickly under a system of huge grants to individuals or corporations. Many wise and good men honestly believed that they would benefit the country at the same time that they enriched themselves by acquiring vast tracts of virgin wilderness, and then proceeding to people them. There was a rage for land speculation and land companies of every kind. The private correspondence of almost all the public men of the period, from Washington, Madison, and Gouverneur Morris down, is full of the subject. Innumerable people of position and influence dreamed of acquiring untold wealth in this manner. Almost every man of note was actually or potentially a land speculator; and in turn almost every prominent pioneer, from Clark and Boone to Shelby and Robertson, was either himself one of the speculators or an agent for those who were. Many people did not understand the laws on the subject, or hoped to evade them; and the hope was as strong in the breast of the hunter who made a "tomahawk claim," by blazing a few trees, and sold it for a small sum, to a newcomer, as in that of the well-to-do schemer, who bought an Indian title for a song, and then got what he could from all outsiders who came in to dwell on the land.

This speculative spirit was a powerful stimulus to the settlement not only of Kentucky, but of middle Tennessee. Henderson's claim included the Cumberland country, and when North Carolina annulled his rights, she promised him a large but indefinitely located piece of land in their place. He tried to undersell the State in the land market, and undoubtedly his offers had been among the main causes that induced Robertson and his associates to go to the Cumberland when they did. But at the time it was uncertain whether

Cumberland lay in Virginia or North Carolina, as the line was not run by the surveyors until the following spring; and Robertson went up to see Clark, because it was rumored that the latter had the disposal of Virginia "cabin rights," under which each man could, for a small sum, purchase a thousand acres, on condition of building a cabin and raising a crop. However, as it turned out, he might have spared himself the journey, for the settlement proved to be well within the Carolina boundary.

In the fall very many men came out to the new settlement, guided thither by Robertson and Mansker; the former persuading a number who were bound to Kentucky to go to the Cumberland instead. Cold weather of extraordinary severity set in during November; for this was the famous "hard winter" of '79-80, during which the Kentucky settlers suffered so much. They were not molested by Indians, and reached the Bluffs about Christmas. The river was frozen solid, and they all crossed the ice in a body; when in midstream the ice jarred, and—judging from the report—the jar or crack must have gone miles up and down the stream; but the ice only settled a little and did not break. By January 1st, there were over two hundred people scattered on both sides of the river.

The settlers who came by water passed through much greater peril and hardship. By a stroke of good fortune the journal kept by John Donelson, the leader of the expedition, has been preserved. Donelson's flotilla, after being joined by a number of other boats, especially at the mouth of the Clinch, consisted of some thirty craft, all told—flatboats, dugouts, and canoes. There were probably two or three hundred people, perhaps many more, in the company; among them, as the journal records, "James Robertson's lady and children," the latter to the number of five. The chief boat, the flag-ship of the flotilla, was the *Adventure*, a great scow, in which there were over thirty men, besides the families of some of them.

They embarked at Holston, Long Island, on December 22d, but falling water and heavy frosts detained them two months, and the voyage did not really begin until they left Cloud Creek on February 27, 1780. The first ten days were uneventful. The *Adventure* spent an afternoon and night on a shoal, until the water fortunately rose and, all the men getting out, the clumsy scow was floated off. Another boat was driven on the point of an island and sunk, her crew being nearly drowned; whereupon the rest of the flotilla put to shore, the sunken boat was raised and bailed out, and most of her cargo recovered. At one landing-place a man went out to hunt, and got lost, not being taken up again for three days, though "many guns were fired to fetch him in," and the four-pounder on the *Adventure* was discharged for the same purpose. A negro became "much frosted in his feet and legs, of which he died." Where the river was wide a strong wind and high sea forced the whole flotilla to lay to, for the sake of the smaller craft. This happened on March 7th, just before coming to the uppermost Chickamauga town; and that night the wife of one Ephraim Peyton, who had himself gone with Robertson overland, was delivered of a child. She was in a boat whose owner was named Jonathan Jennings.

The next morning they soon came to an Indian village on the south shore. The Indians made signs of friendliness, and two men started toward them in a canoe which the *Adventure* had in tow, while the flotilla drew up on the opposite side of the river. But a half-breed and some Indians jumping into a pirogue, paddled out to meet the two messengers and advised them to return to their comrades, which they did. Several canoes then came off from the shore to the flotilla. The Indians who were in them seemed friendly and were pleased with the presents they received; but while these were being distributed the whites saw a number of other canoes putting off, loaded with armed warriors, painted black and red. The half-breed instantly told the Indians roundabout to paddle to the shore, and warned the whites to push off at once, at the same time giving them some instructions about the river. The armed Indians went down along the shore for some time as if to intercept them; but at last they were seemingly left behind.

In a short time another Indian village was reached, where the warriors tried in vain to lure the whites ashore; and as the boats were hugging the opposite bank, they were suddenly fired at by a party in ambush, and one man slain. Immediately afterward a much more serious tragedy occurred. There was with the flotilla a boat containing twenty-eight men, women, and children, among whom the smallpox had broken out. To guard against infection, it was agreed that it should keep well in the rear; being warned each night by the sound of a horn when it was time to go into camp.

As this forlorn boat-load of unfortunates came along, far behind the others, the Indians, seeing their defenseless position, sallied out in their canoes and butchered or captured all who were aboard. Their cries were distinctly heard by the rearmost of the other craft, who could not stem the current and come to their rescue. But a dreadful retribution fell on the Indians; for they were infected with the disease of their victims, and for some months virulent smallpox raged among many of the bands of Creeks and Cherokees. When stricken by the disease, the savages first went into the sweat-houses, and when heated to madness, plunged into the cool streams, and so perished in multitudes.

When the boats entered the Narrows they had lost sight of the Indians on shore, and thought they had left them behind. A man, who was in a canoe, had gone aboard one of the larger boats with his family, for the sake of safety while passing through the rough water. His canoe was towed alongside, and in the rapids it was overturned, and the cargo lost. The rest of the company, pitying his distress over the loss of all his wordly goods, landed, to see if they could not help him recover some of his property. Just as they got out on the shore to walk back, the Indians suddenly appeared almost over them, on the high cliffs opposite, and began to fire, causing a hurried retreat to the boats. For some distance the Indians lined the bluffs, firing from the heights into the boats below. Yet only four people were wounded, and they not dangerously. One of them was a girl named Nancy Gower. When, by the sudden onslaught of the Indians, the crew of the boat in which she was were thrown into dismay, she took the helm and steered, exposed to the fire of the savages. A ball went through the upper part of one of her thighs, but she neither flinched nor uttered any cry; and it was not known that she was wounded until, after the danger was past, her mother saw the blood soaking through her clothes. She recovered, married one of the frontiersmen, and lived for fifty years afterward, long enough to see all the wilderness filled with flourishing and populous States.

One of the clumsy craft, however, did not share the good

fortune that befell the rest, in escaping with so little loss and damage. Jonathan Jennings's boat, in which was Mrs. Peyton, with her new-born baby, struck on a rock at the upper end of the whirl, the swift current rendering it impossible for the others to go to his assistance; and they drifted by, leaving him to his fate. The Indians soon turned their whole attention to him, and from the bluffs opened a most galling fire upon the disabled boat. He returned it as as he could, keeping them somewhat in check, for he was a most excellent marksman. At the same time he directed his two negroes, a man and women, his nearly grown son, and a young man who was with him, to lighten the boat by throwing his goods into the river. Before this was done, the negro man, the son, and the other young man most basely jumped into the river, and swam ashore. It is satisfactory to record that at least two of the three dastards met the fate they deserved. The negro was killed in the water, and the other two captured, one of them being afterward burned at the stake, while the other, it is said, was ultimately released. Meanwhile, Mrs. Jennings, assisted by the negro woman and Mrs. Peyton, actually succeeded in shoving the lighted boat off the rock, though their clothes were cut in many places by the bullets; and they rapidly drifted out of danger. The poor little baby was killed in the hurry and confusion; but its mother, not eighteen hours from childbed, in spite of the cold, wet, and exertion, kept in good health. Sailing by night as well as day, they caught up with the rest of the flotilla before dawn on the second morning afterward, the men being roused from their watch-fires by the cries of "help poor Jennings," as the wretched and worn-out survivors in the disabled boat caught the first glimpse of the lights on shore.

Having successfully run the gantlet of the Chickamauga banditti, the flotilla was not again molested by the Indians, save once when the boats that drifted near shore were fired on by a roving war-party, and five men wounded. They ran over the great Muscle Shoals in about three hours without accident, though the boats scraped on the bottom here and there. The swift, broken water surged into high waves, and roared through the piles of driftwood that covered the points of the small islands, round which the current ran in every direction; and those among the men who were unused to river-work were much relieved when they found themselves in safety.

On the 20th of the month they reached the Ohio. On the 24th, they entered the mouth of the Cumberland. The *Adventure,* the heaviest of all the craft, got much help from a small squaresail that was set in the bow.

Two days afterward, the hungry party killed some buffalo, and feasted on the lean meat, and the next day they shot a swan "which was very delicious," as Donelson recorded. Their meal was exhausted and they could make no more bread; but buffalo were plenty, and they hunted them steadily for their meat; and they also made what some of them called "Shawnee salad" from a kind of green herb that grew in the bottoms.

On the last day of the month they met Colonel Richard Henderson, who had just come out and was running the line between Virginia and North Carolina. The crews were so exhausted that the progress of the boats became very slow, and it was not until April 24th that they reached the Big Salt Lick, and found Robertson awaiting them. The long, toilsome, and perilous voyage had been brought to a safe end.

There were then probably nearly five hundred settlers on the Cumberland, one-half of them being able-bodied men in the prime of life. The central station, the capital of the little community, was that at the Bluffs, where Robertson built a little stockaded hamlet and called it Nashborough (after A. Nash, governor of North Carolina); it was of the usual type of small frontier forted town.

True to their customs and traditions, and to their race-capacity for self-rule, the settlers determined forthwith to organize some kind of government under which justice might be done among themselves, and protection afforded against outside attack. Not only had the Indians begun their ravages, but turbulent and disorderly whites were also causing trouble. Robertson, who had been so largely instrumental in founding the Watauga settlement, and giving it laws, naturally took the lead in organizing this, the second community which he had caused to spring up in the wilderness. He summoned a meeting of delegates from the various stations, to be held at Nashborough; Henderson being foremost in advocating the adoption of the plan.

In fact, Henderson, the treaty-maker and land speculator, whose purchase first gave the whites clear color of title to the valleys of the Kentucky and Cumberland, played somewhat the same part, though on a smaller scale, in the settlement made by Robertson as in that made by Boone. He and the Virginian commissioner Walker had surveyed the boundary-line and found that the Cumberland settlements were well to the south of it. He then claimed the soil as his under the Cherokee deed and disposed of it to the settlers who contracted to pay ten dollars a thousand acres. This was but a fraction of the State price, so the settlers were all eager to hold under Henderson's deed; one of the causes of their coming out had been the chance of getting land so cheap. But Henderson's claim was annulled by the legislature, and the satisfaction-piece of two hundred thousand acres allotted him was laid off elsewhere; so his contracts with the settlers came to nothing, and they eventually got title in the usual way from North Carolina. They suffered no loss in the matter, for they had merely given Henderson promises to pay when his title was made good.

The settlers, by their representatives, met together at Nashborough, and on May 1, 1780, entered into articles of agreement or a compact of government. It was doubtless drawn up by Robertson, with perhaps the help of Henderson, and was modelled upon what may be called the "constitution" of Watauga, with some hints from that of Transylvania. The settlers ratified the deeds of their delegates on May 13th, when they signed the articles, binding themselves to obey them to the number of two hundred and fifty-six men. The signers practically guaranteed one another their rights in the land, and their personal security against wrong-doers; those who did not sign were treated as having no rights whatever—a proper and necessary measure, as it was essential that the naturally lawless elements should be forced to acknowledge some kind of authority.

The compact provided that the affairs of the community should be administered by a Court or Committee of twelve, Judges, Triers, or General Arbitrators, to be elected in the different stations by vote of all the freemen in them who were over twenty-one years of age. Three of the Triers were to come from Nashborough, two from Mansker's, two from

Bledsoe's, and one from each of five other named stations. Whenever the freemen of any station were dissatisfied with their Triers, they could at once call a new election, at which others might be chosen in their stead. The Triers had no salaries, but the Clerk of the Court was allowed some very small fees, just enough to pay for the pens, ink, and paper, all of them scarce commodities. The Court had jurisdiction in all cases of conflict over land titles, a land-office being established and an entry-taker appointed. Over half of the compact was devoted to the rules of the land-office. The Court, acting by a majority of its members, was to have jurisdiction for the recovery of debt or damages, and to be allowed to tax costs. Three Triers were competent to make a court to decide a case where the debt or damage was a hundred dollars or less, and there was no appeal from their decision. For a large sum an appeal lay to the whole Court. The Court appointed whomsoever it pleased to see decisions executed. It had power to punish all offenses against the peace of the community, all misdemeanors and criminal acts, provided only that its decisions did not go so far as to affect the life of the criminal. If the misdeed of the accused was such as to be dangerous to the State, or one "for which the benefit of clergy was taken away by law," he was to be bound and sent under guard to some place where he could be legally dealt with. The Court levied fines, payable in money or provisions, entered up judgments and awarded executions, and granted letters of administration upon estates of deceased persons, and took bonds "payable to the chairman of the Committee." The expenses were to be paid proportionately by the various settlers. It was provided, in view of the Indian incursions, that the militia officers elected at the various stations should have power to call out the militia when they deemed it necessary to repel or pursue the enemy. They were also given power to fine such men as disobeyed them, and to impress horses, if need be; if damaged, the horses were to be paid for by the people of the station in the proportion the Court might direct. It was expressly declared that the compact was designed as a "temporary method of restraining the licentious," that the settlement did not desire to be exempt from the ratable share of the expense for the Revolutionary War, and earnestly asked that North Carolina would immediately make it part of the State, erecting it into a county. Robertson was elected chairman of the Court and colonel of the militia, being thus made both civil and military commandant of the settlement. In common with other Triers, he undertook the solemnization of marriages; and these were always held legal, which was fortunate, as it was a young and vigorous community, of which the members were much given to early wedlock.

Thus a little commonwealth, a self-governing State, was created. It was an absolute democracy, the majority of freemen of full age in each stockade having power in every respect, and being able not only to elect, but to dismiss their delegates at any moment. Their own good sense and a feeling of fair play could be depended upon to protect the rights of the minority, especially as a minority of such men would certainly not tolerate anything even remotely resembling tyranny. They had formed a representative government in which the legislative and judicial functions were not separated, and were even to a large extent combined with the executive. They had proceeded in an eminently practical manner, having modelled their system on what was to them the familiar governmental unit of the county with its county court and county militia officers. They made the changes that their peculiar position required, grafting the elective and representative systems on the one they adopted, and, of course, enlarging the scope of the Court's action. Their compact was thus in some sort of an unconscious reproduction of the laws and customs of the old-time court-leet, profoundly modified to suit the peculiar needs of backwoods life, the intensely democratic temper of the pioneers, and, above all, the military necessities of their existence. They had certain theories of liberty and justice; but they were too shrewd and hard-headed to try to build up a government on an entirely new foundation when they had, ready to hand, materials with which they were familiar. They knew by experience the workings of the county system; all they did was to alter the immediate channel from which the Court drew its powers, and to adapt the representation to the needs of a community where constant warfare obliged the settlers to gather in little groups, which served as natural units.

For some months the whites who first arrived dwelt in

peace. But in the spring, hunting and war parties from various tribes started to harass the settlers. They began to commit murders, kill the stock, and drive off the horses in April, and their ravages continued unceasingly throughout the year.

These accumulated disasters wrought the greatest discouragement among the settlers. Many left the country, and most. of the remainder, when midsummer was past, began to urge that they should all go back in a body to the old settlements. The panic became very great. One by one the stockades were deserted, until finally all the settlers who remained were gathered in Nashborough and Freeland's. The Cumberland country would have been abandoned to the Indians, had Robertson not shown himself to be exactly the man for whom the crisis called.

Robertson was not a dashing, brilliant Indian fighter and popular frontier leader, like Sevier. He had rather the qualities of Boone, with the difference that he was less a wandering hunter and explorer, and better fitted to be head of a settled community. He was far-seeing, tranquil, resolute, unshaken by misfortune and disaster; a most trustworthy man, with a certain severe fortitude of temper. All people naturally turned to him in time of panic, when the ordinarily bold and daring became cowed and confused. The straits to which the settlers were reduced, and their wild clamor for immediate flight, the danger from the Indians, the death of his own son, all combined failed to make him waver one instant in his purpose. He strongly urged on the settlers the danger of flight through the wilderness. He did not attempt to make light of the perils that confronted them if they remained, but he asked them to ponder well if the beauty and fertility of the land did not warrant some risk being run to hold it, now that it was won. They were at last in a fair country, fitted for the homes of their children. Now was the time to keep it. If they abandoned it they would lose all the advantages they had gained, and would be forced to suffer the like losses and privations if they ever wished to retake possession of it or of any similar tract of land. He, at least, would not turn back, but would stay to the bitter end.

His words and his steadfast bearing gave heart to the settlers, and they no longer thought of flight. As their corn had failed them they got their food from the woods. Some gathered quantities of walnuts, hickory-nuts, and shellbarks, and the hunters wrought havoc among the vast herds of game.

The hunters were very accurate marksmen; game was plenty, and not shy, and so they got up close and rarely wasted a shot. Moreover, their small-bore rifles took very little powder—in fact, the need of excessive economy in the use of ammunition when on their long hunting trips was one of the chief reasons for the use of small bores. They therefore used comparatively little ammunition. Nevertheless, by the beginning of winter both powder and bullets began to fail. In this emergency Robertson again came to the front to rescue the settlement he had founded and preserved. He was accustomed to making long, solitary journeys through the forest, unmindful of the Indians; he had been one of the first to come from North Carolina to Watauga; he had repeatedly been on perilous missions to the Cherokees; he had the previous year gone north to the Illinois country to meet Clark. He now announced that he would himself go to Kentucky and bring back the needed ammunition; and at once set forth on his journey, across the long stretches of snow-powdered barrens, and desolate, Indian-haunted woodland.

Robertson passed unharmed through the wilderness to Kentucky. There he procured plenty of powder, and without delay set out on his return journey to the Cumberland. As before, he travelled alone through the frozen woods, trusting solely to his own sharp senses for his safety.

In the evening of January 15, 1781, he reached Freeland's station, and was joyfully received by the inmates. They supped late, and then sat up for some time, talking over many matters. When they went to bed all were tired, and neglected to take the usual precautions against surprise; moreover, at that season they did not fear molestation. They slept heavily, none keeping watch. Robertson alone was wakeful and suspicious; and even during his light slumbers his keen and long trained senses were on the alert.

At midnight all was still. The moon shone brightly down on the square blockhouses and stockaded yard of the lonely little frontier fort; its rays lit up the clearing, and by contrast darkened the black shadow of the surrounding forest. None of the sleepers within the log walls dreamed of danger. Yet their peril was imminent. An Indian war band was lurking

near by, and was on the point of making an effort to carry
Freeland's station by an attack in the darkness. In the dead
of the night the attempt was made. One by one the warriors
left the protection of the tangled wood-growth, slipped silently
across the open space, and crouched under the heavy timber
pickets of the palisades, until all had gathered together.
Though the gate was fastened with a strong bar and chain,
the dexterous savages finally contrived to open it.

In so doing they made a slight noise, which caught Robertson's quick ear, as he lay on his buffalo-hide pallet. Jumping up, he saw the gate open, and dusky figures gliding into
the yard with stealthy swiftness. At his cry of "Indians,"
and the report of his piece, the settlers sprang up, every man
grasping the loaded arm by which he slept. From each log
cabin the rifles cracked and flashed; and, though the Indians
were actually in the yard, they had no cover, and the sudden
and unexpected resistance caused them to hurry out much
faster than they had come in. Robertson shot one of their
number, and they in return killed a white man who sprang
out-of-doors at the first alarm. When they were driven out,
the gate was closed after them; but they fired through the
loopholes, especially into one of the blockhouses where the
chinks had not been filled with mud, as in the others. They
thus killed a negro, and wounded one or two other men; yet
they were soon driven off. Robertson's return had been at a
most opportune moment. As so often before and afterward,
he had saved the settlement from destruction.

Other bands of Indians joined the war-party, and they
continued to hover about the stations, daily inflicting loss and
damage on the settlers. They burned down the cabins and
fences, drove off the stock, and killed the hunters, the women,
and children who ventured outside the walls, and the men
who had gone back to their deserted stockades.

On the second day of April another effort was made by a
formidable war-party to get possession of one of the two
remaining stations—Freeland's and Nashborough—and thus,
at a stroke, drive the whites from the Cumberland district.
This time Nashborough was the point aimed at. After the
failure of this attempt, the Indians did not, for some years,
make any formidable attack on any of the larger stations.
Though the most dangerous of all foes on their own ground,

their extreme caution, and dislike of suffering punishment, prevented them from ever making really determined efforts to carry a fort openly by storm; moreover, these stockades were really very defensible against men unprovided with artillery, and there is no reason for supposing that any troops could have carried them by fair charging, without suffering altogether disproportionate loss. The red tribes acted in relation to the Cumberland settlements exactly as they had previously done toward those on the Kentucky and Watauga. They harassed the settlers from the outset; but they did not wake up to the necessity for a formidable and combined campaign against them until it was too late for such a campaign to succeed. If, at the first, any one of these communities had been forced to withstand the shock of such Indian armies as were afterward brought against it, it would, of necessity, have been abandoned.

Throughout '81 and '82 the Cumberland settlers were worried beyond description by a succession of small war-parties. Many of the settlers were killed, many others left for Kentucky, Illinois, or Natchez, or returned to their old homes among the Alleghanies; and in 1782 the inhabitants, who had steadily dwindled in numbers, became so discouraged that they again mooted the question of abandoning the Cumberland district in a body. Only Robertson's great influence prevented this being done; but by word and example he finally persuaded them to remain. The following spring brought the news of peace with Great Britain. A large inflow of new settlers began with the new year, and though the Indian hostilities still continued, the Cumberland country throve apace, and by the end of 1783 the old stations had been rebuilt and many new ones founded. Some of the settlers began to live out on their clearings. Rude little corn-mills and "hominy pounders" were built beside some of the streams. The piles of furs and hides that had accumulated In the stockades were sent back to the coast country on pack-horses. After this year there was never any danger that the settlements would be abandoned.

Chapter XII

The End of the Revolutionary
Wars and the Inrush
of Settlers

W HEN the first Continental Congress began its sittings,
the only frontiersmen west of the mountains, and beyond the limits of continuous settlement within the
old Thirteen Colonies, were the two or three hundred citizens
of the little Watauga commonwealth. When peace was declared with Great Britain, the backwoodsmen had spread westward, in groups, almost to the Mississippi, and they had increased in number to some twenty-five thousand souls, of
whom a few hundred dwelt in the bend of the Cumberland,
while the rest were about equally divided between Kentucky
and Holston.

This great westward movement of armed settlers was essentially one of conquest, no less than of colonization. Thronging in with their wives and children, their cattle, and their few
household goods, they won and held the land in the teeth of
fierce resistance, both from the Indian claimants of the soil
and from the representatives of a mighty and arrogant European power. The chain of events by which the winning was
achieved is perfect; had any link therein snapped, it is likely
that the final result would have been failure. The wide wanderings of Boone and his fellow hunters made the country
known, and awakened in the minds of the frontiersmen a
keen desire to possess it. The building of the Watauga commonwealth by Robertson and Sevier gave a base of operations, and furnished a model for similar communities to follow. Lord Dunmore's war made the actual settlement possible,
for it cowed the Northern Indians, and restrained them from
seriously molesting Kentucky during its first and most feeble

171

years. Henderson and Boone made their great treaty with
the Cherokees in 1775, and then established a permanent
colony far beyond all previous settlements, entering into final
possession of the new country. The victory over the Cherokees in 1776 made safe the line of communication along the
Wilderness Road, and secured the chance for further expansion. Clark's campaigns gained the Illinois, or northwestern regions. The growth of Kentucky then became very rapid; and
in its turn this, and the steady progress of the Watauga settlements, rendered possible Robertson's successful effort to
plant a new community still farther west, on the Cumberland.

The backwoodsmen pressed in on the line of least resistance,
first taking possession of the debatable hunting-grounds lying
between the Algonquins of the North and the Appalachian confederacies of the South. Then they began to encroach on the
actual tribal territories. Every step was accompanied by stubborn and bloody fighting with the Indians. The forest tribes
were exceedingly formidable opponents; it is not too much to
say that they formed a far more serious obstacle to the
American advance than would have been offered by an equal
number of the best European troops. Their victories over
Braddock, Grant, and St. Clair, gained in each case with a
smaller force, conclusively proved their superiority, on their
own ground, over the best regulars, disciplined and commanded in the ordinary manner. Almost all of the victories,
even of the backwoodsmen, were won against inferior numbers of Indians.* The red men were fickle of temper, and large

---

* That the contrary impression prevails is due to the boastful vanity
which the backwoodsmen often shared with the Indians, and to the gross
ignorance of the average writer concerning these border wars. Many
of the accounts in the popular histories are sheer inventions. Thus, in
the "Chronicles of Border Warfare," by Alex. S. Withers (Clarksburg,
Va., 1831, p. 301), there is an absolutely fictitious account of a feat of
the Kentucky Colonel Scott, who is alleged to have avenged St. Clair's
defeat by falling on the victorious Indians while they were drunk, and
killing two hundred of them. This story has not even a foundation in
fact; there was not so much as a skirmish of the sort described. As Mann
Butler—a most painstaking and truthful writer—points out, it is made
up out of the whole cloth, thirty years after the event; it is a mere
invention to soothe the mortified pride of the whites. Gross exaggeration
of the Indian numbers and losses prevails even to this day. Mr. Edmund
Kirke, for instance, usually makes the absolute or relative numbers of the
Indians from five to twenty-five times as great as they really were. Still,
it is hard to blame backwoods writers for such slips in the face of the
worse misdeeds of the average historian of the Greek and Roman wars
with barbarians.

bodies could not be kept together for a long campaign, nor, indeed, for more than one special stroke; the only piece of strategy any of their chiefs showed was Cornstalk's march past Dunmore to attack Lewis; but their tactics and discipline in the battle itself were admirably adapted to the very peculiar conditions of forest warfare. Writers who speak of them as undisciplined, or as any but most redoubtable antagonists, fall into an absurd error. An old Indian fighter, who, at the close of the last century, wrote, from experience, a good book on the subject, summed up the case very justly when he said: "I apprehend that the Indian discipline is as well calculated to answer the purpose in the woods of America as the British discipline is in Flanders; and British discipline in the woods is the way to have men slaughtered, with scarcely any chance of defending themselves." A comparison of the two victories gained by the backwoodsmen—at the Great Kanawha, over the Indians, and at Kings Mountain over Ferguson's British and Tories—brings out clearly the formidable fighting capacity of the red men. At the Kanawha the Americans outnumbered their foes, at Kings Mountain they were no more than equal; yet in the former battle they suffered twice the loss they did in the latter, inflicted much less damage in return, and did not gain nearly so decisive a victory.

The Indians were urged on by the British, who furnished them with arms, ammunition, and provisions, and sometimes also with leaders and with bands of auxiliary white troops, French, British, and Tories. It was this that gave to the Revolutionary contest its twofold character, making it on the part of the Americans a struggle for independence in the East, and in the West a war of conquest, or rather a war to establish, on behalf of all our people, the right of entry into the fertile and vacant regions beyond the Alleghanies. The grievances of the backwoodsmen were not the same as the grievances of the men of the seacoast. The Ohio valley and the other Western lands of the French had been conquered by the British, not the Americans. Great Britain had succeeded to the policy as well as the possession of her predecessor, and, strange to say, had become almost equally hostile to the colonists of her own stock. As France had striven for half a century, so England now in her turn strove, to bar out the settlers of English race from the country beyond the Alleghanies.

The British Crown, Parliament, and people were a unit in wishing to keep woodland and prairie for the sole use of their own merchants, as regions tenanted only by Indian hunters and French trappers and traders. They became the guardians and allies of all the Indian tribes. On the other hand, the American backwoodsmen were resolute in their determination to go in and possess the land. The aims of the two sides thus clashed hopelessly. Under all temporary and apparent grounds of quarrel lay this deep-rooted jealousy and incompatibility of interests. Beyond the Alleghanies the Revolution was fundamentally a struggle between England, bent on restricting the growth of the English race, and the Americans, triumphantly determined to acquire the right to conquer the continent.

Had not the backwoodsmen been successful in the various phases of the struggle, we would certainly have been cooped up between the sea and the mountains. If in 1774 and '76 they had been beaten by the Ohio tribes and the Cherokees, the border ravaged, and the settlements stopped or forced back as during what the colonists called Braddock's War, there is every reason to believe that the Alleghanies would have become our Western frontier. Similarly, if Clark had failed in his efforts to conquer and hold the Illinois and Vincennes, it is overwhelmingly probable that the Ohio would have been the boundary between the Americans and the British. Before the Revolution began, in 1774, the British Parliament had, by the Quebec Act, declared the country between the Great Lakes and the Ohio to be part of Canada; and under the provisions of this act the British officers continued to do as they had already done—that is, to hold adverse possession of the land, scornfully heedless of the claims of the different colonies. The country was *de facto* part of Canada; the Americans tried to conquer it exactly as they tried to conquer the rest of Canada; the only difference was that Clark succeeded, whereas Arnold and Montgomery failed.

Of course, the conquest by the backwoodsmen was by no means the sole cause of our acquisition of the West. The sufferings and victories of the Westerners would have counted for nothing had it not been for the success of the American arms in the East, and for the skill of our three treaty-makers at Paris—Jay, Adams, and Franklin, but above all the two former, and especially Jay. On the other hand, it was the actual occupation and holding of the country that gave our diplomats their vantage-ground. When the treaty was made, in 1782, the commissioners of the United States represented a people already holding the whole Ohio valley, as well as the Illinois. The peace of 1783, as far as our Western limits were affected, did nothing more than secure us undisturbed possession of lands from which it had proved impossible to oust us. We were in reality given nothing more than we had by our own prowess gained; the inference is strong that we got what we did get only because we had won and held it.

With the ending of the Revolutionary War, the rush of settlers to these Western lands assumed striking proportions. The peace relieved the pressure which had hitherto restrained this movement, on the one hand, while on the other it tended to divert into the new channel of pioneer work those bold spirits whose spare energies had thus far found an outlet on stricken fields. To push the frontier westward in the teeth of the forces of the wilderness was fighting work, such as suited well enough many a stout soldier who had worn the blue and buff of the Continental line, or who, with his fellow rough-riders, had followed in the train of some grim partisan leader.

The great growth of the West took place in Kentucky. The Kentucky country was by far the most widely renowned for its fertility; it was much more accessible and more firmly held, and its government was on a more permanent footing than was the case in the Wabash, Illinois, and Cumberland regions. In consequence, the majority of the men who went West to build homes fixed their eyes on the vigorous young community which lay north of the Ohio, and which already aspired to the honors of statehood.

The immigrants came into Kentucky in two streams, following two different routes—the Ohio River, and Boone's old Wilderness Trail. Those who came overland, along the latter road, were much fewer in number than those who came by water; and yet they were so numerous that the trail at times was almost thronged, and much care had to be taken in order to find camping-places where there was enough feed for the horses. The people who travelled this Wilderness Road went in the usual backwoods manner, on horseback, with laden pack-trains, and often with their herds and flocks. Young men went out alone or in parties, and groups of families from the same neighborhood often journeyed together. They struggled over the narrow, ill-made roads which led from the different back settlements, until they came to the last outposts of civilization east of the Cumberland Mountains: scattered blockhouses, whose owners were by turns farmers, tavern-keepers, hunters, and Indian fighters. Here they usually waited until a sufficient number had gathered together to furnish a band of riflemen large enough to beat off any prowling-party of red marauders; and then set off to traverse by slow stages the mountains and vast forests which lay between them and the nearest Kentucky station. The time of the journey depended, of course, upon the composition of the travelling-party, and upon the mishaps encountered; a party of young men on good horses might do it in three days, while a large band of immigrants, who were hampered by women, children, and cattle, and dogged by ill luck, might take three weeks. Ordinarily, six or eight days were sufficient. Before starting, each man laid in a store of provisions for himself and his horse—perhaps thirty pounds of flour, half a bushel of corn-meal, and three bushels of oats. There was no meat, unless game was shot. Occasionally, several travellers clubbed together and carried a tent; otherwise, they slept in the open. The trail was very bad, especially at first, when it climbed between the gloomy and forbidding cliffs that walled in Cumberland Gap. Even when undisturbed by Indians, the trip was accompanied by much fatigue and exposure; and, as always in frontier travelling, one of the perpetual annoyances was the necessity for hunting up strayed horses.

The chief highway was the Ohio River; for to drift down-stream in a scow was easier and quicker, and no more dangerous, than to plod through thick mountain forests. More-over, it was much easier for the settler who went by water to carry with him his household goods and implements of husbandry; and even such cumbrous articles as wagons, or, if he was rich and ambitious, the lumber wherewith to build a frame house. All kinds of craft were used, even bark canoes and pirogues, or dugouts; but the keel-boat, and especially the flat-bottomed scow, with square ends, were the ordinary means of conveyance. They were of all sizes. The passengers and their live stock were, of course, huddled together so as to take up as little room as possible. Sometimes the immigrants built or bought their own boat, navigated it themselves, and sold it or broke it up on reaching their destination. At other times they merely hired a passage. A few of the more enterprising boat-owners speedily introduced a regular emigrant service, making trips at stated times from Pittsburg, or perhaps Limestone, and advertising the carriage capacity of their boats and the times of starting. The trip from Pittsburg to Louisville took a week or ten days; but in low water it might last a month.

The newcomers were mainly Americans from all the States of the Union; but there were also a few people from nearly every country in Europe, and even from Asia. The industrious and the adventurous, the homestead winners and the land speculators, the criminal fleeing from justice and the honest man seeking a livelihood or a fortune, all alike prized the wild freedom and absence of restraint so essentially characteristic of their new life—a life in many ways very pleasant, but one which on the border of the Indian country sank into mere savagery.

Kentucky was "a good poor man's country," provided the poor man was hardy and vigorous. The settlers were no longer in danger of starvation, for they already raised more flour than they could consume. Neither was there as yet anything approaching to luxury. But between these two extremes there was almost every grade of misery and well-being, according to the varying capacity shown by the different settlers in grappling with the conditions of their new life. Among the foreign-born immigrants success depended in part upon race; a contemporary Kentucky observer estimated that, of twelve families of each nationality, nine German, seven Scotch, and four Irish prospered, while the others failed. The German women worked just as hard as the men, even in the fields, and both sexes were equally saving. Naturally, such thrifty immigrants did well materially; but they never took any position of leadership or influence in the community until they had assimilated themselves in speech and customs to their American neighbors. The Scotch were frugal and industrious; for good or for bad they speedily became indistinguishable from the native-born. The greater proportion of failures among the Irish, brave and vigorous though they were, was due to

their quarrelsomeness, and their fondness for drink and litigation; besides, remarks this Kentucky critic, "they soon take
to the gun, which is the ruin of everything." None of these
foreign-born elements were of any very great importance in
the development of Kentucky; its destiny was shaped and
controlled by its men of native stock.

In such a population there was, of course, much loosening
of the bands, social, political, moral, and religious, which knit
a society together. A great many of the restraints of their
old life were thrown off, and there was much social adjustment
and readjustment before their relations to one another under
the new conditions became definitely settled. But there came
early into the land many men of high purpose and pure life
whose influence upon their fellows, though quiet, was very
great. Moreover, the clergyman and the school-teacher, the
two beings who had done so much for colonial civilization on
the seaboard, were already becoming important factors in the
life of the frontier communities. Austere Presbyterian ministers
were people of mark in many of the towns. The Baptist
preachers lived and worked exactly as did their flocks; their
dwellings were little cabins with dirt floors and, instead of bed-
steads, skin-covered pole-bunks; they cleared the ground, split
rails, planted corn, and raised hogs on equal terms with their
parishioners. After Methodism cut loose from its British
connections in 1785, the time of its great advance began, and
the circuit-riders were speedily eating bear meat and buffalo
tongues on the frontier.

Rough log schools were springing up everywhere beside the
rough log meeting-houses, the same building often serving for
both purposes. The school-teacher might be a young surveyor out of work for the moment, a New Englander, fresh
from some academy in the northeast, an Irishman with a
smattering of learning, or perhaps an English immigrant of the
upper class, unfit for and broken down by the work of a new
country. The boys and girls were taught together, and at
recess played together—tag, pawns, and various kissing games.
The rod was used unsparingly, for the elder boys proved bois-
terous pupils. A favorite mutinous frolic was to "bar out" the
teacher, taking possession of the schoolhouse and holding it
against the master with sticks and stones until he had either
forced an entrance or agreed to the terms of the defenders.

Sometimes this barring out represented a revolt against tyranny; often it was a conventional, and half-acquiesced-in, method of showing exuberance of spirit, just before the Christmas holidays. In most of the schools the teaching was necessarily of the simplest, for the only books might be a Testament, a primer, a spelling-book, and a small arithmetic.

In such a society, simple, strong, and rude, both the good features and the bad were nakedly prominent; and the views of observers in reference thereto varied accordingly as they were struck by one set of characteristics or another. One traveller would paint the frontiersmen as little better than the Indians against whom they warred, and their life as wild, squalid, and lawless; while the next would lay especial and admiring stress on their enterprise, audacity, and hospitable open-handedness. Though much alike, different portions of the frontier stock were beginning to develop along different lines. The Holston people, both in Virginia and North Carolina, were by this time comparatively little affected by immigration from without those States, and were, on the whole, homogeneous; but the Virginians and Carolinians of the seaboard considered them rough, unlettered, and not of very good character. One travelling clergyman spoke of them with particular disfavor; he was probably prejudiced by their indifference to his preaching, for he mentions with much dissatisfaction that the congregations he addressed "though small, behaved extremely bad." The Kentuckians showed a mental breadth that was due largely to the many different sources from which even the predominating American elements in the population sprang. The Cumberland people seemed to travellers the wildest and rudest of all, as was but natural, for these fierce and stalwart settlers were still in the midst of a warfare as savage as any ever waged among the cave-dwellers of the Stone Age.

Chapter XIII

The Indian Wars

A FTER the close of the Revolution there was a short,
uneasy lull in the eternal border warfare between the
white men and the red. The Indians were, for the
moment, daunted by a peace which left them without allies;
and the feeble Federal Government attempted for the first
time to aid and control the West by making treaties with the
most powerful frontier tribes. Congress raised a tiny regular
army, and several companies were sent to the upper Ohio
to garrison two or three small forts which were built upon
its banks. Commissioners (one of whom was Clark himself)
were appointed to treat with both the Northern and Southern Indians. Councils were held in various places. In 1785,
and early in 1786, utterly fruitless treaties were concluded
with Shawnees, Wyandots, and Delawares, at one or other
of the little forts.

About the same time, in the late fall of 1785, another treaty,
somewhat more noteworthy, but equally fruitless, was concluded with the Cherokees at Hopewell, on Keowee, in South
Carolina. In this treaty, the commissioners promised altogether too much. They paid little heed to the rights and needs
of the settlers. Neither did they keep in mind the power-
lessness of the Federal Government to enforce against these
settlers what their treaty promised the Indians. The pioneers
along the upper Tennessee and the Cumberland had made various arrangements with bands of the Cherokees, sometimes
acting on their own initiative, and sometimes on behalf of
the State of North Carolina. Many of these different agreements were entered into by the whites with honesty and good
faith, but were violated at will by the Indians. Others were
violated by the whites, or were repudiated by the Indians as

180

well, because of some real or fancied unfairness in the making. Under them large quantities of land had been sold or allotted, and hundreds of homes had been built on the lands thus won by the whites or ceded by the Indians. As with all Indian treaties, it was next to impossible to say exactly how far these agreements were binding, because no persons, not even the Indians themselves, could tell exactly who had authority to represent the tribes. The commissioners paid little heed to these treaties, and drew the boundary so that quantities of land which had been entered under regular grants, and were covered by the homesteads of the frontiersmen, were declared to fall within the Cherokee line. Moreover, they even undertook to drive all settlers off these lands.

Of course, such a treaty excited the bitter anger of the frontiersmen, and they scornfully refused to obey its provisions. They hated the Indians, and, as a rule, were brutally indifferent to their rights, while they looked down on the Federal Government as impotent. Nor was the ill will to the treaty confined to the rough borderers. Many men of means found that land grants which they had obtained in good faith and for good money were declared void. Not only did they denounce the treaty, and decline to abide by it, but they denounced the motives of the commissioners, declaring, seemingly without justification, that they had ingratiated themselves with the Indians to further land speculations of their own.

As the settlers declined to pay any heed to the treaty, the Indians naturally became as discontented with it as the whites. In the following summer the Cherokee chiefs made solemn complaint that, instead of retiring from the disputed ground, the settlers had encroached yet farther upon it, and had come to within five miles of the beloved town of Chota. The chiefs added that they had now made several such treaties, each of which established boundaries that were immediately broken, and that indeed it had been their experience that after a treaty the whites settled even faster on their lands than before. Just before this complaint was sent to Congress the same chiefs had been engaged in negotiations with the settlers themselves who advanced radically different claims. The fact was that in this unsettled time the bond of governmental authority was almost as lax among the whites as among the Indians, and the leaders on each side who wished for peace were hopelessly unable to restrain their fellows who did not. Under such circumstances, the sword, or rather the tomahawk, was ultimately the only possible arbiter.

The Federal Government still feebly hoped for peace; and in the vain endeavors to avoid irritating the Indians forbade all hostile expeditions into the Indian country—though these expeditions offered the one hope of subduing the savages and preventing their inroads. By 1786, the settlers generally, including all their leaders, such as Clark, had become convinced that the treaties were utterly futile, and that the only right policy was one of resolute war.

In truth the war was unavoidable. The claims and desires of the two parties were irreconcilable. Treaties and truces were palliatives which did not touch the real underlying trouble. The white settlers were unflinchingly bent on seizing the land over which the Indians roamed, but which they did not in any true sense own or occupy. In return, the Indians were determined at all costs and hazards to keep the men of chain and compass, and of axe and rifle, and the forest-felling settlers who followed them, out of their vast and lonely hunting-grounds. Nothing but the actual shock of batttle could decide the quarrel. The display of overmastering, overwhelming force might have cowed the Indians; but it was not possible for the United States, or for any European power, ever to exert or display such force far beyond the limits of the settled country. In consequence, the warlike tribes were not then, and never have been since, quelled, save by actual hard fighting, until they were overawed by the settlement of all the neighboring lands.

Nor was there any alternative to these Indian wars. It is idle folly to speak of them as being the fault of the United States Government; and it is even more idle to say that they could have been averted by treaty. Here and there, under exceptional circumstances or when a given tribe was feeble and unwarlike, the whites might gain the ground by a treaty entered into of their own free will by the Indians, without the least duress; but this was not possible with warlike and powerful tribes when once they realized that they were threatened with serious encroachment on their hunting-grounds. Moreover, looked at from the standpoint of the ultimate result, there was little real difference to the Indian whether the land was taken by treaty or by war. In the end the Delaware fared no better at the hands of the Quaker than the Wampanoag at the hands of the Puritan; the methods were far more humane in the one case than in the other, but the outcome was the same in both. No treaty could be satisfactory to the whites, no treaty served the needs of humanity and civilization, unless it gave the land to the Americans as unreservedly as any successful war.

As a matter of fact, the lands we have won from the Indians have been won as much by treaty as by war; but it was almost always war, or else the menace and possibility of war, that secured the treaty. In these treaties we have been more than just to the Indians; we have been abundantly generous, for we have paid them many times what they were entitled to; many times what we would have paid any civilized people whose claim was as vague and shadowy as theirs. By war or threat of war, or purchase, we have won from great civilized nations, from France, Spain, Russia, and Mexico, immense tracts of country already peopled by many tens of thousands of families; we have paid many millions of dollars to these nations for the land we took; but for every dollar thus paid to these great and powerful civilized commonwealths, we have paid ten, for lands less valuable, to the chiefs and warriors of the red tribes. No other conquering and colonizing nation has ever treated the original savage owners of the soil with such generosity as has the United States. Nor is the charge that the treaties with the Indians have been broken, of weight itself; it depends always on the individual case. Many of the treaties were kept by the whites and broken by the Indians; others were broken by the whites themselves; and sometimes those who broke them did very wrong indeed, and sometimes they did right. No treaties, whether between civilized nations or not, can ever be regarded as binding in perpetuity; with changing conditions, circumstances may arise which render it not only expedient, but imperative and honorable, to abrogate them.

Whether the whites won the land by treaty, by armed conquest, or, as was actually the case, by a mixture of both, mattered comparatively little so long as the land was won. It was all-important that it should be won, for the benefit of civilization and in the interests of mankind. It is, indeed, a warped, perverse, and silly morality which would forbid a course of conquest that has turned whole continents into the seats of mighty and flourishing civilized nations. All men of sane and wholesome thought must dismiss with impatient contempt the plea that these continents should be reserved for the use of scattered savage tribes, whose life was but a few degrees less meaningless, squalid, and ferocious than that of the wild beasts with whom they held joint ownership. It is as idle to apply to savages the rules of international morality which obtain between stable and cultured communities, as it would be to judge the fifth-century English conquest of Britain by the standards of to-day. Most fortunately, the hard, energetic, practical men who do the rough pioneer work of civilization in barbarous lands, are not prone to false sentimentality. The people who are, are the people who stay at home. Often these stay-at-homes are too selfish and indolent, too lacking in imagination, to understand the race-importance of the work which is done by their pioneer brethren in wild and distant lands; and they judge them by standards which would only be applicable to quarrels in their own townships and parishes. Moreover, as each new land grows old, it misjudges the yet newer lands, as once it was itself misjudged. The home-staying Englishman of Britain grudges to the Africander his conquest of Matabeleland; and so the home-staying American of the Atlantic States dislikes to see the Western miners and cattlemen win for the use of their people the Sioux hunting-grounds. Nevertheless, it is the men actually on the borders of the longed-for ground, the men actually in contact with the savages, who in the end shape their own destinies.

The most ultimately righteous of all wars is a war with savages, though it is apt to be also the most terrible and inhuman. The rude, fierce settler who drives the savage from the land lays all civilized mankind under a debt to him. American and Indian, Boer and Zulu, Cossack and Tartar, New Zealander and Maori—in each case the victor, horrible though many of his deeds are, has laid deep the foundations for the future greatness of a mighty people. The consequences of struggles for territory between civilized nations seem small by comparison. Looked at from the standpoint of the ages, it is of little moment whether Lorraine is part of Germany or of France, whether the northern Adriatic cities pay homage to Austrian Kaiser or Italian King; but it is of incalculable importance that America, Australia, and Siberia should pass out of the hands of their red, black, and yellow aboriginal owners, and become the heritage of the dominant world races.

Yet the very causes which render this struggle between savagery and the rough front rank of civilization so vast and elemental in its consequence to the future of the world, also tend to render it in certain ways peculiarly revolting and barbarous. It is primeval warfare, and it is waged as war was waged in the ages of bronze and of iron. All the merciful humanity that even war has gained during the last two thousand years is lost. It is a warfare where no pity is shown to noncombatants, where the weak are harried without ruth, and the vanquished maltreated with merciless ferocity. A sad and evil feature of such warfare is that the whites, the representatives of civilization, speedily sink almost to the level of their barbarous foes, in point of hideous brutality. The armies are neither led by trained officers nor made up of regular troops— they are composed of armed settlers, fierce and wayward men, whose ungovernable passions are unrestrained by discipline, who have many grievous wrongs to redress, and who look on their enemies with a mixture of contempt and loathing, of dread and intense hatred. When the clash comes between these men and their sombre foes, too often there follow deeds of enormous, of incredible, of indescribable horror. It is impossible to dwell without a shudder on the monstrous woe and misery of such a contest.

Chapter XIV

The Navigation of the Mississippi; Separatist Movements and Spanish Intrigues

THE lusty young commonwealths which were springing into life on the Ohio and its tributaries knew that commerce with the outside world was essential to their full and proper growth. The high, forest-clad ranges of the Appalachians restricted and hampered their mercantile relations with the older States, and, therefore, with the Europe which lay beyond; while the giant river offered itself as a huge trade artery to bring them close to all the outer world, if only they were allowed its free use.

However, the Westerners wished more than the privilege of sending downstream the products of their woods and pastures and tilled farms. They had already begun to cast longing eyes on the fair Spanish possessions. Spain was still the greatest of colonial powers.

In wealth, in extent, and in population, both native and European—her colonies surpassed even those of England; and by far the most important of her possessions were in the New World. For two centuries her European rivals— English, French, and Dutch—had warred against her in America, with the net result of taking from her a few islands in the West Indies. On the American mainland her possessions were even larger than they had been in the age of the great Conquistadores—the age of Cortes, Pizarro, De Soto, and Coronado.

It was not alone the attitude of the frontiersmen toward Spain that was novel, and based upon a situation for which there was little precedent. Their relations with one another, with their brethren on the seaboard, and with the Federal Government, likewise had to be adjusted without much chance of profiting by antecedent experience. Many phases of these relations between the people who stayed at home and those who wandered off to make homes, between the frontiersmen, as they formed young States, and the Central Government representing the old States, were entirely new, and were ill understood by both parties.

The Union was as yet imperfect. The jangling colonies had been welded together, after a fashion, in the slow fire of the Revolutionary War; but the old lines of cleavage were still distinctly marked. All civil wars loosen the bands of orderly liberty, and leave in their train disorder and evil. Hence, those who cause them must rightly be held guilty of the gravest wrong-doing; unless they are not only pure of purpose, but sound of judgment, and unless the result shows their wisdom. As yet the success had only been in tearing down; there remained the harder and all-important task of building up.

This task of building up was accomplished, and the acts of the men of the Revolution were thus justified. It was the after result of the Revolution, not the Revolution itself, which gave to the governmental experiment inaugurated by the Second Continental Congress its unique and lasting value. It was this result which marks most clearly the difference between the careers of the English-speaking and the Spanish-speaking peoples on this continent. The wise statesmanship typified by such men as Washington and Marshall, Hamilton, Jay, John Adams, and Charles Cotesworth Pinckney, prevailed over the spirit of separatism and anarchy. Seven years after the war ended, the Constitution went into effect, and the United States became in truth a nation. Had we not thus become a nation, had the separatists won the day, and our country become the seat of various antagonistic States and confederacies, then the Revolution by which we won liberty and independence would have been scarcely more memorable or noteworthy than the wars which culminated in the separation of the Spanish-American colonies from Spain; for we would thereby have proved that we did not deserve either liberty or independence.

The Revolutionary War itself had certain points of similarity with the struggles of which men like Bolivar were the heroes; where the parallel totally fails is in what followed. There were features in which the campaigns of the Mexicans and South American insurgent leaders resembled at least the partisan warfare so often waged by American Revolutionary generals; but with the deeds of the great constructive statesmen of the United States there is nothing in the career of any Spanish-American community to compare. It was the power to build a solid and permanent Union, the power to construct a mighty nation out of the wreck of a crumbling confederacy, which drew a sharp line between the Americans of the North and the Spanish-speaking races of the South.

In their purposes and in the popular sentiment to which they have appealed, our separatist leaders of every generation have borne an ominous likeness to the horde of dictators and half-military, half-political adventurers who for three-quarters of a century have wrought such harm in the lands between the Argentine and Mexico; but the men who brought into being and preserved the Union have had no compeers in Southern America. The North American colonies wrested their independence from Great Britain as the colonies of South America wrested theirs from Spain; but whereas the United States grew with giant strides into a strong and orderly nation, Spanish America has remained split into a dozen turbulent states, and has become a by-word for anarchy and weakness.

The separatist feeling has at times been strong in almost every section of the Union, although in some regions it has been much stronger than in others. Calhoun and Pickering, Jefferson and Gouverneur Morris, Wendell Phillips and William Taney, Aaron Burr and Jefferson Davis—these and many other leaders of thought and action, East and West, North and South, at different periods of the nation's growth, and at different stages of their own careers, have, for various reasons, and with widely varying purity of motive, headed or joined in separatist movements. Many of these men were actuated by high-minded, though narrow, patriotism; and those who, in the culminating catastrophe of all the separatist agitations, appealed to the sword, proved the sincerity of their convictions by their resolute courage and self-sacrifice. Nevertheless, they warred against the right, and strove mightily to bring about the downfall and undoing of the nation.

Yet, evil though the separatist movements were, they were at times imperfectly justified by the spirit of sectional distrust and bitterness rife in portions of the country which, at the moment, were themselves loyal to the Union. This was especially true of the early separatist movements in the West. Unfortunately, the attitude toward the Westerners of certain portions of the population in the older States, and especially in the northeastern States, was one of unreasoning jealousy and suspicion; and though this mental attitude rarely crystallized into hostile deeds, its very existence, and the knowledge that it did exist, embittered the men of the West. Moreover, the people among whom these feelings were strongest were, unfortunately, precisely those who, on the questions of the Union and the Constitution, showed the broadest and most far-seeing statesmanship. New England, the towns of the Middle States and Maryland, the tidewater region of South Carolina, and certain parts of Virginia, were the seats of the soundest political thought of the day. The men who did this sane, wholesome political thinking were quite right in scorning and condemning the crude unreason, often silly, often vicious, which characterized so much of the political thought of their opponents. The strength of these opponents was largely derived from the ignorance and suspicion of the raw country districts, and from the sour jealousy with which the backwoodsmen regarded the settled regions of the seaboard.

But when these sound political thinkers permitted their distrust of certain sections of the country to lead them into doing injustice to those sections, they, in their turn, deserved the same condemnation which should be meted to so many of their political foes. When they allowed their judgment to become so warped by their dissatisfaction with the traits inevitably characteristic of the earlier stages of frontier development, that they became opposed to all extension of the frontier; when they allowed their liking for the well-ordered society of their own districts to degenerate into indifference to or dislike of the growth of the United States toward continental greatness; then they themselves sank into the position of men who in cold selfishness sought to mar the magnificent destiny of their own people.

In the northeastern States, and in New England especially, this feeling showed itself for two generations after the close of the Revolutionary War. On the whole, the New Englanders have exerted a more profound and wholesome influence upon the development of our common country than has ever been exerted by any other equally numerous body of our people. They have led the nation in the path of civil liberty and sound governmental administration. But too often they have viewed the nation's growth and greatness from a narrow and provincial standpoint, and have grudgingly acquiesced in, rather than led the march toward, continental supremacy. In shaping the nation's policy for the future, their sense of historic perspective seemed imperfect. They could not see the all-importance of the valley of the Ohio, or of the valley of the Columbia, to the republic of the years to come. The value of a county in Maine offset, in their eyes, the value of these vast, empty regions. Indeed, in the days immediately succeeding the Revolution, their attitude toward the growing West was worse than one of mere indifference; it was one of alarm and dislike. They for the moment adopted toward the West a position not wholly unlike that which England had held toward the American colonies as a whole. They came dangerously near repeating, in their feeling toward their younger brethren on the Ohio, the very blunder committed in reference to themselves by their elder brethren in Britain. For some time they seemed, like the British, unable to grasp the grandeur of their race's imperial destiny. They hesitated to throw themselves with hearty enthusiasm into the task of building a nation with a continent as its base. They rather shrank from the idea as implying a lesser weight of their own section in the nation; not yet understanding that to an American the essential thing was the growth and well-being of America, while the relative importance of the locality where he dwelt was a matter of small moment.

While many of the people on the Eastern seaboard thus took an indefensible position in reference to the Trans-Alleghany settlements, in the period immediately succeeding the Revolution, there were large bodies of the population of these same settlements, including very many of their popular leaders, whose own attitude toward the Union was, if anything, even more blameworthy. They were clamorous about their rights, and were not unready to use veiled threats of disunion when they deemed these rights infringed; but they showed little appreciation of their own duties to the Union.

While giving unlimited praise to the men so clear-sighted, and of such high thought, that from the beginning they foresaw the importance of the Union, and strove to include all the West therein, we must beware of blaming overmuch those whose vision was less acute. The experiment of the Union was as yet inchoate; its benefits were prospective; and loyalty to it was loyalty to a splendid idea the realization of which lay in the future rather than in the present. All honor must be awarded to the men who, under such conditions, could be loyal to so high an ideal; but we must not refuse to see the many strong and admirable qualities in some of the men who looked less keenly into the future. It would be merely folly to judge a man, who, in 1787, was lukewarm or even hostile to the Union, by the same standard we should use in testing his son's grandson a century later.

When we deal, not with the leading statesmen of the frontier communities, but with the ordinary frontier folk themselves, there is need to apply the same tests used in dealing with the rude, strong peoples of bygone ages. The standard by which international, and even domestic, morality is judged, must vary for different countries under widely different conditions, for exactly the same reasons that it must vary for different periods of the world's history. We cannot expect the refined virtues of a highly artificial civilization from frontiersmen who, for generations, have been roughened and hardened by the same kind of ferocious wilderness toil that once fell to the lot of their remote barbarian ancestors.

The Kentuckian, from his clearing in the great forest, looked with bold and greedy eyes at the Spanish possessions, much as Markman, Goth, and Frank had once peered through their marshy woods at the Roman dominions. He possessed the virtues proper to a young and vigorous race; he was trammelled by few misgivings as to the rights of the men whose lands he coveted; he felt that the future was for the stouthearted, and not for the weakling. He was continually hampered by the advancing civilization of which he was the vanguard, and of which his own sons were destined to form an important part. He rebelled against the restraints imposed by his own people behind him exactly as he felt impelled to attack the alien peoples in front of him. He did not care very much what form the attack took. On the whole, he preferred that it should be avowed war, whether waged under the stars and stripes or under some flag new-raised by himself and his fellow adventurers of the border. In default of such a struggle, he was ready to serve under alien banners, either those of some nation at the moment hostile to Spain, or else those of some insurgent Spanish leader.

In the last resort the question of the navigation of the Mississippi had to be decided between the governments of Spain and the United States; and it was chiefly through the latter that the Westerners could, indirectly, but most powerfully, make their influence felt. In the long and intricate negotiations carried on toward the close of the Revolutionary War between the representatives of Spain, France, and the United States, Spain had taken high ground in reference to this and to all other Western questions, and France had supported her in her desire to exclude the Americans from all rights in the vast regions beyond the Alleghanies. At that time the delegates from the Southern, no less than from the Northern, States, in the Continental Congress, showed much weakness in yielding to this attitude of France and Spain. On the motion of those from Virginia, all the delegates, with the exception of those from North Carolina, voted to instruct Jay, then minister to Spain, to surrender outright the free navigation of the Mississippi. Later, when he was one of the commissioners to treat for peace, they practically repeated the blunder by instructing Jay and his colleagues to assent to whatever France proposed. With rare wisdom and courage, Jay repudiated these instructions. The chief credit for the resulting diplomatic triumph, almost as essential as the victory at Yorktown itself to our national well-being, belongs to him, and by his conduct he laid the men of the West under an obligation which they never acknowledged during his lifetime.

Shortly after his return to America he was made secretary of foreign affairs, and was serving as such when, in the spring of 1785, Don Diego Gardoqui arrived in Philadelphia, bearing a commission from his Catholic Majesty to Congress. He and Jay could come to no agreement, and the negotiations were finally broken off. Before this happened, in the fall of 1786,

Jay, in entire good faith, had taken a step which aroused furious anger in the West. Like so many other statesmen of the day, he did not realize how fast Kentucky had grown, and deemed the navigation question one which would not be of real importance to the West for two decades to come. He absolutely refused to surrender our right to navigate the Mississippi; but, not regarding it as of immediate consequence, he proposed both to Congress and Gardoqui that in consideration of certain concessions by Spain we should agree to forbear to exercise this right for twenty or twenty-five years. The delegates from the Northern States assented to Jay's views; those from the Southern States strongly opposed them. In 1787, after a series of conferences between Jay and Gardoqui, which came to naught, the Spaniard definitely refused to entertain Jay's proposition. Even had he not refused, nothing could have been done, for under the confederation a treaty had to be, ratified by the votes of nine States, and there were but seven which supported the policy of Jay.

The news of Jay's attempted negotiations with Gardoqui, distorted and twisted, threw the backwoodsmen into a frenzy. There was never any real danger that Jay's proposition would be adopted; but the Westerners did not know this. In all the considerable settlements on the Western waters, committees of correspondence were elected to remonstrate and petition Congress against any agreement to close the Mississippi. Even those who had no sympathy with the separatist movement warned Congress that if any such agreement were entered into it would probably entail the loss of the Western country.

There was justification for the original excitement; there was none whatever for its continuance after Jay's final report to Congress, in April, 1787, and after the publication by Congress of its resolve never to abandon its claim to the Mississippi. Jay, in this report, took what was unquestionably the rational position. He urged that the United States was undoubtedly in the right; and that it should either insist upon a treaty with Spain, by which all conflicting claims would be reconciled, or else simply claim the right, and if Spain refused to grant it, promptly declare war.

In this summer of 1787 there rose to public prominence in the Western country a man whose influence upon it was destined to be malign in intention rather than in actual fact.

James Wilkinson, by birth a Marylander, came to Kentucky in 1784. He had done his duty respectably as a soldier in the Revolutionary War, for he possessed sufficient courage and capacity to render average service in subordinate positions, though at a later date he showed abject inefficiency as commander of any army. He was a good-looking, plausible, energetic man, gifted with a taste for adventure, with much proficiency in low intrigue, and with a certain address in influencing and managing bodies of men. He also spoke and wrote well, according to the rather florid canons of the day. In character he can only be compared to Benedict Arnold, though he entirely lacked Arnold's ability and brilliant courage. He had no conscience and no scruples; he had not the slightest idea of the meaning of the word honor; he betrayed his trust from the basest motives, and he was too inefficient to make his betrayal effective. He was treacherous to the Union while it was being formed and after it had been formed; and his crime was aggravated by the sordid meanness of his motives, for he eagerly sought opportunities to barter his own infamy for money. In all our history there is no more despicable character.

Wilkinson was a man of broken fortune when he came to the West. In three years he made a good position for himself, in matters commercial and political, and his restless, adventurous nature and thirst for excitement and intrigue prompted him to try the river trade, with its hazards and its chances of great gain. In June, 1787, he went down the Mississippi to New Orleans with a loaded flatboat, and sold his cargo at a high profit, thanks to the understanding he immediately established with the Spanish governor. Don Esteban Miro. Doubtless he started with the full intention of entering into some kind of corrupt arrangement with the Louisiana authorities, leaving the precise nature of the arrangement to be decided by events.

The relations that he so promptly established with the Spaniards were both corrupt and treacherous; that is, he undoubtedly gave and took bribes, and promised to intrigue against his own country for pecuniary reward; but exactly what the different agreements were, and exactly how far he tried or intended to fulfil them, is, and must always remain, uncertain. He persuaded the Spaniards to give him money for using his influence to separate the West from the Union, which was one of the chief objects of Spanish diplomacy. He was obliged to try to earn the money by leading the separatist intrigues in Kentucky, but it is doubtful if he ever had enough straightforwardness in him to be a thoroughgoing villain. All he cared for was the money; if he could not get it otherwise, he was quite willing to do any damage he could to his country, even when he was serving it in a high military position. But if it was easier, he was perfectly willing to betray the people who had bribed him.

However, he was an adept in low intrigue; and though he speedily became suspected by all honest men, he covered his tracks so well that it was not until after his death, and after the Spanish archives had been explored, that his guilt was established.

He returned to Kentucky after some months' absence. He had greatly increased his reputation, and as substantial results of his voyage he showed permits to trade, and some special and exclusive commercial privileges, such as supplying the Mexican market with tobacco, and depositing it in the king's store, at New Orleans. The Kentuckians were much excited by what he had accomplished. He bought goods himself and received goods from other merchants on commission; and a year after his first venture he sent a flotilla of heavy-laden flatboats down the Mississippi, and disposed of their contents at a high profit in New Orleans.

The power this gave Wilkinson, the way he had obtained it, and the use he made of it, gave an impetus to the separatist party in Kentucky. But the separatist feeling, and the desire to sunder the West from the East, and join hands with Spain or Britain, were not confined to Kentucky. In the State of Franklin, for instance, the settlers were equally indifferent to the advantages of the Union. In a letter, written in 1788 to the Creek chief McGillivray, Robertson frankly set forth his belief that the West should separate from the Union and join some foreign power, writing: "In all probability we cannot long remain in our present state, and if the British, or any commercial nation which may be in possession of the Mississippi, would furnish us with trade and receive our produce, there cannot be a doubt but the people on the west side of the Appalachian Mountains will open their eyes to their real interests." At the same time Sevier was writing to Gardoqui, offering to put his insurrectionary State of Franklin, then at its last gasp, under the protection of Spain.

In Kentucky Wilkinson devoted himself to working for separation from both Virginia and the United States, and for an alliance with Spain. He was on intimate terms with the separatist leaders of all shades, and broached his views to them as far as he thought fit. His turgid oratory was admired in the backwoods, and he was much helped by his skill in the baser kinds of political management. He speedily showed all the familiar traits of the demagogue—he was lavish in his hospitality, and treated young and old, rich and poor, with jovial good-fellowship; so that all the men of loose habits, the idle men who were ready for any venture, and the men of weak character and fickle temper swore by him, and followed his lead, while not a few straightforward, honest citizens were blinded by his showy ability and professions of disinterestedness.

It is impossible to say exactly how far his different allies among the separatist leaders knew his real designs or sympathized with them. Their loosely knit party was at the moment united for one ostensible purpose—that of separation from Virginia. The measures they championed were in effect revolutionary, as they wished to pay no regard to the action either of Virginia herself, or of the Federal Government. They openly advocated Kentucky's entering into a treaty with Spain on her own account. Their leaders must certainly have known Wilkinson's real purposes, even though vaguely. The probability is that they did not, either to him or in their own minds, define their plans with clearness, but awaited events before deciding on a definite policy. Meantime by word and act they pursued a course which might be held to mean, as occasion demanded, either mere insistence upon Kentucky's admission to the Union as a separate State, or else a movement for complete independence with a Spanish alliance in the background.

While Miro was corresponding with Wilkinson and arranging for pensioning both him and Sebastian, Gardoqui was busy at New York. His efforts at negotiation were fruitless; for his instructions positively forbade him to yield the navigation of the Mississippi, or to allow the rectification of the boundary-lines as claimed by the United States, while the representatives of the latter refused to treat at all unless both of these points were conceded. Jay he found to be particularly intractable, and in one of his letters he expressed the hope that he would be replaced by Richard Henry Lee, whom Gardoqui considered to be in the Spanish interest. He never understood the people with whom he was dealing. He was sure that they could all be reached by underhand and corrupt influences of some kind, if he could only find out where to put on the pressure. The perfect freedom with which many loyal men talked to and before him puzzled him; and their characteristically American habit of indulging in gloomy forebodings as to the nation's future—when they were not insisting that the said future would be one of unparalleled magnificence—gave him wild hopes that it might prove possible to corrupt them.

Madison, Knox, Clinton, and other men of position under the Continental Congress, including Brown, the delegate from Kentucky, were among those who conferred freely with Gardoqui. In speaking with several of them, including Madison and Brown, he broached the subject of Kentucky's possible separation from the Union and alliance with Spain; and Madison and Brown discussed his statements between themselves. So far there was nothing out of the way in Brown's conduct; but after one of these conferences he wrote to Kentucky in terms which showed that he was willing to entertain Gardoqui's proposition if it seemed advisable to do so.

His letter, which was intended to be private, but which was soon published, was dated July 10, 1788. It advocated immediate separation from Virginia without regard to constitutional methods, and also ran in part as follows: "In private conferences which I have had with Mr. Gardoqui, the Spanish Minister, I have been assured by him in the most explicit terms that if Kentucky will declare her independence and empower some proper person to negotiate with him, that he has authority and will engage to open the navigation of the Mississippi for the exportation of their produce on terms of mutual advantage. But this privilege never can be extended to them while part of the United States. . . . I have thought proper to communicate [this] to a few confidential friends in this district, with his permission, not doubting but that they will make a prudent use of the information."

The publication of Brown's letter and the boldness of the separatist party spurred to renewed effort the Union men, one of whom, Colonel Thomas Marshall, an uncle of Humphrey Marshall and father of the great chief justice, sent a full account of the situation to Washington. The more timid and wavering among the disunionists drew back; and the agitation was dropped when the new National Government began to show that it was thoroughly able to keep order at home, and enforce respect abroad.

These separatist movements were general in the West, on the Holston and Cumberland, as well as on the Ohio, during the troubled years immediately succeeding the Revolution; and they were furthered by the intrigues of the Spaniards. But the antipathy of the backwoodsmen to the Spaniards was too deep-rooted for them ever to effect a real combination. Ultimately, the good sense and patriotism of the Westerners triumphed; and the American people continued to move forward with unbroken front toward their mighty future.

Chapter XV

The State of Franklin

THE separatist spirit was strong throughout the West. Different causes, such as the unchecked ravages of the Indians, or the refusal of the right to navigate the Mississippi, produced or accentuated different manifestations; but the feeling itself was latent everywhere. Its most striking manifestation occurred not in Kentucky, but in what is now the State of Tennessee; and was aimed not at the United States, but at the parent State of North Carolina.

In Kentucky, the old frontiersmen were losing their grip on the governmental machinery of the district. The great flood of immigration tended to swamp the pioneers; and the leading parts in the struggle for statehood were played by men who had come to the country about the close of the Revolutionary War, and who were often related by ties of kinship to the leaders of the Virginia legislatures and conventions.

On the waters of the upper Tennessee matters were entirely different. Immigration had been slower, and the people who did come in were usually of the type of those who had first built their stockaded hamlets on the banks of the Watauga. The leaders of the early pioneers were still the leaders of the community, in legislation as in warfare. Moreover, North Carolina was a much weaker and more turbulent State than Virginia, so that a separatist movement ran less risk of interference. Chains of forest-clad mountains severed the State proper from its Western outposts. Many of the pioneer leaders were from Virginia—backwoodsmen who had drifted south along the trough-like valleys. These, of course, felt little loyalty to North Carolina. The others, who were North Carolinians by birth, had cast their lot, for good or for evil, with the frontier communities, and were inclined to side with them in any contest with the parent State.

North Carolina herself was at first quite as anxious to get rid of the frontiersmen as they were to go. The State was very poor, and regarded the Western settlements as mere burdensome sources of expense. In the innumerable Indian wars, debts were contracted by the little pioneer communities with the faith that the State would pay them; but the payment was made grudgingly or not at all, and no measures were taken to provide for the protection of the frontier in the future. No provisions were made for the extension of the jurisdiction of the State courts over the Western counties, and they became a refuge for outlaws, who could be dealt with only as the Indians were—that is, by the settlers acting on their own initiative, without the sanction of law. In short, the settlers were left to themselves, to work out their own salvation as they best might, in peace or war; and as they bore most of the burdens of independence, they began to long for the privileges.

In June, 1784, the State legislature passed an act ceding to the Continental Congress all the Western lands, that is, all of what is now Tennessee. It was provided that the sovereignty of North Carolina over the ceded lands should continue in full effect until the United States accepted the gift; and that the act should lapse and become void unless Congress accepted within two years.

The Western members were present and voted in favor of the cession, and immediately afterward they returned to their homes and told the frontier people what had been done. There was a general feeling that some step should be taken forthwith to prevent the whole district from lapsing into anarchy. The frontiersmen did not believe that Congress, hampered as it was and powerless to undertake new responsibilities, could accept the gift until the two years were nearly gone; and meanwhile North Carolina would in all likelihood pay them little heed, so that they would be left a prey to the Indians without and to their own wrongdoers within. It was incumbent on them to organize for their own defense and preservation. The three counties on the upper Tennessee proceeded to take measures accordingly. The Cumberland people, however, took no part in the movement, and showed hardly any interest in it; for they felt as alien to the men of the Holston valley as to those of North Carolina proper, and watched the conflict with a tepid absence of friendship for, or hostility toward, either side. They had long practically managed their own affairs, and though they suffered from the lack of a strong central authority on which to rely, they did not understand their own wants, and were inclined to be hostile to any effort for betterment of the National Government.

The first step taken by the frontiersmen in the direction of setting up a new state was very characteristic, as showing the military structure of the frontier settlements. To guard against Indian inroad and foray, and to punish them by reprisals, all the able-bodied, rifle-bearing males were enrolled in the militia; and the divisions of this militia were territorial. The soldiers of each company represented one cluster of rough little hamlets or one group of scattered log houses. The company, therefore, formed a natural division for purposes of representation. It was accordingly agreed that "each captain's company" in the counties of Washington, Lincoln, and Greene should choose two delegates, who should all assemble as committees in their respective counties to deliberate upon some general plan of action. The committees met and recommended the election of deputies with full powers to a convention held at Jonesboro.

This convention, of forty deputies or thereabouts, met at Jonesboro, on August 23, 1784, and appointed John Sevier president. The delegates were unanimous that the three counties represented should declare themselves independent of North Carolina, and passed a resolution to this effect. They also resolved that the three counties should form themselves into an association, and should enforce all the laws of North Carolina not incompatible with beginning the career of a separate state, and that Congress should be petitioned to countenance them, and advise them in the matter of their constitution. In addition, they made a provision for admitting to their state the neighboring portions of Virginia, should they apply, and should the application be sanctioned by the State of Virginia, "or other power having cognizance thereof." This last reference was, of course, to Congress, and was significant. Evidently, the mountaineers ignored the doctrine of

State sovereignty. The power which they regarded as paramount was that of the nation. The adhesion they gave to any government was somewhat shadowy; but such as it was, it was yielded to the United States, and not to any one State. They wished to submit their claim for independence to the judgment of Congress, not to the judgment of North Carolina; and they were ready to admit into their new state the western part of Virginia, on the assent, not of both Congress and Virginia, but of either Congress or Virginia.

The convention adjourned after providing for the calling of a new convention, to consist of five delegates from each county, who should give a name to the state, and prepare for it a constitution. The members of this constitutional convention were to be chosen by counties, and not by captain's companies.

There was much quarreling over the choice of members for the constitutional convention, the parties dividing on the lines indicated in the vote on the question of immediate independence. When the convention did meet in November, it broke up in confusion. At the same time North Carolina, becoming alarmed, repealed her cession act; and thereupon Sevier himself counselled his fellow citizens to abandon the movement for a new state. However, they felt they had gone too far to back out. The convention came together again in December, and took measures looking toward the assumption of full statehood. In the constitution they drew up they provided, among other things, for a Senate and a House of Commons, to form the legislative body, which should itself choose the governor. By an extraordinary resolution, they further provided that the government should go into effect, and elections be held, at once; and yet that in the fall of 1785 a new convention should convene at which the very constitution under which the government had been carried on would be submitted for revision, rejection, or adoption.

Elections for the legislature were accordingly held, and in March, 1785, the two houses of the new State of Franklin met, and chose Sevier as governor. Courts were organized, and military and civil officials of every grade were provided, those holding commissions under North Carolina being continued in office in almost all cases.

In November, 1785, the convention to provide a permanent

constitution for the State met at Greenville. There was already much discontent with the Franklin government. The differences between its adherents and those of the old North Carolina government were accentuated by bitter faction fights among the rivals for popular leadership, backed by their families and followers. Bad feeling showed itself at this convention, the rivalry between Sevier and Tipton being pronounced. Tipton was one of the mountain leaders, second in influence only to Sevier, and his bitter personal enemy. At the convention a brand-new constitution was submitted by a delegate named Samuel Houston. The adoption of the new constitution was urged by a strong minority. The most influential man of the minority party was Tipton.

This written constitution, with its bill of rights prefixed, was a curious document. It provided that the new State should be called the Commonwealth of Frankland. Full religious liberty was established, so far as rites of worship went; but no one was to hold office unless he was a Christian who believed in the Bible, in Heaven, in Hell, and in the Trinity. There were other classes prohibited from holding office—immoral men and Sabbath-breakers, for instance, and clergymen, doctors, and lawyers. The exclusion of lawyers from law-making bodies was one of the darling plans of the ordinary sincere rural demagogue of the day. At that time lawyers, as a class, furnished the most prominent and influential political leaders; and they were, on the whole, the men of most mark in the communities. A narrow, uneducated, honest countryman, especially in the backwoods, then looked upon a lawyer usually with smothered envy and admiration, but always with jealousy, suspicion, and dislike; much as his successors to this day look upon bankers and railroad men. It seemed to him a praiseworthy thing to prevent any man whose business it was to study the law from having a share in making the law.

The proposed constitution showed the extreme suspicion felt by the common people for even their own elected lawmakers. It made various futile provisions to restrain them, such as providing that, "except on occasions of sudden necessity," laws should only become such after being enacted by two successive legislatures, and that a Council of Safety should be elected to look after the conduct of all the other public officials. Universal suffrage for all freemen was provided; the legislature was to consist of but one body; and almost all offices were made elective. Taxes were laid to provide a State university. The constitution was tediously elaborate and minute in its provisions.

However, its only interest is its showing the spirit of the local "reformers" of the day and place in the matters of constitution-making and legislation. After a hot debate and some tumultuous scenes, it was rejected by the majority of the convention, and in its stead, on Sevier's motion, the North Carolina constitution was adopted as the groundwork for the new government. This gave umbrage to Tipton and his party, who for some time had been discontented with the course of affairs in Franklin, and had been grumbling about them.

The new constitution—which was in effect simply the old constitution with unimportant alterations—went into being, and under it the Franklin legislature convened at Greenville, which was made the permanent capital of the new State. The Commons met in the court-house, a clapboarded building of unhewn logs, without windows, the light coming in through the door and through the chinks between the timbers. The Senate met in one of the rooms of the town tavern. The backwoods legislators lodged at this tavern or at some other, at the cost of fourpence a day, the board being a shilling for the man, and sixpence for his horse, if the horse only ate hay; a half-pint of liquor or a gallon of oats cost sixpence. Life was very rude and simple; no luxuries, and only the commonest comforts, were obtainable.

The State of Franklin had now been in existence over a year, and during this period the officers holding under it had exercised complete control in the three insurrectionary counties. They had passed laws, made treaties, levied taxes, recorded deeds, and solemnized marriages. In short, they had performed all the functions of civil government, and Franklin had assumed in all respects the position of an independent commonwealth.

But, in the spring of 1786, the discontent which had smouldered burst into a flame. Tipton and his followers openly espoused the cause of North Carolina, and were joined, as time waned, by the men who for various reasons were dissatisfied with the results of the trial of independent statehood.

They held elections, at the Sycamore Shoals and elsewhere, to choose representatives to the North Carolina legislature, John Tipton being elected senator. They organized the entire local government over again in the interest of the old State.

The two rival governments clashed in every way. County courts of both were held in the same counties; the militia were called out by both sets of officers; taxes were levied by both legislatures. The Franklin courts were held at Jonesboro, the North Carolina courts at Buffalo, ten miles distant; and each court in turn was broken up by armed bands of the opposite party. Criminals throve in the confusion, and the people refused to pay taxes to either party. Brawls, with their brutal accompaniments of gouging and biting, were common. Sevier and Tipton themselves, on one occasion when they by chance met, indulged in a rough-and-tumble fight before their friends could interfere.

Throughout the year 1786 the confusion gradually grew worse. A few days after the Greenville convention met, the legislature of North Carolina passed an act in reference to the revolt. It declared that, at the proper time, the Western counties would be erected into an independent State, but that this time had not yet come; until it did, they would be well cared for, but must return to their ancient allegiance, and appoint and elect their officers under the laws of North Carolina. A free pardon and oblivion of all offenses was promised. Following this act came a long and tedious series of negotiations. Franklin sent ambassadors to argue her case before the legislature of the mother State; the governors and high officials exchanged long-winded letters and proclamations, and the rival legislatures passed laws intended to undermine each other's influence. The Franklin Assembly tried menace, and threatened to fine any one who acted under a commission from North Carolina. The legislature of the latter State achieved more by promises, having wisely offered to remit all taxes for the two troubled years to any one who would forthwith submit to her rule.

Neither side was willing to force the issue to trial by arms if it could be helped; and there was a certain pointlessness about the struggle, inasmuch as the differences between the contending parties were really so trifling. The North Carolinians kept protesting that they would be delighted to see

Franklin set up as an independent State, as soon as her territory contained enough people; and the Franklin leaders in return were loud in their assurances of respect for North Carolina and of desire to follow her wishes. But neither would yield the points immediately at issue.

One of the main reasons for discontent with the parent State was the delay in striking an advantageous treaty with the Indians, and the Franklin people hastened to make up for this delay by summoning the Cherokees to a council. Many of the chiefs, who were already under solemn agreement with the United States and North Carolina, refused to attend; but, as usual with Indians, they could not control all their people, some of whom were present at the time appointed. With the Indians who were thus present the whites went through the form of a treaty under which they received large cessions of Cherokee lands. The ordinary results of such a treaty followed. The Indians who had not signed promptly repudiated, as unauthorized and ineffective, the action of the few who had; and the latter asserted that they had been tricked into signing, and were not aware of the true nature of the document to which they had affixed their marks. The whites heeded these protests not at all, but kept the land they had settled.

In fact, the attitude of the Franklin people toward the Cherokees was one of mere piracy. The backwoodsmen lusted for the possessions of the Indian, as the buccaneers of the Spanish main had once lusted for the possessions of the Spaniard. There was but little more heed paid to the rights of the assailed in one case than in the other.

Yet in its results, and viewed from the standpoint of applied ethics, the conquest and settlement by the whites of the Indian lands was necessary to the greatness of the race and to the well-being of civilized mankind. It was as ultimately beneficial as it was inevitable. Huge tomes might be filled with arguments as to the morality or immorality of such conquests. But these arguments appeal chiefly to the cultivated men in highly civilized communities who have neither the wish nor the power to lead warlike expeditions into savage lands. Such conquests are commonly undertaken by those reckless and daring adventurers who shape and guide each race's territorial growth. They are sure to come when a masterful people, still

in its raw barbarian prime, finds itself face to face with the
weaker and wholly alien race which holds a coveted prize in
its feeble grasp.

Many good persons seem prone to speak of all wars of conquest as necessarily evil. This is, of course, a short-sighted
view. In its after-effects a conquest may be fraught either
with evil or with good for mankind, according to the comparative worth of the conquering and conquered peoples. It
is useless to try to generalize about conquests simply as such
in the abstract; each case or set of cases must be judged by
itself. The world would have halted had it not been for the
Teutonic conquests in alien lands; but the victories of Moslem
over Christian have always proved a curse in the end. Nothing but sheer evil has come from the victories of Turk and
Tartar. This is true generally of the victories of barbarians
of low racial characteristics over gentler, more moral, and more
refined peoples, even though these people have, to their shame
and discredit, lost the vigorous fighting virtues. Yet it remains no less true that the world would probably have gone
forward very little, indeed would probably not have gone
forward at all, had it not been for the displacement or submersion of savage and barbaric peoples as a consequence of
the armed settlement in strange lands of the races who hold in
their hands the fate of the years. Every such submersion or
displacement of an inferior race, every such armed settlement
or conquest by a superior race, means the infliction and suffering of hideous woe and misery. It is a sad and dreadful
thing that there should be of necessity such throes of agony;
and yet they are the birth-pangs of a new and vigorous people. That they are in truth birth-pangs does not lessen the
grim and hopeless woe of the race supplanted; of the race
outworn or overthrown. The wrongs done and suffered cannot be blinked. Neither can they be allowed to hide the results
to mankind of what has been achieved.

It is not possible to justify the backwoodsmen by appeal to
principles which we would accept as binding on their descendants, or on the mighty nation which has sprung up and flourished in the soil they first won and tilled. All that can be
asked is that they shall be judged as other wilderness conquerors, as other slayers and quellers of savage peoples, are
judged. The same standards must be applied to Sevier and

his hard-faced horse-riflemen that we apply to the Greek colonist of Sicily and the Roman colonist of the valley of the Po; to the Cossack rough-rider who won for Russia the vast and melancholy Siberian steppes, and to the Boer who guided his ox-drawn wagon-trains to the hot grazing-lands of the Transvaal; to the founders of Massachusetts and Virginia, of Oregon and icy Saskatchewan; and to the men who built up those far-off commonwealths whose coasts are lapped by the waters of the great South Sea.

The aggressions by the Franklin men on the Cherokee lands bore bloody fruit in 1786. The young warriors, growing ever more alarmed and angered at the pressure of the settlers, could not be restrained. They shook off the control of the old men, who had seen the tribe flogged once and again by the whites, and knew how hopeless such a struggle was. The Chickamauga banditti watched from their eyries to pounce upon all boats that passed down the Tennessee, and their war bands harried the settlements far and wide, being joined in their work by parties from the Cherokee towns proper. Stock was stolen, cabins were burned, and settlers murdered. The stark riflemen gathered for revenge, carrying their long rifles and riding their rough mountain horses. Counter-inroads were carried into the Indian country. On one, when Sevier himself led, two or three of the Indian towns were burned and a score or so of warriors killed. As always, it proved comparatively easy to deal a damaging blow to these Southern Indians, who dwelt in well-built log towns; while the widely scattered, shifting, wigwam villages of the forest nomads of the North rarely offered a tangible mark at which to strike. Of course, the retaliatory blows of the whites, like the strokes of the Indians, fell as often on the innocent as on the guilty. During this summer, to revenge the death of a couple of settlers, a backwoods colonel, with the appropriate name of Outlaw, fell on a friendly Cherokee town and killed two or three Indians, besides plundering a white man, a North Carolina trader, who happened to be in the town. Nevertheless, throughout 1786 the great majority of the Cherokees remained quiet.

Early in 1787, however, they felt the strain so severely that they gathered in a great council and deliberated whether they should not abandon their homes and move far out into the

Western wilderness; but they could not yet make up their minds to leave their beloved mountains. The North Carolina authorities wished to see them receive justice, but all they could do was to gather the few Indian prisoners who had been captured in the late wars and return them to the Cherokees. The Franklin government had opened a land-office and disposed of all the lands between the French Broad and the Tennessee, which territory North Carolina had guaranteed the Cherokees; and when, on the authority of the governor of North Carolina, his representative ordered the settlers off the invaded land, they treated his command with utter defiance. Not only the Creeks, but even the distant Choctaws and Chickasaws, became uneasy and irritated over the American encroachments, while the French traders who came up the Tennessee preached war to the Indians, and the Spanish Government ordered all the American traders to be expelled from among the Southern tribes unless they would agree to take commissions from Spain and throw off their allegiance to the United States.

In 1787, the State of Franklin began to totter to its fall. In April, Sevier, hungering for help or friendly advice, wrote to the gray statesman after whom his State was named. The answer did not come for several months, and when it did come it was not very satisfactory. The old sage repeated that he knew too little of the circumstances to express an opinion, but he urged a friendly understanding with North Carolina, and he spoke with unpalatable frankness on the subject of the Indians. At that very time he was writing to a Cherokee chief who had come to Congress in the vain hope that the Federal authorities might save the Cherokees from the reckless backwoodsmen; he had promised to try to obtain justice for the Indians, and he was in no friendly mood toward the backwoods aggressors.

"Prevent encroachments on Indian lands," Franklin wrote to Sevier—Sevier, who, in a last effort to rally his followers, was seeking a general Indian war to further these very encroachments—"and remember that they are the more unjustifiable because the Indians usually give good bargains in the way of purchase, while a war with them costs more than any possible price they may ask." This advice was based on Franklin's usual principle of merely mercantile morality; but he was writing to a people who stood in sore need of just the teaching he could furnish and who would have done well to heed it. They were slow to learn that while sober, debt-paying thrift, love of order, and industry, are perhaps not the loftiest virtues and are certainly not in themselves all-sufficient, they yet form an indispensable foundation, the lack of which is but ill supplied by other qualities even of a very noble kind.

In September, 1787, the legislature met, for the last time, at Greenville. When, in March, 1788, the term of Sevier as governor came to an end, there was no one to take his place, and the officers of North Carolina were left in undisputed possession of whatever government authority there was.

The North Carolina Assembly which met in November, 1787, had been attended by regularly elected members from all the Western counties, Tipton being among them; while the far-off log hamlets on the banks of the Cumberland sent Robertson himself. This assembly once more offered full pardon and oblivion of past offenses to all who would again become citizens; and the last adherents of the insurrectionary government reluctantly accepted the terms. Franklin had been in existence for three years, during which time she had exercised all the powers and functions of independent statehood. During the first year her sway in the district was complete; during the next she was forced to hold possession in common with North Carolina; and then, by degrees, her authority lapsed altogether.

Sevier was left in dire straits by the falling of the State he had founded; for not only were the North Carolina authorities naturally bitter against him, but he had to count on the personal hostility of Tipton. In his distress, he wrote to one of the opposing party, not personally unfriendly to him, that he had been dragged into the Franklin movement by the people of the country; that he wished to suspend hostilities, and was ready to abide by the decision of the North Carolina legislature, but that he was determined to share the fate of those who had stood by him, whatever it might be. About the time that his term as governor expired, a writ, issued by the North Carolina courts, was executed against his estate. The sheriff seized all his negro slaves, as they worked on his Nolichucky farm, and bore them for safe-keeping to Tipton's household, a rambling cluster of stout log buildings, on Sinking Creek of the Watauga. Sevier raised a hundred and fifty men and marched to take them back, carrying a light field-piece. Tipton's friends gathered, thirty or forty strong, and a siege began. Sevier hesitated to push matters to extremity by charging home. For a couple of days there was some skirmishing and two or three men were killed or wounded. Then the county lieutenant of Sullivan, with a hundred and eighty militia, came to Tipton's rescue. They surprised Sevier's camp at dawn on the last day of February, while the snow was falling heavily; and the Franklin men fled in mad panic, only one or two being slain. Two of Sevier's sons were taken prisoners, and Tipton was with difficulty dissuaded from hanging them. This scrambling fight marked the ignoble end of the State of Franklin. Sevier fled to the uttermost part of the frontier, where no writs ran, and the rough settlers were devoted to him. Here he speedily became engaged in the Indian war.

Early in the spring of 1788, the Indians renewed their ravages. The Chickamaugas were the leaders, but there were among them a few Creeks, and they were also joined by some of the Cherokees proper, goaded to anger by the encroachments of the whites on their lands. Many of the settlers were killed, and the people on the frontier began to gather into their stockades and blockhouses. The alarm was great. One murder was of peculiar treachery and atrocity. A man named John Kirk, lived on a clearing on Little River, seven miles south of Knoxville. One day, when he was away from home, an Indian named Slim Tom, well known to the family, and believed to be friendly, came to the cabin and asked for food. The food was given him and he withdrew. But he had come merely as a spy; and, seeing that he had to deal only with helpless women and children, he returned with a party of Indians who had been hiding in the woods. They fell on the wretched creatures, and butchered them all, eleven in number, leaving the mangled bodies in the courtyard. The father and eldest boy were absent and thus escaped. It would have been well had the lad been among the slain, for his coarse and brutal nature was roused to a thirst for indiscriminate revenge, and shortly afterward he figured as chief actor in a deed of retaliation as revolting and inhuman as the original crime.

At the news of the massacres the frontiersmen gathered as was their custom, mounted and armed, and ready either to follow the marauding-parties or to make retaliatory inroads on their own account. Sevier, their daring leader, was among them, and to him they gave the command. He struck a town on Hiawassee and destroyed it, killing a number of the warriors. This feat, and two or three others like it, made the frontiersmen flock to his standard; but before any great number were embodied under him, he headed a small party on a raid which was sullied by a deed of atrocious treachery and cruelty. He led some forty men to Chilhowa on the Tennessee; opposite a small town of Cherokees, who were well known to have been friendly to the whites. Among them were several chiefs, including an old man named Corn Tassel, who for years had been foremost in the endeavor to keep the peace, and to prevent raids on the settlers. They put out a white flag; and the whites then hoisted one themselves. On the strength of this, one of the Indians crossed the river, and, on demand of the whites, ferried them over. Sevier put the Indians in a hut, and then a horrible deed of infamy was perpetrated. Among Sevier's troops was young John Kirk, whose mother, sisters, and brothers had been so foully butchered by the Cherokee Slim Tom and his associates. Young Kirk's brutal soul was parched with longing for revenge, and he was, both in mind and heart, too nearly kin to his Indian foes greatly to care whether his vengeance fell on the wrongdoers or on the innocent. He entered the hut where the Cherokee chiefs were confined and brained them with his tomahawk, while his comrades looked on without interfering. Sevier's friends asserted that at the moment he was absent but this was no excuse. He knew well the fierce blood-lust of his followers, and it was criminal negligence on his part to leave to their mercy the friendly Indians who had trusted to his good faith; and, moreover, he made no effort to punish the murderer.

As if to show the futility of the plea that Sevier was powerless, a certain Captain Gillespie successfully protected a captive Indian from militia violence at this very time. He had come into the Indian country with one of the parties which

intended to join Sevier, and while alone he captured a Cherokee. When his troops came up they immediately proposed to
kill the Indian, and told him they cared nothing for his remon-
strances; whereupon he sprang from his horse, cocked his
rifle, and told them he would shoot dead the first man who
raised a hand to molest the captive. They shrank back, and
the Indian remained unharmed.

As for young Kirk, all that need be said is that he stands
in the same category with Slim Tom, the Indian murderer.
He was a fair type of the low-class, brutal white borderer,
whose inhumanity almost equalled that of the savage. But
Sevier must be judged by another standard. He was a member of the Cincinnati, a correspondent of Franklin, a follower
of Washington. He sinned against the light, and must be
condemned accordingly. He sank to the level of a lieutenant
of Alva, Guise, or Tilly, to the level of a crusading noble of
the Middle Ages. It would be unfair to couple even this crime
with those habitually committed by Sidney and Sir Peter
Carew, Shan O'Neil and Fitzgerald, and the other dismal
heroes of the hideous wars waged between the Elizabethan
English and the Irish. But it is not unfair to compare this
border warfare in the Tennessee mountains with the border
warfare of England and Scotland two centuries earlier. There
is no blinking the fact that in this instance Sevier and his followers stood on the same level of brutality with "keen Lord
Evers," and on the same level of treachery with the "assured"
Scots at the battle of Ancrum Moor.

Even on the frontier, and at that time, the better class of
backwoodsmen expressed much horror at the murder of the
friendly chiefs. Sevier had planned to march against the
Chickamaugas with the levies that were thronging to his banner; but the news of the murder provoked such discussion
and hesitation that his forces melted away. He was obliged
to abandon his plan, partly owing to this disaffection among
the whites, and partly owing to what one of the backwoodsmen, in writing to General Martin, termed "the severity of
the Indians," —a queer use of the word severity which ob-
tains to this day in out-of-the-way places through the Alleghanies, where people style a man with a record for desperate
fighting a "severe man," and speak of big, fierce dogs, able
to tackle a wolf, as "severe" dogs.

Elsewhere throughout the country the news of the murder excited great indignation. The Continental Congress passed resolutions condemning acts which they had been powerless to prevent and were powerless to punish. The justices of the court of Abbeville County, South Carolina, with Andrew Pickens at their head, wrote "to the people living on Nolechucke, French Broad, and Holstein," denouncing in unmeasured terms the encroachments and outrages of which Sevier and his backwoods troopers had been guilty. The governor of North Carolina, as soon as he heard the news, ordered the arrest of Sevier and his associates—doubtless as much because of their revolt against the State as because of the atrocities they had committed against the Indians.

In their panic many of the Indians fled across the mountains and threw themselves on the mercy of the North and South Carolinians, by whom they were fed and protected. Others immediately joined the Chickamaugas in force, and the frontier districts of the Franklin region were harried with vindictive ferocity. The strokes fell most often and most heavily on the innocent. Half of the militia were called out, and those who most condemned the original acts of aggression committed by their neighbors were obliged to make common cause with these neighbors, so as to save their own lives and the lives of their families. The officers of the district ordered a general levy of the militia to march against the Indian towns, and in each county the backwoodsmen began to muster.

Sevier was the natural leader of the Holston riflemen in such a war; and the bands of frontiersmen insisted that he should take the command whenever it was possible. Sevier swam well in troubled waters, and he profited by the storm he had done so much to raise. Again and again during the summer of 1788 he led his bands of wild horsemen on forays against the Cherokee towns, and always with success. He followed his usual tactics, riding hard and long, pouncing on the Indians in their homes before they suspected his presence, or intercepting and scattering their war-parties; and he moved with such rapidity that they could not gather in force sufficient to do him harm. Not only was the fame of his triumphs spread along the frontier, but vague rumors reached even the old settled States of the seaboard, rumors that told of the slight loss suffered by his followers, of the headlong hurry of

his marches, of the fury with which his horsemen charged in
the skirmishes, of his successful ambuscades and surprises,
and of the heavy toll he took in slain warriors and captive
women and children, who were borne homeward to exchange
for the wives and little ones of the settlers who had themselves been taken prisoners.

Sevier's dashing and successful leadership wiped out in the
minds of the backwoodsmen the memory of all his shortcomings and misdeeds; even the memory of that unpunished murder of friendly Indians which had so largely provoked the
war. The representatives of the North Carolina government
and his own personal enemies were less forgetful. The governor of the State had given orders to seize him because of
his violation of the laws and treaties in committing wanton
murder on friendly Indians; and a warrant to arrest him for
high treason was issued by the courts.

As long as "Nolichucky Jack" remained on the border,
among the rough Indian fighters whom he had so often led
to victory, he was in no danger. But in the fall, late in October, he ventured back to the longer settled districts. A council
of officers with Martin presiding and Tipton present as one
of the leading members, had been held at Jonesboro, and had
just broken up when Sevier and a dozen of his followers rode
into the squalid little town. He drank freely and caroused
with his friends; and he soon quarrelled with one of the other
side who denounced him freely and justly for the murder of
Corn Tassel and the other peaceful chiefs. Finally they all
rode away, but when some miles out of town Sevier got into
a quarrel with another man; and after more drinking and
brawling he went to pass the night at a house, the owner of
which was his friend. Meanwhile one of the men with whom
he had quarrelled informed Tipton that his foe was in his
grasp. Tipton gathered eight or ten men and early next morning surprised Sevier in his lodgings.

Sevier could do nothing but surrender, and Tipton put him
in irons and sent him across the mountains to Morgantown,
in North Carolina, where he was kindly treated and allowed
much liberty. Most of the inhabitants sympathized with him,
having no special repugnance to disorder, and no special sympathy even for friendly Indians. Meanwhile, a dozen of his
friends, with his two sons at their head, crossed the moun-

tains to rescue their beloved leader. They came into Morgantown while court was sitting and went unnoticed in the crowds. In the evening, when the court adjourned and the crowds broke up, Sevier's friends managed to get near him with a spare horse; he mounted and they all rode off at speed. By daybreak they were out of danger. Nothing further was attempted against him. A year later he was elected a member of the North Carolina legislature; after some hesitation he was allowed to take his seat, and the last trace of the old hostility disappeared.

Neither the North Carolinians, nor any one else, knew that there was better ground for the charge of treason against Sevier than had appeared in his overt actions. He was one of those who had been in correspondence with Gardoqui on the subject of an alliance between the Westerners and Spain. His newborn State had died; he was being prosecuted for high treason; he was ready to go to any lengths against North Carolina; and he clutched at the chance of help from the Spaniard. At the time North Carolina was out of the Union, so that Sevier committed no offense against the Federal Government.

Gardoqui was much interested in the progress of affairs in Franklin; and in the effort to turn them to the advantage of Spain he made use of James White, the Indian agent who was in his pay. He wrote home that he did not believe Spain could force the backwoodsmen out of Franklin (which he actually claimed as Spanish territory), but that he had secret advices that they could easily be brought over to the Spanish interest by proper treatment. When the news came of the fight between Sevier's and Tipton's men, he judged the time to be ripe, and sent White to Franklin to sound Sevier and bring him over; but he did not trust White enough to give him any written directions, merely telling him what to do and furnishing him with three hundred dollars for his expenses. The mission was performed with such guarded caution that only Sevier and a few of his friends ever knew of the negotiations, and these kept their counsel well.

Sevier was in the mood to grasp a helping hand stretched out from no matter what quarter. He had no organized government back of him; but he was in the midst of his successful

Cherokee campaigns, and he knew the reckless Indian fighters would gladly follow him in any movement, if he had a chance of success. He felt that if he were given money and arms, and the promise of outside assistance, he could yet win the day. He jumped at Gardoqui's cautious offers; though careful not to promise to subject himself to Spain, and doubtless with no idea of playing the part of Spanish vassal longer than the needs of the moment required.

In July, he wrote to Gardoqui, eager to strike a bargain with him; and in September sent him two letters by the hand of his son, James Sevier, who accompanied White when the latter made his return journey to the Federal capital. One letter, which was not intended to be private, formally set forth the status of Franklin with reference to the Indians, and requested the representatives of the Catholic king to help keep the peace with the Southern tribes. The other letter was the one of importance. In it he assured Gardoqui that the Western people had grown to know that their hopes of prosperity rested on Spain, and that the principal people of Franklin were anxious to enter into an alliance with, and obtain commercial concessions from, the Spaniards. He importuned Gardoqui for money and for military aid, assuring him that the Spaniards could best accomplish their ends by furnishing these supplies immediately, especially as the struggle over the adoption of the Federal Constitution made the time opportune for revolt.

Gardoqui received White and James Sevier with much courtesy, and was profuse, though vague, in his promises. He sent them both to New Orleans that Miro might hear and judge of their plans. Nevertheless, nothing came of the project, and doubtless only a few people in Franklin ever knew that it existed. As for Sevier, when he saw that he was baffled, he suddenly became a Federalist and an advocate of a strong central government; and this, doubtless, not because of love for Federalism, but to show his hostility to North Carolina, which had at first refused to enter the new Union. This particular move was fairly comic in its abrupt unexpectedness.

Thus the last spark of independent life flickered out in Franklin proper. The people who had settled on the Indian borders were left without government, North Carolina regarding them as trespassers on the Indian territory. They accord-

ingly met and organized a rude governmental machine, on the
model of the commonwealth of Franklin; and the wild little
State existed as a separate and independent republic until the
new Federal Government included it in the territory south of
the Ohio.

Chapter XVI

Kentucky's Struggle for Statehood

WHILE the social condition of the communities on the Cumberland and the Tennessee had changed very slowly, in Kentucky the changes had been rapid.

Colonel William Fleming, one of the heroes of the battle of the Great Kanawha, and a man of note on the border, visited Kentucky on surveying business in the winter of 1779-80. His journal shows the state of the new settlements as seen by an unusually competent observer; for he was an intelligent, well-bred, thinking man. Away from the immediate neighborhood of the few scattered log hamlets, he found the wilderness absolutely virgin. The easiest way to penetrate the forest was to follow the "buffalo paths," which the settlers usually adopted for their own bridle trails, and finally cut out and made into roads. Game swarmed. There were multitudes of swans, geese, and ducks on the river; turkeys and the small furred beasts, such as coons, abounded. Big game was almost as plentiful. Colonel Fleming shot, for the subsistence of himself and his party, many buffalo, bear, and deer, and some elk. His attention was drawn by the great flocks of paroquets, which appeared even in winter, and by the big, boldly colored, ivory-billed woodpeckers—birds which have long drawn back to the most remote swamps of the hot Gulf coast, fleeing before man precisely as the buffalo and elk have fled.

Like all similar parties he suffered annoyance from the horses straying. He lost much time in hunting up the strayed beasts, and frequently had to pay the settlers for helping find them. There were no luxuries to be had for any money, and even such common necessaries as corn and salt were scarce and dear. Half a peck of salt cost a little less than eight pounds, and a bushel of corn the same. The surveying-party, when

219

not in the woods, stayed at the cabins of the more prominent settlers, and had to pay well for board and lodging, and for washing, too.

Fleming was much struck by the misery of the settlers. At the Falls they were sickly, suffering with fever and ague; many of the children were dying. Boonesborough and Harrodsburg were very dirty, the inhabitants were sickly; and the offal and dead beasts lay about, poisoning the air and the water. During the winter no more corn could be procured than was enough to furnish an occasional hoe-cake. The people sickened on a steady diet of buffalo-bull beef, cured in smoke without salt, and prepared for the table by boiling. The buffalo was the standby of the settlers; they used his flesh as their common food, and his robe for covering; they made moccasins of his hide, fiddle-strings of his sinews, and combs of his horns. They spun his winter coat into yarn, and out of it they made coarse cloth, like wool. They made a harsh linen from the bark of the rotted nettles. They got sugar from the maples. There were then, Fleming estimated, about three thousand souls in Kentucky. The Indians were everywhere, and all men lived in mortal terror of their lives; no settlement was free from the dread of the savages.

Half a dozen years later all this was changed. The settlers had fairly swarmed into the Kentucky country, and the population was so dense that the true frontiersmen, the real pioneers, were already wandering off to Illinois and elsewhere; every man of them desiring to live on his own land, by his own labor, and scorning to work for wages. The unexampled growth had wrought many changes; not the least was the way in which it lessened the importance of the first hunter-settlers and hunter-soldiers. The great herds of game had been woefully thinned, and certain species, as the buffalo, practically destroyed. The killing of game was no longer the chief industry, and the flesh and hides of wild beasts were no longer the staples of food and clothing. The settlers already raised crops so large that they were anxious to export the surplus. They no longer clustered together in palisaded hamlets. They had cut out trails and roads in every direction from one to another of the many settlements. The scattered clearings on which they generally lived dotted the forest everywhere, and the towns, each with its straggling array of log cabins, and its occasional frame houses, did not differ materially from those in the remote parts of Pennsylvania and Virginia. The gentry were building handsome houses, and their amusements and occupations were those of the up-country planters of the seaboard.

The Indians were still a scourge to the settlements; but, though they caused much loss of life, there was not the slightest danger of their imperilling the existence of the settlements as a whole, or even of any considerable town or group of clearings. Kentucky was no longer all a frontier. In the thickly peopled districts life was reasonably safe, though the frontier proper was harried and the remote farms jeopardized and occasionally abandoned, while the river route and the Wilderness Road were beset by the savages. Where the country was at all well settled, the Indians did not attack in formidable war bands, like those that had assailed the forted villages in the early years of their existence; they skulked through the woods by twos and threes, and pounced only upon the helpless or the unsuspecting.

Nevertheless, if the warfare was not dangerous to the life and growth of the commonwealth, it was fraught with undreamed-of woe and hardship to individual settlers and their families. On the outlying farms no man could tell when the blow would fall. Thus, in one backwoodsman's written reminiscences, there is a brief mention of a settler named Israel Hart, who, during one May night, in 1787, suffered much from a toothache. In the morning he went to a neighbor's, some miles away through the forest, to have his tooth pulled, and when he returned he found his wife and his five children dead and cut to pieces. Incidents of this kind are related in every contemporary account of Kentucky; and though they commonly occurred in the thinly peopled districts, this was not always the case. Teamsters and travellers were killed on the highroads near the towns—even in the neighborhood of the very town where the constitutional convention was sitting.

In all new-settled regions in the United States, so long as there was a frontier at all, the changes in the pioneer population proceeded in a certain definite order, and Kentucky furnished an example of the process. Throughout our history as a nation the frontiersmen have always been mainly native Americans, and those of European birth have been speedily beaten into the usual frontier type by the wild forces against which they waged unending war. As the frontiersmen conquered and transformed the wilderness, so the wilderness in its turn created and preserved the type of man who overcame it. Nowhere else on the continent has so sharply defined and distinctively American a type been produced as on the frontier, and a single generation has always been more than enough for its production. The influence of the wild country upon the man is almost as great as the effect of the man upon the country. The frontiersman destroys the wilderness, and yet its destruction means his own. He passes away before the coming of the very civilization whose advance-guard he has been. Nevertheless, much of his blood remains, and his striking characteristics have great weight in shaping the development of the land. The varying peculiarities of the different groups of men who have pushed the frontier westward at different times and places remain stamped with greater or less clearness on the people of the communities that grow up in the frontier's stead.*

In Kentucky, as in Tennessee and the western portions of the seaboard States, and as later in the great West, different types of settlers appeared successively on the frontier. The hunter or trapper came first. Sometimes he combined with hunting and trapping the functions of an Indian trader, but ordinarily the American, as distinguished from the French or Spanish frontiersman, treated the Indian trade as something purely secondary to his more regular pursuits. In Kentucky and Tennessee the first comers from the East were not traders at all, and were hunters rather than trappers. Boone was a type of this class, and Boone's descendants went westward generation by generation until they reached the Pacific.

Close behind the mere hunter came the rude hunter-settler. He pastured his stock on the wild range, and lived largely by his skill with the rifle. He worked with simple tools and he did his work roughly. His squalid cabin was destitute of the commonest comforts; the blackened stumps and dead,

---

* Frederick Jackson Turner: "The Significance of the Frontier in American History." A suggestive pamphlet, published by the State Historical Society of Wisconsin.

girdled trees stood thick in his small and badly tilled field. He was adventurous, restless, shiftless, and he felt ill at ease and cramped by the presence of more industrious neighbors. As they pressed in roundabout him he would sell his claim, gather his cattle and his scanty store of tools and household goods, and again wander forth to seek uncleared land. The Lincolns, the forebears of the great President, were a typical family of this class.

Most of the frontiersmen of these two types moved fitfully westward with the frontier itself, or near it, but in each place where they halted, or where the advance of the frontier was for the moment stayed, some of their people remained to grow up and mix with the rest of the settlers.

The third class consisted of the men who were thrifty as well as adventurous, the men who were even more industrious than restless. These were they who entered in to hold the land, and who had handed it on as an inheritance to their children and their children's children. Often, of course, these settlers of a higher grade found that for some reason they did not prosper, or heard of better chances still farther in the wilderness, and so moved onward, like their less thrifty and more uneasy brethren, the men who half cleared their lands and half built their cabins. But, as a rule, these better-class settlers were not mere lifelong pioneers. They wished to find good land on which to build, and plant, and raise their big families of healthy children, and when they found such land they wished to make thereon their permanent homes. They did not share the impulse which kept their squalid, roving fellows of the backwoods ever headed for the vague beyond. They had no sympathy with the feeling which drove these humbler wilderness-wanderers always onward, and made them believe, wherever they were, that they would be better off somewhere else, that they would be better off in that somewhere which lay in the unknown and untried. On the contrary, these thriftier settlers meant to keep whatever they had once grasped. They got clear title to their lands. Though they first built cabins, as soon as might be they replaced them with substantial houses and barns. Though they at first girdled and burnt the standing timber, to clear the land, later they tilled it as carefully as any farmer of the seaboard States. They composed the bulk of the population, and formed the backbone and body of the State. The McAfees may be taken as a typical family of this class.

Yet a fourth class was composed of the men of means, of the well-to-do planters, merchants, and lawyers, of the men whose families already stood high on the Atlantic slope. The Marshalls were such men; and there were many other families of the kind in Kentucky. Among them were an unusually large proportion of the families who came from the fertile limestone region of Botetourt County in Virginia, leaving behind them, in the hands of their kinsmen, their roomy, comfortable houses, which stand to this day. These men soon grew to take the leading places in the new commonwealth. They were of good blood—using the words as they should be used, as meaning blood that had flowed through the veins of generations of self-restraint and courage and hard work, and careful training in mind and in the manly virtues. Their inheritance of sturdy and self-reliant manhood helped them greatly; their blood told in their favor as blood generally does tell when other things are equal. If they prized intellect they prized character more; they were strong in body and mind, stout of heart, and resolute of will. They felt that pride of race which spurs a man to effort, instead of making him feel that he is excused from effort. They realized that the qualities they inherited from their forefathers ought to be further developed by them as their forefathers had originally developed them. They knew that their blood and breeding, though making it probable that they would with proper effort succeed, yet entitled them to no success which they could not fairly earn in open contest with their rivals.

Such were the different classes of settlers who successively came into Kentucky, as into other Western lands. There were, of course, no sharp lines of cleavage between the classes. They merged insensibly into one another, and the same individual might at different times stand in two or three. As a rule, the individuals composing the first two were crowded out by their successors, and, after doing the roughest of the pioneer work, moved westward with the frontier; but some families were of course continually turning into permanent abodes what were merely temporary halting-places of the greater number.

With the change in population came the corresponding

change in intellectual interests and in material pursuits. The axe was the tool, and the rifle the weapon, of the early settlers; their business was to kill the wild beasts, to fight the savages, and to clear the soil; and the enthralling topics of conversation were the game and the Indians, and, as the settlements grew, the land itself. As the farms became thick, and towns throve, and life become more complex, the chances for variety in work and thought increased likewise. The men of law sprang into great prominence, owing in part to the interminable litigation over the land titles. The more serious settlers took about as much interest in matters theological as in matters legal; and the congregations of the different churches were at times deeply stirred by quarrels over questions of church discipline and doctrine. Most of the books were either text-books of the simpler kinds or else theological.

Except when there was an Indian campaign, politics and the river commerce formed the two chief interests for all Kentuckians, but especially for the well-to-do.

In spite of all the efforts of the Spanish officials, the volume of trade on the Mississippi grew steadily. Six or eight years after the close of the Revolution the vast stretches of brown water, swirling ceaselessly between the melancholy forests, were already furrowed everywhere by the keeled and keelless craft. The hollowed log in which the Indian paddled; the same craft, the pirogue, only a little more carefully made, and on a little larger model, in which the creole trader carried his load of paints and whiskey and beads and bright cloths to trade for the peltries of the savage; the rude little scow in which some backwoods farmer drifted downstream with his cargo, the produce of his own toil; the keel-boats which, with square-sails and oars, plied up as well as down the river; the flotilla of huge flat-boats, the property of some rich merchant, laden deep with tobacco and flour, and manned by crews who were counted rough and lawless even in the rough and lawless backwoods—all these and others, too, were familiar sights to every traveller who descended the Mississippi from Pittsburg to New Orleans, or who was led by business to journey from Louisville to St. Louis or to Natchez or New Madrid.

The fact that the river commerce throve was partly the cause and partly the consequence of the general prosperity of Kentucky. The pioneer days, with their fierce and squalid struggle for bare life, were over. If men were willing to work, and escaped the Indians, they were sure to succeed in earning a comfortable livelihood in a country so rich. "The neighbors are doing well in every sense of the word," wrote one Kentuckian to another; "they get children and raise crops." Like all other successful and masterful people the Kentuckians fought well and bred well, and they showed by their actions their practical knowledge of the truth that no race can ever hold its own unless its members are able and willing to work hard with their hands.

The general prosperity meant rude comfort everywhere; and it meant a good deal more than rude comfort for the men of greatest ability. By the time the river commerce had become really considerable, the rich merchants, planters, and lawyers had begun to build two-story houses of brick or stone, like those in which they had lived in Virginia. They were very fond of fishing, shooting, and riding, and were lavishly hospitable. They sought to have their children well taught, not only in letters, but in social accomplishments like dancing; and at the proper season they liked to visit the Virginian watering-places, where they met "genteel company" from the older States, and lodged in good taverns in which "a man could have a room and a bed to himself."

An agreement entered into about this time between one of the Clarks and a friend shows that Kentuckians were already beginning to appreciate the merits of neat surroundings even for a rather humble town house. This particular house, together with the stable and lot, was rented for "one cow" for the first eight months, and two dollars a month after that —certainly not an excessive rate; and it was covenanted that everything should be kept in good repair, and particularly that the grassplots around the house should not be "trod on or tore up."

All Kentuckians took a great interest in politics, as is the wont of self-asserting, independent freemen, living under a democratic government. But the gentry and men of means and the lawyers very soon took the lead in political affairs. A larger proportion of these classes came from Virginia than was the case with the rest of the population, and they shared the eagerness and aptitude for political life generally shown by the leading families of Virginia. In many cases they were kin to these families; not, however, as a rule, to the families of the tidewater region, the aristocrats of colonial days, but to the families—so often of Presbyterian Irish stock—who rose to prominence in western Virginia at the time of the Revolution. In Kentucky, all men mixed together, no matter from what State they came, the wrench of the break from their home ties having shaken them so that they readily adapted themselves to new conditions, and easily assimilated with one another. As for their differences of race origin, these had ceased to influence their lives even before they came to Kentucky. They were all Americans, in feeling as well as in name, by habit as well as by birth; and the position they took in the political life of the West was determined partly by the new conditions surrounding them, and partly by the habits bred in them through generations of life on American soil.

One man who would naturally have played a prominent part in Kentucky politics, failed to do so from a variety of causes. This was George Rogers Clark. He was by preference a military rather than a civil leader; he belonged by choice and habit to the class of pioneers and Indian fighters whose influence was waning; his remarkable successes had excited much envy and jealousy, while his subsequent ignominious failure had aroused contempt; and, finally, he was undone by his fondness for strong drink. He drew himself to one side, though he chafed at the need, and in his private letters he spoke with bitterness of the "big little men," the ambitious nobodies, whose jealousy had prompted them to destroy him by ten thousand lies; and, making a virtue of necessity, he plumed himself on the fact that he did not meddle with politics, and sneered at the baseness of his fellow citizens, whom he styled "a swarm of hungry persons gaping for bread."

Benjamin Logan, who was senior colonel and county lieu-tenant of the District of Kentucky, stood second to Clark in the estimation of the early settlers, the men who, riding their own horses and carrying their own rifles, had so often fol-lowed both commanders on their swift raids against the Indian towns. Logan naturally took the lead in the first serious move-ment to make Kentucky an independent State. In its begin-nings this movement showed a curious parallelism to what was occurring in Franklin at the same time, though when

once fairly under way the difference between the cases became very strongly marked. In each case the prime cause in
starting the movement was trouble with the Indians. In each,
the first steps were taken by the commanders of the local
militia, and the first convention was summoned on the same
plan, a member being elected by every militia company. The
companies were territorial as well as military units, and the
early settlers were all, in practice as well as in theory, embodied in the militia. Thus in both Kentucky and Franklin the
movements were begun in the same way by the same class of
Indian-fighting pioneers; and the method of organization
chosen shows clearly the rough military form which at that
period settlement in the wilderness, in the teeth of a hostile
savagery, always assumed.

In 1784, fear of a formidable Indian invasion—an unwar-
ranted fear, as the result showed—became general in
Kentucky, and in the fall Logan summoned a meeting of the
field-officers to discuss the danger and to provide against it.
When the officers gathered and tried to evolve some plan of
operations, they found that they were helpless. They were
merely the officers of one of the districts of Virginia; they
could take no proper steps of their own motion, and Virginia
was too far away and her interests had too little in common
with theirs, for the Virginian authorities to prove satisfactory
substitutes for their own. Confronted by such a condition
of affairs, the militia officers issued a circular letter to the
people of the district, recommending that on December 24,
1784, a convention should be held at Danville further to
consider the subject, and that this convention should consist
of delegates elected one from each militia company.

The recommendation was well received by the people of
the district; and on the appointed date the convention met at
Danville. Colonel William Fleming, the old Indian fighter and
surveyor, was again visiting Kentucky, and he was chosen
president of the convention. After some discussion the members concluded that, while some of the disadvantages under
which they labored could be remedied by the action of the
Virginia legislature, the real trouble was deep-rooted, and
could only be met by separation from Virginia and the erection
of Kentucky into a State. There was, however, much opposition to this plan, and the convention wisely decided to dissolve,

after recommending to the people to elect, by counties, members who should meet in convention at Danville in May for the express purpose of deciding on the question of addressing to the Virginia Assembly a request for separation.

The convention assembled accordingly, Logan being one of the members, while it was presided over by Colonel Samuel McDowell, who, like Fleming, was a veteran Indian fighter and hero of the Great Kanawha. Up to this point the phases through which the movement for statehood in Kentucky had passed were almost exactly the same as the phases of the similar movement in Franklin. But the two now entered upon diverging lines of progression. In each case the home government was willing to grant the request for separation, but wished to affix a definite date to their consent, and to make the fulfilment of certain conditions a prerequisite. In each case there were two parties in the district desiring separation, one of them favoring immediate and revolutionary action, while the other, with much greater wisdom and propriety, wished to act through the forms of law and with the consent of the parent State. In Kentucky, the latter party triumphed. Moreover, while up to the time of this meeting of the May convention the leaders in the movement had been the old Indian fighters, after this date the lead was taken by men who had come to Kentucky only after the great rush of immigrants began. The new men were not backwoods hunter-warriors, like Clark and Logan, Sevier, Robertson, and Tipton. They were politicians of the Virginia stamp. They founded political clubs, one of which, the Danville Club, became prominent, and in them they discussed with fervid eagerness the public questions of the day, the members showing a decided tendency toward the Jeffersonian school of political thought.

The convention, which met at Danville, in May, 1785, decided unanimously that it was desirable to separate, by constitutional methods, from Virginia, and to secure admission as a separate State into the Federal Union. Accordingly, it directed the preparation of a petition to this effect, to be sent to the Virginia legislature, and prepared an address to the people in favor of the proposed course of action. Then, in a queer spirit of hesitancy, instead of acting on its own responsibility, as it had both the right and power to do, the convention decided that the issuing of the address, and the ratification of its own actions generally, should be submitted to another convention, which was summoned to meet at the same place in August of the same year. The people of the district were as yet by no means a unit in favor of separation, and this made the convention hesitate to take any irrevocable step.

One of the members of this convention was Judge Caleb Wallace, a recent arrival in Kentucky, and a representative of the new school of Kentucky politicians. He was a friend and ally of Brown and Innes. He was also a friend of Madison, and to him he wrote a full account of the reasons which actuated the Kentuckians in the step they had taken. He explained that he and the people of the district generally felt that they did not "enjoy a greater portion of liberty than an American colony might have done a few years ago had she been allowed a representation in the British Parliament." He complained bitterly that some of the taxes were burdensome and unjust, and that the money raised for the expenses of government all went to the East, to Virginia proper, while no corresponding benefits were received; and insisted that the seat of government was too remote for Kentucky ever to get justice from the rest of the State. Therefore, he said, he thought it would be wiser to part in peace rather than remain together in discontented and jealous union. But he frankly admitted that he was by no means sure that the people of the district possessed sufficient wisdom and virtue to fit them for successful self-government, and he anxiously asked Madison's advice as to several provisions which it was thought might be embodied in the constitution of the new State.

In the August convention, Wilkinson sat as a member, and he succeeded in committing his colleagues to a more radical course of action than that of the preceding convention. The resolutions they forwarded to the Virginia legislature asked the immediate erection of Kentucky into an independent State, and expressed the conviction that the new commonwealth would undoubtedly be admitted into the Union. This, of course, meant that Kentucky would first become a power outside and independent of the Union; and no provision was made for entry into the Union beyond the expression of a hopeful belief that it would be allowed.

Such a course would have been in the highest degree unwise; and the Virginians refused to allow it to be followed. Their legislature, in January, 1786, provided that a new convention should be held in Kentucky in September, 1786, and that, if it declared for independence, the State should come into being after the 1st of September, 1787, provided, however, that Congress, before June 1, 1787, consented to the erection of the new State and agreed to its admission into the Union. It was also provided that another convention should be held, in the summer of 1787, to draw up a constitution for the new State.

Virginia thus, with great propriety, made the acquiescence of Congress a condition precedent to the formation of the new State. Wilkinson immediately denounced this condition and demanded that Kentucky declare herself an independent State forthwith, no matter what Congress or Virginia might say. All the disorderly, unthinking, and separatist elements followed his lead. Had his policy been adopted the result would probably have been a civil war; and at the least there would have followed a period of anarchy and confusion, and a condition of things similar to that obtaining at this very time in the territory of Franklin. The most enlightened and far-seeing men of the district were alarmed at the outlook; and a vigorous campaign in favor of orderly action was begun, under the lead of men like the Marshalls. There were thus two well-defined parties, and there were hot contests for seats in the convention.

Virginia had so far acted wisely; but now she in her turn showed unwisdom, for her legislature passed a new act, providing for another convention to be held in August, 1787, the separation from Virginia only to be consummated if Congress, prior to July 4, 1788, should agree to the erection of the State and provide for its admission to the Union. When news of this act, with its requirement of needless and tedious delay, reached the Kentucky convention, it adjourned for good, with much chagrin.

Wilkinson and the other separatist leaders took advantage of this very natural chagrin to inflame the minds of the people against both Virginia and Congress. It was at this time that the Westerners became deeply stirred by exaggerated reports of the willingness of Congress to yield the right to navigate the Mississippi; and the separatist chiefs fanned their discontent by painting the danger as real and imminent, although they must speedily have learned that it had already ceased to exist. Moreover, there was much friction between the Federal and Virginian authorities and the Kentucky militia officers in reference to the Indian raids. The Kentuckians showed a disposition to include all Indians, good and bad alike, in the category of foes. On the other hand, the home authorities were inclined to forbid the Kentuckians to make the offensive return forays which could alone render successful their defensive warfare against the savages. All these causes combined to produce much irritation, and the separatists began to talk rebellion. One of their leaders, Innes, in a letter to the governor of Virginia, threatened that Kentucky would revolt not only from the parent State, but from the Union, if heed were not paid to her wishes and needs.

However, at this time Wilkinson started on his first trading voyage to New Orleans, and the district was freed from his very undesirable presence. He was the mainspring of the movement in favor of lawless separation; for the furtive, restless, unscrupulous man had a talent for intrigue which rendered him dangerous at a crisis of such a kind. In his absence the feeling cooled. The convention met in September, 1787, and acted with order and propriety, passing an act which provided for statehood upon the terms and conditions laid down by Virginia. The act went through by a nearly unanimous vote, only two members dissenting, while three or four refused to vote either way. Both Virginia and the Continental Congress were notified of the action taken.

With Wilkinson's return to Kentucky, after his successful trading trip to New Orleans, the disunion agitation once more took formidable form. The news of his success excited the cupidity of every mercantile adventurer, and the whole district became inflamed with desire to reap the benefits of the rich river trade; and, naturally, the people formed the most exaggerated estimate of what these benefits would be. Chafing at the way the restrictions imposed by the Spanish officials hampered their commerce, the people were readily led by Wilkinson and his associates to consider the Federal authorities as somehow to blame because these restrictions were not removed.

The discontent was much increased by the growing fury of

the Indian ravages. There had been a lull in the murderous woodland warfare during the years immediately succeeding the close of the Revolution, but the storm had again gathered. The hostility of the savages had grown steadily. By the summer of 1787 the Kentucky frontier was suffering much. In their anger the Kentuckians denounced the Federal Government for not aiding them, the men who were loudest in their denunciations being the very men who were most strenuously bent on refusing to adopt the new constitution, which alone could give the National Government the power to act effectually in the interest of the people.

While the spirit of unrest and discontent was high, the question of ratifying or rejecting this new Federal Constitution came up for decision. The Wilkinson party, and all the men who believed in a weak central government, or who wished the Federal tie dissolved outright, were, of course, violently opposed to ratification. Many weak or short-sighted men, and the doctrinaires and theorists—most of the members of the Danville political club, for instance—announced that they wished to ratify the Constitution, but only after it had been amended. As such prior amendment was impossible, this amounted merely to playing into the hands of the separatists; and the men who followed it were responsible for the by no means creditable fact that most of the Kentucky members in the Virginia convention voted against ratification. Three of them, however, had the patriotism and foresight to vote in favor of the Constitution.

Another irritating delay in the march toward statehood now occurred. In June, 1788, the Continental Congress declared that it was expedient to erect Kentucky into a State. But immediately afterward news came that the Constitution had been ratified by the necessary nine States, and that the new government was, therefore, practically in being. This meant the dissolution of the old confederation, so that there was no longer any object in admitting Kentucky to membership, and Congress thereupon very wisely refused to act further in the matter. Unfortunately, Brown, who was the Kentucky delegate in Congress, was one of the separatist leaders. He wrote home an account of the matter, in which he painted the refusal as due to the jealousy felt by the East for the West. As a matter of fact, the delegates from all the States, except

Virginia, had concurred in the action taken. Brown suppressed this fact, and used language carefully calculated to render the Kentuckians hostile to the Union.

Naturally, all this gave an impetus to the separatist movement. The district held two conventions, in July and again in November, during the year 1788; and in both of them the separatist leaders made determined efforts to have Kentucky forthwith erect herself into an independent State. In uttering their opinions and desires they used vague language as to what they would do when once separated from Virginia. It is certain that they bore in mind, at the time at least, the possibility of separating outright from the Union and entering into a close alliance with Spain. The moderate men, headed by those who were devoted to the national idea, strenuously opposed this plan; they triumphed, and Kentucky merely sent a request to Virginia for an act of separation in accordance with the recommendations of Congress.

It was in connection with these conventions that there appeared the first newspaper ever printed in this new West; the West which lay no longer among the Alleghanies, but beyond them. It was a small weekly sheet, called the *Kentucke Gazette,* and the first number appeared in August, 1787. The editor and publisher was one John Bradford, who brought his printing-press down the river on a flatboat; and some of the type were cut out of dogwood. In politics, the paper sided with the separatists and clamored for revolutionary action by Kentucky.

The purpose of the extreme separatist was, unquestionably, to keep Kentucky out of the Union and turn her into a little independent nation—a nation without a present or a future, an English-speaking Uruguay or Ecuador. The back of this separatist movement was broken by the action of the fall convention of 1788, which settled definitely that Kentucky should become a State of the Union. All that remained was to decide on the precise terms of the separation from Virginia. There was at first a hitch over these, the Virginia legislature making terms to which the district convention of 1789 would not consent; but Virginia then yielded the points in dispute, and the Kentucky convention of 1790 provided for the admission of the State to the Union in 1792, and for holding a constitutional convention to decide upon the form of government, just before the admission.

Thus Kentucky was saved from the career of ignoble dishonor to which she would have been doomed by the success of the disunion faction. She was saved from the day of small things. Her interests became those of a nation which was bound to succeed greatly or to fail greatly. Her fate was linked for weal or for woe with the fate of the mighty Republic.

Chapter XVII

The Southwest Territory

D URING the years 1788 and 1789 there was much dis-
quiet and restlessness throughout the southwestern
territory, the land lying between Kentucky and the
Southern Indians. The disturbances caused by the erection
of the State of Franklin were subsiding, the authority of North
Carolina was re-established over the whole territory, and by
degrees a more assured and healthy feeling began to prevail
among the settlers; but as yet their future was by no means
certain, nor was their lot irrevocably cast in with that of their
fellows in the other portions of the Union.

Congress had tried hard to bring about peace with the
Southern Indians, both by sending commissioners to them
and by trying to persuade the three Southern States to enter
into mutually beneficial treaties with them. A successful effort
was also made to detach the Chickasaws from the others, and
keep them friendly with the United States. Congress as usual
sympathized with the Indians against the intruding whites, although it was plain that only by warfare could the red men be
permanently subdued.

The Cumberland people felt the full weight of the warfare,
the Creeks being their special enemies. Robertson himself
lost a son and a brother in the various Indian attacks. To
him fell the task of trying to put a stop to the ravages. He
was the leader of his people in every way, their commander in
war and their spokesman when they sought peace; and early
in 1788 he wrote a long letter on their behalf to the Creek chief
McGillivray. After disclaiming all responsibility for or connection with the Franklin men, he said that the settlers for
whom he spoke had not had the most distant idea that any
Indians would object to their settling on the Cumberland, in

a country that had been purchased outright at the Henderson treaty. He further stated that he had believed the Creek chief would approve of the expedition to punish the marauders at the Muscle Shell Shoals, inasmuch as the Creeks had repeatedly assured him that these marauders were refractory people who would pay no heed to their laws and commands. Robertson knew this to be a good point, for as a matter of fact the Creeks, though pretending to be peaceful, had made no effort to suppress these banditti, and had resented by force of arms the destruction of their stronghold.

Robertson then came to his personal wrongs. His quaintly worded letter runs in part: "I had the mortification to see one of my children Killed and uncommonly Massacred . . . from my earliest youth I have endeavored to arm myself with a sufficient share of Fortitude to meet anything that Nature might have intended, but to see an innocent child so Uncommonly Massacred by people who ought to have both sense and bravery has in a measure unmanned me. . . . I have always striven to do justice to the red people; last fall, trusting in Cherokee friendship, I with utmost difficulty prevented a great army from marching against them. The return is very inadequate to the services I have rendered them as last summer they killed an affectionate brother and three days ago an innocent child." The letter concludes with an emphatic warning that the Indians must expect heavy chastisement if they do not stop their depredations.

Robertson looked on his own woes and losses with much of the stoicism for which his Indian foes were famed. He accepted the fate of his son with a kind of grim stolidity; and did not let it interfere with his efforts to bring about a peace. Writing to his friend General Martin, he said: "On my return home [from the North Carolina legislature, to which he was a delegate] I found distressing times in the country. A number of persons have been killed since; among those unfortunate persons were my third son. . . . We sent Captains Hackett and Ewing to the Creeks who have brought very favorable accounts, and we do not doubt but a lasting peace will be shortly concluded between us and that nation. The Cherokees we shall flog, if they do not behave well." He wished to make peace if he could; but if that was impossible, he was ready to make war with the same stern acceptance of fate.

The letter then goes on to express the opinion that, if Congress does not take action to bring about a peace, the Creeks will undoubtedly invade Georgia with some five thousand warriors, for McGillivray has announced that he will consent to settle the boundary question with Congress, but will do nothing with Georgia. The letter shows, with rather startling clearness, how little Robertson regarded the Cumberland people and the Georgians as being both in the same nation; he saw nothing strange in one portion of the country concluding a firm peace with an enemy who was about to devastate another portion.

Robertson wrote several times to McGillivray, alone or in conjunction with another veteran frontier leader, Colonel Anthony Bledsoe. Various other men of note on the border, both from Virginia and North Carolina, wrote likewise. To these letters McGillivray responded promptly in a style rather more polished though less frank than that of his correspondents. His tone was distinctly more warlike and less conciliatory than theirs. He avowed, without hesitation, that the Creeks and not the Americans had been the original aggressors, saying that "my nation has waged war against your people for several years past; but that we had no motive of revenge, nor did it proceed from any sense of injuries sustained from your people, but being warmly attached to the British and being under their influence our operations were directed by them against you in common with other Americans." He then acknowledged that after the close of the war the Americans had sent overtures of peace, which he had accepted—although as a matter of fact the Creeks never ceased their ravages—but complained that Robertson's expedition against the Muscle Shoals again brought on war. But now that vengeance had been taken, McGillivray declared that a stable peace would be secured, and he expressed "considerable concern" over the "tragical end" of Robertson's slain kinsfolk. As for the Georgians, he announced that if they were wise and would agree to an honorable peace he would bury the red hatchet, and if not then he would march against them whenever he saw fit. Writing again at the end of the year, he reiterated his assurances of the peaceful inclinations of the Creeks, though their troubles with Georgia were still unsettled.

Nevertheless, these peaceful protestations produced absolutely no effect upon the Indian ravages, which continued with unabated fury. Many instances of revolting brutality and aggression by the whites against the Cherokees took place in Tennessee, both earlier and later than this, and in eastern Tennessee at this very time; but the Cumberland people, from the earliest days of their settlement, had not sinned against the red men, while as regards all the Tennesseeans, the Creeks throughout this period appeared always, and the Cherokees appeared sometimes, as the wrong-doers, the men who began the long and ferocious wars of reprisal.

Robertson's companion, Bledsoe, was among the many settlers who suffered death in the summer of 1788. He was roused from sleep by the sound of his cattle running across the yard in front of the twin log houses occupied by himself and his brother and their families. As he opened the door he was shot by Indians, who were lurking behind the fence, and one of his hired men was also shot down. The savages fled, and Bledsoe lived through the night, while the other inmates of the house kept watch at the loopholes until day broke and the fear was passed. Under the laws of North Carolina at that time, all the lands went to the sons of a man dying intestate, and Bledsoe's wealth consisted almost exclusively in great tracts of land. As he lay dying in his cabin, his sister suggested to him that unless he made a will he would leave his seven daughters penniless; and so the will was drawn; and the old frontiersman signed it just before he drew his last breath, leaving each of his children provided with a share of his land.

During these two years many people were killed, both in the settlements, on the trail through the woods, and on the Tennessee River, as they drifted downstream in their boats. Among many attacks on the boats that went down the Tennessee it happens that a full record has been kept of one. A North Carolinian, named Brown, had served in the Revolutionary War with the troop of Light-Horse Harry Lee, and had received in payment a land certificate. Under this certificate he entered several tracts of Western land, including some on the Cumberland; and in the spring of 1788 he started by boat down the Tennessee, to take possession of his claims. He took with him his wife and his seven children; and three or four young men also went along. When they reached the Chickamauga towns the Indians swarmed out toward them in canoes. On Brown's boat was a swivel, and with this and the rifles of the men they might have made good their defense, but as soon as the Indians saw them preparing for resistance they halted and hailed the crew, shouting that they were peaceful and that in consequence of the recent Holston treaties war had ceased between the white man and the red. Brown was not used to Indians; he was deceived, and before he made up his mind what to do the Indians were alongside, and many of them came aboard. They then seized the boat and massacred the men, while the mother and children were taken ashore and hurried off in various directions by the Indians who claimed to have captured them. One of the boys, Joseph, long afterward wrote an account of his captivity. He was not treated with deliberate cruelty, though he suffered now and then from the casual barbarity of his captors, and toiled like an ordinary slave. Once he was doomed to death by a party of Indians, who made him undress, so as to avoid bloodying his clothes; but they abandoned this purpose through fear of his owner, a half-breed and a dreaded warrior, who had killed many whites.

After about a year's captivity, Joseph and his mother and sisters were all released, though at different times. Their release was brought about by Sevier. When, in the fall of 1788, a big band of Creeks and Cherokees took Gillespie's station, on Little River, a branch of the upper Tennessee, they carried off a score of women and children. The four highest chiefs, headed by one with the appropriate name of Bloody Fellow, left behind a note addressed to Sevier and Martin, in which they taunted the whites with their barbarities, and especially with the murder of the friendly Cherokee chief Tassel, and warned them to move off the Indian land. In response, Sevier made one of his swift raids, destroyed an Indian town on the Coosa River, and took prisoners a large number of Indian women and children. These were well treated, but were carefully guarded, and were exchanged for the white women and children who were in captivity among the Indians. The Browns were among the fortunate people who were thus rescued from the horrors of Indian slavery. It is small wonder that the rough frontier people, whose wives and little ones, friends and neighbors, were in such manner rescued by Nolichucky Jack, should have looked with leniency on their daring leader's short-comings, even when these shortcomings took the form of failure to prevent or punish the massacre of friendly Indians.

Soon after the Constitution went into effect the National Government made a vigorous effort to conclude peace on a stable basis. Commissioners were sent to the Southern Indians. Under their persuasion McGillivray and the leading kings and chiefs of the Muscogee confederacy came to New York and there entered into a solemn treaty. In this treaty the Creeks acknowledged the United States, to the exclusion of Spain, as the sole power with which they could treat; they covenanted to keep faith and friendship with the Americans; and in return for substantial payments and guaranties they agreed to cede some lands to the Georgians, though less than was claimed under the treaty of Galphinton.

This treaty was solemnly entered into by the recognized chiefs and leaders of the Creeks; and the Americans fondly hoped that it would end hostilities. It did nothing of the kind. Though the terms were very favorable to the Indians, so much so as to make the frontiersmen grumble, the Creeks scornfully repudiated the promises made on their behalf by their authorized representatives. Their motive in going to war, and keeping up the war, was not so much anger at the encroachments of the whites as the eager thirst for glory, scalps, and plunder, to be won at the expense of the settlers. The war-parties raided the frontier as freely as ever. The simple truth was that the Creeks could be kept quiet only when cowed by physical fear. If the white men did not break the treaties, then the red men did. It is idle to dispute about the rights or wrongs of the contests. Two peoples, in two stages of culture which were separated by untold ages, stood face to face; one or the other had to perish, and the whites went forward from sheer necessity.

Throughout these years of Indian warfare the influx of settlers into the Holston and Cumberland regions steadily continued. Early in 1790, North Carolina finally ceded, and the National Government finally accepted, what is now Tennessee; and in May, Congress passed a law for the government of this Territory southwest of the River Ohio, as they chose to call it. This law followed on the general lines of the Ordinance of 1787, for the government of the Northwest; but there was one important difference. North Carolina had made her cession conditional upon the non-passage of any law tending to emancipate slaves. At that time such a condition was inevitable; but it doomed the Southwest to suffer under the curse of negro bondage.

William Blount, of North Carolina, was appointed governor of the Territory, and at once proceeded to his new home to organize the civil government. He laid out Knoxville as his capital, where he built a good house with a lawn in front. On his recommendation, Sevier was appointed brigadier-general for the Eastern District and Robertson for the Western—the two districts known as Washington and Miro, respectively.

Blount was the first man of leadership in the West who was of Cavalier ancestry; for though so much is said of the Cavalier type in the Southern States it was everywhere insignificant in numbers, and comparatively few of the Southern men of mark have belonged to it. Blount was really of Cavalier blood. He was descended from a royalist baronet, who was roughly handled by the Cromwellians, and whose three sons came to America. One of them settled in North Carolina, near Albemarle Sound, and from him came the new governor of the southwestern Territory. Blount was a good-looking, well-bred man, with cultivated tastes; but he was also a man of force and energy, who knew well how to get on with the backwoodsmen, so that he soon became popular among them.

The West had grown with astonishing rapidity during the seven years following the close of the Revolutionary War. In 1790, there were in Kentucky nearly seventy-four thousand, and in the Southwest Territory nearly thirty-six thousand souls. In the Northwest Territory the period of rapid growth had not yet begun, and the old French inhabitants still formed the majority of the population.

The changes during these seven years had been vital. In the West, as elsewhere through the Union, the years succeeding the triumphant close of the Revolution were those which determined whether the victory was or was not worth winning. To throw off the yoke of the stranger was useless and worse than useless if we showed ourselves unable to turn to good account the freedom we had gained. Unless we could build up a great nation, and unless we possessed the power and self-restraint to frame an orderly and stable government, and to live under its laws when framed, the long years of warfare against the armies of the king were wasted and went for naught.

At the close of the Revolution the West was seething with sedition. There were three tasks before the Westerners; all three had to be accomplished, under pain of utter failure. It was their duty to invade and tame the shaggy wilderness; to drive back the Indians and their European allies, and to erect free governments which should form parts of the indissoluble Union. If the spirit of sedition, of lawlessness, and of wild individualism and separatism had conquered, then our history would merely have anticipated the dismal tale of the Spanish-American republics.

Viewed from this standpoint the history of the West during these eventful years has a special and peculiar interest. The inflow of the teeming throng of settlers was the most striking feature; but it was no more important than the half-seen struggle in which the Union party finally triumphed over the restless strivers for disunion. The extent and reality of the danger are shown by the numerous separatist movements. The intrigues in which so many of the leaders engaged with Spain, for the purpose of setting up barrier States, in some degree feudatory to the Spaniards; the movement in Kentucky for violent separation from Virginia, and the more secret movement for separation from the United States; the turbulent career of the commonwealth of Franklin; the attitude of isolation of interest from all their neighbors assumed by the Cumberland settlers—all these various movements and attitudes were significant of the looseness of the Federal tie, and were ominous of the anarchic violence, weakness, and misrule which would have followed the breaking of that tie.

The career of Franklin gave the clearest glimpse of what might have been; for it showed the gradual breaking down of law and order, the rise of factions ready to appeal to arms for success, the bitter broils with neighboring States, the reckless readiness to provoke war with the Indians, unheeding their rights or the woes such wars caused other frontier communities, and finally the entire willingness of the leaders to seek foreign aid when their cause was declining. Had not the Constitution been adopted, and a more perfect union been thus called into being, the history of the State of Franklin would have been repeated in fifty communities from the Alleghanies to the Pacific coast; only these little States, instead of dying in the bud, would have gone through a rank flowering period of bloody and aimless revolutions, of silly and ferocious warfare against their neighbors, and of degrading alliance with the foreigner. From these and a hundred other woes the West no less than the East was saved by the knitting together of the States into a nation.

This knitting process passed through its first and most critical stage, in the West, during the period intervening between the close of the war for independence, and the year which saw the organization of the Southwest into a Territory ruled under the laws, and by the agent, of the National Government. During this time no step was taken toward settling the question of boundary-lines with our British and Spanish neighbors; that remained as it had been, the Americans never abandoning claims which they had not yet the power to enforce, and which their antagonists declined to yield. Neither were the Indian wars settled; on the contrary, they had become steadily more serious, though for the first time a definite solution was promised by the active interference of the National Government. But a vast change had been made by the inflow of population; and an even vaster by the growing solidarity of the Western settlements with one another, and with the Central Government. The settlement of the Northwest, so different in some of its characteristics from the settlement of the Southwest, had begun. Kentucky was about to become a State of the Union. The Territories north and south of it were organized as part of the domain of the United States. The West was no longer a mere wilderness dotted with cabins and hamlets, whose backwoods builders were held by but the loosest tie of allegiance to any government, even their own. It had become an integral part of the mighty American Republic.

Chapter XVIII

Tennessee Becomes a State

THE Territory of the United States of America South of the River Ohio" was the official title of the tract of land which had been ceded by North Carolina to the United States, and which a few years later became the State of Tennessee. William Blount, the newly appointed governor, took charge late in 1790. He made a tour of the various counties, as laid out under authority of the State of North Carolina, rechristening them as counties of the Territory, and summoning before him the persons in each county holding commissions from North Carolina, at the respective court-houses, where he formally notified them of the change. He read to them the act of Congress accepting the cessions of the claims of North Carolina; then he read his own commission from President Washington; and informed them of the provision by North Carolina that Congress should assume and execute the government of the new Territory "in a manner similar to that which they support northwest of the River Ohio." Following this he formally read the ordinance for the government of the Northwestern Territory. He commented upon and explained this proclamation, stating that under it the President had appointed the governor, the judges, and the secretary of the new Territory, and that he himself, as governor, would now appoint the necessary county officers.

The remarkable feature of this address was that he read to the assembled officers in each county, as part of the law apparently binding upon them, Article 6 of the Ordinance of 1787, which provided that there should be neither slavery nor involuntary servitude in the Northwestern Territory. It had been expressly stipulated that this particular provision as regards slavery should not apply to the Southwestern Territory, and of course Blount's omission to mention this fact did not in any way alter the case; but it is a singular thing that he should without comment have read and his listeners without comment have heard, a recital that slavery was abolished in their Territory. It emphasizes the fact that at this time there was throughout the West no very strong feeling on the subject of slavery, and what feeling there was, was if anything, hostile. The adventurous backwoods farmers who composed the great mass of the population in Tennessee, as elsewhere among and west of the Alleghanies, were not a slave-owning people, in the sense that the planters of the seaboard were. They were pre-eminently folk who did their work with their own hands. Master and man chopped and ploughed and reaped and builded side by side, and even the leaders of the community, the militia generals, the legislators, and the judges, often did their share of farm work, and prided themselves upon their capacity to do it well. They had none of that feeling which makes slave-owners look upon manual labor as a badge of servitude. They were often lazy and shiftless, but they never deified laziness and shiftlessness or made them into a cult. The one thing they prized beyond all others was their personal freedom, the right of the individual to do whatsoever he saw fit. Indeed, they often carried this feeling so far as to make them condone gross excesses, rather than insist upon the exercise of even needful authority. They were by no means entirely logical, but they did see and feel that slavery was abhorrent, and that it was utterly inconsistent with the theories of their own social and governmental life. As yet there was no thought of treating slavery as a sacred institution, the righteousness of which must not be questioned. At the Fourth of July celebrations toasts such as "The total abolition of slavery" were not uncommon. It was this feeling which prevented any manifestation of surprise at Blount's apparent acquiescence in a section of the ordinance for the government of the Territory which prohibited slavery.

Nevertheless, though slaves were not numerous, they were far from uncommon, and the moral conscience of the community was not really roused upon the subject. It was hardly possible that it should be roused, for no civilized people who owned African slaves had as yet abolished slavery, and it was too much to hope that the path toward abolition would be pointed out by poor frontiersmen engaged in a life-and-death struggle with hostile savages. The slaveholders were not interfered with until they gradually grew numerous enough and powerful enough to set the tone of thought, and make it impossible to root out slavery save by outside action.

Blount recommended the appointment of Sevier and Robertson as brigadier-generals of militia of the eastern and western districts of the Territory, and issued a large number of commissions to the justices of the peace, militia officers, sheriffs, and clerks of the county courts in the different counties. In his appointments he shrewdly and properly identified himself with the natural leaders of the frontiersmen. He made Sevier and Robertson his right-hand men, and strove always to act in harmony with them, while for the minor military and civil officers he chose the persons whom the frontiersmen themselves desired. In consequence he speedily became a man of great influence for good. The secretary of the Territory reported to the Federal Government that the effect of Blount's character on the frontiersmen was far greater than was the case with any other man, and that he was able to get them to adhere to the principles of order and to support the laws by his influence in a way which it was hopeless to expect from their own respect for governmental authority. Blount was felt by the frontiersmen to be thoroughly in sympathy with them, to understand and appreciate them, and to be heartily anxious for their welfare; and yet at the same time his influence could be counted upon on the side of order, while the majority of the frontier officials in any time of commotion were apt to remain silent and inactive or even to express their sympathy with the disorderly element.

No one but a man of great tact and firmness could have preserved as much order among the frontiersmen as Blount preserved. He was always under fire from both sides. The settlers were continually complaining that they were deserted by the Federal authorities, who favored the Indians, and that Blount himself did not take sufficiently active steps to subdue the savages; while on the other hand the national Administration was continually upbraiding him for being too active against the Indians, and for not keeping the frontiersmen sufficiently peaceable. Under many temptations, and in a situation

that would have bewildered any one, Blount steadfastly followed his course of, on the one hand, striving his best to protect the people over whom he was placed as governor and to
repel the savages, while, on the other hand, he suppressed, so
far as lay in his power, any outbreak against the authorities,
and tried to inculcate a feeling of loyalty and respect for the
National Government. He did much in creating a strong feeling of attachment to the Union among the rough backwoodsmen with whom he had thrown in his lot.

Early in 1791, Blount entered into negotiations with the
Cherokees, and when the weather grew warm he summoned
them to a treaty. They met on the Holston, all of the noted
Cherokee chiefs and hundreds of their warriors being present,
and concluded the treaty of Holston, by which, in consideration
of numerous gifts and of an annuity of a thousand (afterward
increased to fifteen hundred) dollars, the Cherokees at last
definitely abandoned their disputed claims to the various tracts
of land which the whites claimed under various former
treaties. By this treaty with the Cherokees, and by the treaty
with the Creeks entered into at New York the previous summer, the Indian title to most of the present State of Tennessee
was fairly and legally extinguished. However, the western-
most part was still held by the Chickasaws, and certain tracts
in the Southeast by the Cherokees; while the Indian hunting-
grounds in the middle of the Territory were thrust in between
the groups of settlements on the Cumberland and the Holston.

On the ground where the treaty was held Blount proceeded
to build a little town, which he made the capital of the Territory, and christened Knoxville, in honor of Washington's
secretary of war. At this town there was started, in 1791,
under his own supervision, the first newspaper of Tennessee,
known as the Knoxville *Gazette*. It was four or five years
younger than the only other newspaper of the then far West,
the Kentucky *Gazette*. The paper gives an interesting glimpse
of many of the social and political conditions of the day. In
political tone it showed Blount's influence very strongly, and
was markedly in advance of most of the similar papers of
the time, including the Kentucky *Gazette;* for it took a firm
stand in favor of the National Government, and against every
form of disorder, of separatism, or of mob law. As with all
of the American papers of the day, even in the backwoods,

there was much interest taken in European news, and a prominent position was given to long letters, or extracts from seaboard papers, containing accounts of the operations of the English fleets and the French armies, or of the attitude of the European governments. Like most Americans, the editorial writers of the paper originally sympathized strongly with the French Revolution; but the news of the beheading of Marie Antoinette, and the recital of the atrocities committed in Paris, worked a reaction among those who loved order, and the Knoxville *Gazette* ranged itself with them, taking for the time being strong grounds against the French, and even incidentally alluding to the Indians as being more bloodthirsty than any man "not a Jacobin." The people largely shared these sentiments. In 1793, at the Fourth of July celebration at Jonesboro there was a public dinner and ball, as there was also at Knoxville; Federal troops were paraded and toasts were drunk to the President, to the judges of the Supreme Court, to Blount, to General Wayne, to the friendly Chickasaw Indians, to Sevier, to the ladies of the Southwestern Territory, to the American arms, and, finally, "to the true liberties of France and a speedy and just punishment of the murderers of Louis XVI." The word "Jacobin" was used as a term of reproach for some time.

The paper was at first decidedly Federalist in sentiment. No sympathy was expressed with Genet or with the efforts undertaken by the Western allies of the French minister to organize a force for the conquest of Louisiana; and the Tennessee settlers generally took the side of law and order in the earlier disturbances in which the Federal Government was concerned. At the Fourth of July celebration in Knoxville in 1795, one of the toasts was: "The four western counties of Pennsylvania—may they repent their folly and sin no more"; the Tennesseans sympathizing as little with the Pennsylvania whiskey revolutionists as four years later they sympathized with the Kentuckians and Virginians in their nullification agitation against the alien and sedition laws. Gradually, however, the tone of the paper changed, as did the tone of the community, at least to the extent of becoming Democratic and anti-Federal; for the people felt that the Easterners did not sympathize with them either in their contests with the Indians or in their desire to control the Mississippi and the farther West. They grew to regard with particular vindictiveness the Federalists—the aristocrats, as they styled them—of the Southern seaboard States, notably of Virginia and South Carolina.

One pathetic feature of the paper was the recurrence of advertisements by persons whose friends and kinsfolk had been carried off by the Indians, and who anxiously sought any trace of them.

But the *Gazette* was used for the expression of opinions not only by the whites, but occasionally even by an Indian. One of the Cherokee chiefs, the Red Bird, put into the *Gazette,* for two buckskins, a talk to the Cherokee chief of the upper towns, in which he especially warned him to leave alone one William Cocke, "the white man who lived among the mulberry-trees," for, said Red Bird, "the mulberry man talks very strong and runs very fast"; this same Cocke being afterward one of the first two senators from Tennessee. The Red Bird ended his letter by the expression of the rather quaint wish "that all the bad people on both sides were laid in the ground, for then there would not be so many mush men trying to make people to believe they were warriors."

Blount brought his family to Tennessee at once, and took the lead in trying to build up institutions for higher education. After a good deal of difficulty an academy was organized under the title of Blount College, and was opened as soon as a sufficient number of pupils could be gotten together; there were already two other colleges in the Territory, Greeneville and Washington, the latter being the academy founded by Doak. Like almost all other institutions of learning of the day, these three were under clerical control; but Blount College was chartered as a non-denomination institution, the first of its kind in the United States. The clergyman and the lawyer, with the schoolmaster, were still the typical men of letters in all the frontier communities. The doctor was not yet a prominent feature of life in the backwoods, though there is in the *Gazette* an advertisement of one who announces that he intends to come to practice "with a large stock of genuine medicines."

Settlers were thronging into east Tennessee, and many penetrated even to the Indian-harassed western district. In 1794, there being five thousand free male inhabitants, as provided by law, Tennessee became entitled to a Territorial legislature, and the governor summoned the Assembly to meet at Knoxville on August 17th. So great was the danger from the Indians that a military company had to accompany the Cumberland legislators to and from the seat of government. For the same reason the judges on their circuits had to go accompanied by a military guard.

Among the first acts of this Territorial legislature was that to establish higher institutions of learning; John Sevier was made a trustee in both Blount and Greeneville colleges. A lottery was established for the purpose of building the Cumberland Road to Nashville, and another one to build a jail and stocks in Nashville. A pension act was passed for disabled soldiers and for widows and orphans, who were to be given an adequate allowance at the discretion of the county court. A poll-tax of twenty-five cents on all taxable white polls was laid, and on every taxable negro poll fifty cents. Land was taxed at the rate of twenty-five cents a hundred acres, town lots one dollar; while a stud-horse was taxed four dollars. Thus, taxes were laid exclusively upon free males, upon slaves, lands, town lots, and stud-horses—a rather queer combination.

Various industries were started, as the people began to demand not only the necessaries of life, but the comforts and even occasionally the luxuries. Ferries were established at the important crossings, and taverns in the county-seats and small towns.

Various stores were established in the towns, the merchants obtaining most of their goods in the great trade centres of Philadelphia and Baltimore, and thence hauling them by wagon to the frontier. Most of the trade was carried on by barter. There was very little coin in the country, and but few bank-notes. Often the advertisement specified the kind of goods that would be taken and the different values at which they would be received. Thus, the salt-works at Washington, Va., in advertising their salt, stated that they would sell it per bushel for seven shillings and sixpence, if paid in cash or prime furs; at ten shillings, if paid in bear or deer skins, beeswax, hemp, bacon, butter, or beef-cattle; and at twelve shillings if in other trade and country produce, as was usual. The prime furs were mink, coon, muskrat, wildcat, and beaver. Besides this, the stores advertised that they would take for their articles cash, beeswax, and country produce or tallow, hogs' lard in white walnut kegs, butter, pork, new feathers, good horses, and also corn, rye, oats, flax and "old Congress money," the old Congress money being that issued by the Continental Congress and which had depreciated wonderfully in value. They also took certificates of indebtedness either from the State or the nation because of services performed against the Indians, and certificates of land claimed under various rights. The value of some of these commodities was evidently mainly speculative.

All the settlers, or at least all the settlers who had any ambition to rise in the world, were absorbed in land speculations —Blount, Robertson, and the other leaders as much so as anybody. They were continually in correpondence with one another about the purchase of land-warrants, and about laying them out in the best localities. Of course, there was much jealousy and rivalry in the effort to get the best sites. Robertson, being farthest on the frontier, where there was most wild land, had peculiar advantages. Very soon after he settled in the Cumberland district at the close of the Revolutionary War, Blount had entered into an agreement with him for a joint land speculation. Blount was to purchase land claims from both officers and soldiers amounting in all to fifty thousand acres and enter them for the Western Territory, while Robertson was to survey and locate the claims, receiving one-fourth of the whole for his reward. Their connection continued during Blount's term as governor, and Blount's letters to Robertson contain much advice as to how the warrants shall be laid out. Wherever possible they were of course laid outside the Indian boundaries; but, like every one else, Blount and Robertson knew that eventually the Indian lands would come into the possession of the United States, and in view of the utter confusion of the titles, and especially in view of the way the Indians as well as the whites continually broke the treaties and rendered it necessary to make new ones, both Blount and Robertson were willing to place claims on the Indian lands and trust to luck to make the claims good if ever a cession was made. The lands thus located were not lands upon which any Indian village stood. Generally, they were tracts of wilderness through which the Indians occasionally hunted, but as to which there was a question whether they had yet been formally ceded to the government.

Blount also corresponded with many other men on the question of these land speculations, and it is amusing to read the expressions of horror of his correspondents when they read that Tennessee had imposed a land tax. By his activity he became a very large landed proprietor, and when Tennessee was made a State he was taxed on seventy-three thousand two hundred and fifty-two acres in all. The tax was not excessive, being but one hundred and seventy-nine dollars and seventy-two cents. It was, of course, entirely proper for Blount to get possession of the land in this way. The theory of government on the frontier was that each man should be paid a small salary, and be allowed to exercise his private business just as long as it did not interfere with his public duties. Blount's land speculations were similar to those in which almost every other prominent American, in public or private life, was engaged. Neither Congress nor the States had as yet seen the wisdom of allowing the land to be sold only in small parcels to actual occupants, and the favorite kind of speculation was the organization of land companies. Of course, there were other kinds of business in which prominent men took part. Sevier was interested not only in land, but in various mercantile ventures of a more or less speculative kind; he acted as an intermediary with the big importers, who were willing to furnish some of the stores with six months' credit if they could be guaranteed a settlement at the end of that time.

One of the characteristics of all the leading frontiersmen was not only the way in which they combined business enterprises with their work as government officials and as Indian fighters, but the readiness with which they turned from one business enterprise to another. One of Blount's Kentucky correspondents, Thomas Hart, the grandfather of Benton, in his letter to Blount, shows these traits in typical fashion. He was engaged in various land speculations with Blount, and was always writing to him about locating land-warrants, advertising the same as required by law, and the like. He and Blount held some tens of thousands of acres of the Henderson claim, and Hart proposed that they should lay it out in five-hundred-acre tracts, to be rented to farmers, with the idea that each farmer should receive ten cows and calves to start with—a proposition which was, of course, hopeless, as the pioneers would not lease lands when it was so easy to obtain freeholds. In his letters, Hart mentioned cheerfully that though he was sixty-three years old he was just as well able to carry on his manufacturing business, and on occasion to leave it and play pioneer, as he ever had been, remarking that he "never would be satisfied in the world while new countries could be found," and that his intention, now that he had moved to Kentucky, was to push the mercantile business as long as the Indian war continued and money was plenty, and when that failed, to turn his attention to farming and to divide up those of his lands he could not till himself, to be rented by others.

This letter to Blount shows, by the way, as was shown by Madison's correspondent from Kentucky, that the Indian war, scourge though it was to the frontiersmen as a whole, brought some attendant benefits in its wake by putting a stimulus on the trade of the merchants and bringing ready money into the country. It must not be forgotten, however, that men like Hart and Blount, though in some ways they were benefited by the war, were in other ways very much injured, and that, moreover, they consistently strove to do justice to the Indians and to put a stop to hostilities.

In his letters Colonel Hart betrays a hearty, healthy love of life, and capacity to enjoy it, and make the best of it, which fortunately exist in many Kentucky and Tennessee families to this day. He wanted money, but the reason he wanted it was to use it in having a good time for himself and his friends, writing: "I feel all the ardor and spirit for business I did forty years ago, and see myself more capable to conduct it. Oh, if my old friend Uncle Jacob was but living in the country, what pleasure we should have in raking up money and spending it with our friends!" and he closed by earnestly entreating Blount and his family to come to Kentucky, which he assured him was the finest country in the world, with, moreover, "a very pleasant society, for," said he, "I can say with truth that the society of this place is equal, if not superior, to any that can be found in any inland town in the United States, for there is not a day that passes over our heads but I can have half a dozen strange gentlemen to dine with us, and they are from all parts of the Union."

The one overshadowing fact in the history of Tennessee during Blount's term as governor was the Indian warfare.

Hostilities with the Indians were never-ceasing, and, so far as Tennessee was concerned, during these six years it was the Indians, and not the whites, who were habitually the aggressors and wrong-doers. The Indian warfare in the Territory during these years deserves some study because it was typical of what occurred elsewhere. It illustrates forcibly the fact that under the actual conditions of settlement wars were inevitable; for if it is admitted that the land of the Indians had to be taken and that the continent had to be settled by white men, it must be further admitted that the settlement could not have taken place save after war. The whites might be to blame in some cases, and the Indians in others; but under no combination of circumstances was it possible to obtain possession of the country save as the result of war, or of a peace obtained by the fear of war.

As the Federal government took no efficient steps to preserve the peace, either by chastising the Indians or by bridling the ill-judged vengeance of the frontier inhabitants, many of the latter soon grew to hate and despise those by whom they were neither protected nor restrained. On the Georgia frontier the backwoodsmen were very rough and lawless, and were always prone to make aggressions on the red men; nevertheless, even in the case of Georgia, in 1791 and '92, the chief fault lay with the Indians.

In the Tennessee country the wrong was wholly with the Indians. Some of the chiefs of the Cherokees went to Philadelphia at the beginning of the year 1792 to request certain modifications of the treaty of Holston, notably an increase in their annuity, which was granted. The general government had conducted the treaties in good faith and had given the Indians what they asked. The frontiersmen did not molest them in any way or trespass upon their lands; yet their ravages continued without cessation. The authorities at Washington made but feeble efforts to check these outrages, and protect the southwestern settlers.

Naturally, the Tennesseeans, conscious that they had not wronged the Indians, and had scrupulously observed the treaty, grew embittered over the wanton Indian outrages. They were entirely at a loss to explain the reason why the warfare against them was waged with such ferocity. Sevier wrote to Madison, with whom he frequently corresponded: "This country is wholly involved in a war with the Creek and Cherokee Indians, and I am not able to suggest the reasons or the pretended cause of their depredations. The successes of the northern tribes over our late unfortunate armies have created great exultation throughout the whole southern Indians, and the probabilities may be they expect to be equally successful. The Spaniards are making use of all their art to draw over the southern tribes, and I fear may have stimulated them to commence their hostilities. Governor Blount has indefatigably labored to keep these people in a pacific humor, but in vain. War is unavoidable, however ruinous and calamitous it may be." The Federal Government was most reluctant to look facts in the face and acknowledge that the hostilities were serious, and that they were unprovoked by the whites. The secretary of war reported to the President that the offenders were doubtless merely a small banditti of Creeks and Cherokees, with a few Shawnees who possessed no fixed residence, and in groping for a remedy he weakly suggested that inasmuch as many of the Cherokees seemed to be dissatisfied with the boundary-line they had established by treaty it would perhaps be well to alter it. Of course, the adoption of such a measure would have amounted to putting a premium on murder and treachery.

Inability to look facts in the face did not alter the facts. The Indian ravages in the Southern Territory grew steadily more and more serious. The difficulties of the settlers were enormously increased because the United States strictly forbade any offensive measures. The militia were allowed to drive off any war bands found among the settlements with evidently hostile intent; but, acting under the explicit, often-repeated, and emphatic commands of the General Government, Blount was obliged to order the militia under no circumstances to assume the offensive, or to cross into the Indian hunting-grounds beyond the boundaries established by the treaty of Holston. The inhabitants of the Cumberland region, and of the frontier counties generally, petitioned strongly against this, stating that "the frontiers will break if the inroads of the savages are not checked by counter-expeditions." It was a very disagreeable situation for Blount, who, in carrying out the orders of the Federal authorities, had to incur the ill will of the people whom he had been ap-

pointed to govern; but even at the cost of being supposed
to be lukewarm in the cause of the settlers, he loyally endeavored to execute the commands of his superiors. Yet like
every other man acquainted by actual experience with frontier
life and Indian warfare, he knew the folly of defensive war
against Indians.

Such a state of things as that which existed in the Tennessee
Territory could not endure. The failure of the United States
authorities to undertake active offensive warfare and to protect the frontiersmen rendered it inevitable that the frontiersmen should protect themselves; and, under the circumstances, when retaliation began it was certain sometimes to
fall upon the blameless.

When, toward the close of 1792, the ravages became very
serious, Sevier, the man whom the Indians feared more than
any other, was called to take command of the militia. For
a year he confined himself to acting on the defensive, and
even thus he was able to give much protection to the settlements. In September, 1793, however, several hundred Indians,
mostly Cherokees, crossed the Tennessee not thirty miles from
Knoxville. They attacked a small station, within which there
were but thirteen souls, who, after some resistance, surrendered on condition that their lives should be spared; but
they were butchered with obscene cruelty. Sevier immediately
marched toward the assailants, who fled back to the Cherokee
towns. Thither Sevier followed them, and went entirely
through the Cherokee country to the land of the Creeks,
burning the towns and destroying the stores of provisions. He
marched with his usual quickness, and the Indians were never
able to get together in sufficient numbers to oppose him.
When he crossed High Town River there was a skirmish, but
he soon routed the Indians, killing several of their warriors,
and losing himself but three men killed and three wounded.
He utterly destroyed a hostile Creek town, the chief of which
was named Buffalo Horn. He returned late in October, and
after his return the frontiers of eastern Tennessee had a
respite from the Indian ravages. Yet Congress refused to pay
his militia for the time they were out, because they had invaded the Indian country instead of acting on the defensive.

To chastise the upper Cherokee towns gave relief to the
settlements on the Holston, but the chief sinners were the

Chickamaugas of the lower Cherokee towns, and the chief sufferers were the Cumberland settlers. The Cumberland people were irritated beyond endurance, alike by the ravages of these Indians and by the conduct of the United States in forbidding them to retaliate. In September, 1794, they acted for themselves. Early in the month Robertson received certain information that a large body of Creeks and lower Cherokees had gathered at the towns and were preparing to invade the Cumberland settlements. The best way to meet them was by a stroke in advance, and he determined to send an expedition against them in their strongholds. There was no question whatever as to the hostility of the Indians, for at this very time settlers were being killed by war-parties throughout the Cumberland country.

Not only the Federal authorities, but Blount himself, very much disapproved of this expedition; nevertheless, it was right and proper and produced excellent effects. In no other way could the hostile towns have been brought to reason. These counter-attacks served a double purpose. They awed the hostile Cherokees; and they forced the friendly Cherokees, for the sake of their own safety, actively to interfere against the bands of hostile Creeks.

As a result, the Creeks finally sued for peace. [They concluded with the settlers a treaty by which, once again, they surrendered title to their lands.] The concluding stage of the negotiations was marked by an incident which plainly betrayed the faulty attitude of the National Government toward southwestern frontiersmen. With incredible folly, Timothy Pickering, at this time secretary of war, blindly refused to see the necessity of what had been done by Blount and the Tennessee frontiersmen. In behalf of the administration, he wrote a letter to Blount which was as offensive as it was fatuous. He explained that the United States Government was resolved not to have a direct or indirect war with the Creeks; and he closed by reiterating, with futile insistency, that the instruction to the Cherokees not to permit Creek war-parties against the whites to come through their country, did not warrant their using force to stop them. He failed to point out how it was possible, without force, to carry out these instructions.

A more shameful letter was never written, and it was sufficient of itself to show Pickering's conspicuous incapacity for the position he held. The trouble was that he represented, not very unfairly, the sentiment of a large portion of the Eastern and especially the northeastern people. When Blount visited Philadelphia in the summer of 1793, to urge a vigorous national war as the only thing which could bring the Indians to behave themselves, he reported that Washington had an entirely just idea of the whole Indian business, but that Congress generally knew little of the matter and was not disposed to act. His report was correct; and he might have added that the congressmen were no more ignorant, and no more reluctant to do right, than their constituents.

The truth is that the United States Government, during the six years from 1791 to 1796, behaved shamefully to the people who were settled along the Cumberland and Holston. This was the more inexcusable in view of the fact that, thanks to the example of Blount, Sevier, and Robertson, the Tennesseeans, alone among the frontiersmen, showed an intelligent appreciation of the benefits of the Union and a readiness to render it loyal support. The Kentuckians acted far less rationally; yet the government tolerated much misconduct on their part, and largely for their benefit carried on a great national war against the northwestern Indians. In the Southwest almost all that the administration did was to prohibit the frontiersmen from protecting themselves. Peace was finally brought about largely through the effect of Wayne's victory [at the Battle of Fallen Timbers], and the knowledge of the Creeks that they would have to stand alone in any further warfare; but it would not have been obtained at all if Sevier and the other frontier leaders had not carried on their destructive counter-inroads into the Cherokee and upper Creek country, and if under Robertson's orders Nickajack and Running Water had not been destroyed; while the support of the Chickasaws and friendly Cherokees in stopping the Creek war-parties was essential. The southwesterners owed thanks to General Wayne and his army and to their own strong right hands; but they had small cause for gratitude to the Federal Government. They owed still less to the northeasterners, or indeed to any of the men of the Eastern seaboard; the benefits arising from Pinckney's treaty form the only exception. This neglect brought its own punishment. Blount and Sevier were naturally inclined to Federalism, and it was probably only the supineness of the Federal Government in failing to support the southwesterners against the Indians which threw Tennessee, when it became a State, into the arms of the Democratic party.

However, peace was finally wrung from the Indians, and by the beginning of 1796 the outrages ceased. The frontiers, North and South alike, enjoyed a respite from Indian warfare for the first time in a generation; nor was the peace interrupted until fifteen years afterward.

Chapter XIX

Intrigues and Land Speculations—The Treaties of Jay and Pinckney

THROUGHOUT the history of the winning of the West what is noteworthy is the current of tendency rather than the mere succession of individual events. The general movement, and the general spirit behind the movement, became evident in many different forms, and if attention is paid only to some particular manifestation we lose sight of its true import and of its explanation. Particular obstacles retarded or diverted, particular causes accelerated, the current; but the set was always in one direction. The peculiar circumstances of each case must always be taken into account, but it is also necessary to understand that it was but one link in the chain of causation.

Such events as Burr's conspiracy, or the conquest of Texas, cannot be properly understood if we fail to remember that they were but the most spectacular or most important manifestations of what occurred many times. The Texans won a striking victory and performed a feat of the utmost importance in our history; and, moreover, it happened that at the moment the accession of Texas was warmly favored by the party of the slaveholders. Burr had been Vice-President of the United States, and was a brilliant and able man, of imposing personality, whose intrigues in the West attracted an attention altogether disproportionate to their real weight. In consequence, each event is often treated as if it were isolated and stood apart from the general current of Western history; whereas in truth each was but the most striking or important among a host of others. The feats performed by Austin and Houston and the other founders of the Texan Republic were identical in kind with the feats merely attempted, or but partially performed, by the men who, like Morgan, Elijah Clark, and George Rogers Clark, at different times either sought to found colonies in the Spanish-speaking lands under Spanish authority, or else strove to conquer these lands outright by force of arms. Boone settled in Missouri when it was still under the Spanish Government, and himself accepted a Spanish commission. Whether Missouri had or had not been ceded first by Spain to France and then by France to the United States early in the present century, really would not have altered its final destiny, so far at least as concerns the fact that it would ultimately have been independent of both France and Spain, and would have been dominated by an English-speaking people; for when once the backwoodsmen, of whom Boone was the forerunner, became sufficiently numerous in the land they were certain to throw off the yoke of the foreigner; and the fact that they had voluntarily entered the land and put themselves under this yoke would have made no more difference to them than it afterward made to the Texans. So it was with Aaron Burr. His conspiracy was merely one, and by no means the most dangerous, of the various conspiracies in which men like Wilkinson, Sebastian, and many of the members of the early Democratic societies in Kentucky, bore a part. It was rendered possible only by the temper of the people and by the peculiar circumstances which also rendered the earlier conspiracies possible; and it came to naught for the same reasons that they came to naught, and was even more hopeless, because it was undertaken later, when the conditions were less favorable.

The movement deliberately entered into by many of the Kentuckians in the years 1793 and 1794, to conquer Louisiana on behalf of France, must be treated in this way. The leader in this movement was George Rogers Clark. His chance of success arose from the fact that there were on the frontier many men of restless, adventurous, warlike type, who felt a spirit of unruly defiance toward the home government and who greedily eyed the rich Spanish lands. Whether they got the lands by conquest or by colonization, and whether they warred under one flag or another was to them a matter of little moment. Clark's career is of itself sufficient to prove the truth of this. He had already been at the head of a movement to make war against the Spaniards, in defiance of the Central Government, on behalf of the Western settlements. On another occasion he had offered his sword to the Spanish Government, and had requested permission to found in Spanish territory a State which should be tributary to Spain and a barrier against the American advance. He had thus already sought to lead the Westerners against Spain in a warfare undertaken purely by themselves and for their own objects, and had also offered to form, by the help of some of these Westerners, a State which should be a constituent portion of the Spanish dominion. He now readily undertook the task of raising an army of Westerners to overrun Louisiana in the interests of the French Republic. The conditions which rendered possible these various movements were substantially the same, although the immediate causes, or occasions, were different. In any event, the result would ultimately have been the conquest of the Spanish dominions by the armed frontiersmen, and the upbuilding of English-speaking States on Spanish territory.

The expedition which, at the moment, Clark proposed to head, took its peculiar shape from outside causes. At this period Genet was in the midst of his preposterous career as minister from the French Republic to the United States. The various bodies of men who afterward coalesced into the Democratic-Republican party were frantically in favor of the French Revolution, regarding it with a fatuous admiration quite as foolish as the horror with which it affected most of the Federalists. They were already looking to Jefferson as their leader, and Jefferson, though at the time secretary of state under Washington, was secretly encouraging them, and was playing a very discreditable part toward his chief. The ultra-admirers of the French Revolution not only lost their own heads, but turned Genet's as well, and persuaded him that the people were with him and were ready to oppose Washington and the Central Government in the interests of revolutionary France. Genet wished to embroil America with England, and sought to fit out American privateers on the seacoast towns to prey on the English commerce, and to organize on the Ohio River an armed expedition to conquer Louisiana, as Spain was then an ally of England and at war with France. All over the country Genet's admirers formed Democratic societies on the model of the Jacobin Clubs of France. They were, of course, either useless or noxious in such a country and under such a government as that of the United States, and exercised a very mischievous effect. Kentucky was already under the influence of the same forces that were at work in Virginia and elsewhere, and the classes of her people who were politically dominant were saturated with the ideas of those doctrinaire politicians of whom Jefferson was chief. These Jeffersonian doctrinaires were men who, at certain crises, in certain countries, might have rendered great service to the cause of liberty and humanity; but their influence in America was, on the whole, distinctly evil, save that, by a series of accidents, they became the especial champions of the westward extension of the nation, and in consequence were identified with a movement which was all-essential to the national well-being.

Kentucky was ripe for Genet's intrigues, and he found the available leader for the movement in the person of George Rogers Clark. Clark was deeply embittered, not only with the United States Government, but with Virginia, for the Virginia Assembly had refused to pay any of the debts he had contracted on account of the State, and had not even reimbursed him for what he had spent. He had a right to feel aggrieved at the State's penuriousness and her indifference to her moral obligations; and just at the time when he was most angered came the news that Genet was agitating throughout the United States for a war with England, in open defiance of Washington, and that among his plans he included a Western movement against Louisiana. Clark at once wrote to him, expressing intense sympathy with the French objects and offering to undertake an expedition for the conquest of St. Louis and upper Louisiana, if he was provided with the means to obtain provisions and stores. Clark further informed Genet that his country had been utterly ungrateful to him, and that as soon as he received Genet's approbation of what he proposed to do, he would get himself "expatriated." He asked for commissions for officers, and stated his belief that the creoles would rise, that the adventurous Westerners would gladly throng to the contest, and that the army would soon be at the gates of New Orleans.

Genet immediately commissioned Clark as a major-general in the service of the French Republic, and sent out various Frenchmen—Michaux, La Chaise, and others—with civil and military titles, to co-operate with him, to fit out his force as well as possible, and to promise him pay for his expenses. Brown, now one of Kentucky's representatives at Philadelphia, gave these men letters of introduction to merchants in Lexington and elsewhere, from whom they got some supplies; but they found they would have to get most from Philadelphia. Michaux was the agent for the French minister, though nominally his visit was undertaken on purely scientific grounds. Jefferson's course in the matter was characteristic. Openly, he was endeavoring in a perfunctory manner to carry out Washington's policy of strict neutrality in the contest between France and England, but secretly he was engaged in tortuous intrigues against Washington and was thwarting his wishes, so far as he dared, in regard to Genet. It is impossible that he could have been really misled as to Michaux's character and the object of his visits; nevertheless, he actually gave him a letter of introduction to the Kentucky governor, Isaac Shelby. Shelby had shown himself a gallant and capable officer in warfare against both the Indians and the Tories, but he possessed no marked political ability, and was entirely lacking in the strength of character which would have fitted him to put a stop to rebellion and lawlessness. He hated England, sympathized with France, and did not possess sufficient political good sense to appreciate either the benefits of the Central Government or the need of preserving order.

Clark at once proceeded to raise what troops he could, and issued a proclamation signed by himself as major-general of the armies of France, commander-in-chief of the French Revolutionary Legions on the Mississippi. He announced that he proposed to raise volunteers for the reduction of the Spanish posts on the Mississippi and to open the trade of that river, and promised all who would join him from one to three thousand acres of any unappropriated land in the conquered regions, the officers to receive proportionately more. All lawful plunder was to be equally divided according to the customs of war. The proclamation thus frankly put the revolutionary legions on the footing of a gang of freebooters. Each man was to receive a commission proportioned in grade to the number of soldiers he brought to Clark's band. In short, it was a piece of sheer filibustering, not differing materially from one of Walker's filibustering attempts in Central America sixty years later, save that at this time Clark had utterly lost his splendid vigor of body and mind and was unfit for the task he had set himself. At first, however, he met with promises of support from various Kentuckians of prominence, including Benjamin Logan. His agents gathered flatboats and pirogues for the troops and laid in stores of powder, lead, and beef. The nature of some of the provisions shows what a characteristic backwoods expedition it was; for Clark's agent notified him that he had ready "upwards of eleven hundred weight of Bear Meat and about seventy or seventy-four pair of Venison Hams."

The Democratic societies in Kentucky entered into Clark's plans with the utmost enthusiasm, and issued manifestoes against the Central Government which were, in style, of hysterical violence, and, in matter, treasonable. The preparations were made openly, and speedily attracted the attention of the Spanish agents, besides giving alarm to the representatives of the Federal Government and to all sober citizens who had sense enough to see that the proposed expedition was merely another step toward anarchy. St. Clair, the governor of the Northwestern Territory, wrote to Shelby to warn him of what was being done, and Wayne, who was a much more formidable person than Shelby or Clark or any of their backers, took prompt steps to prevent the expedition from starting by building a fort near the mouth of the Ohio, and ordering his lieutenants to hold themselves in readiness for any action he might direct. At the same time the Administration wrote to Shelby telling him what was on foot, and requesting him to see that no expedition of the kind was allowed to march against the domains of a friendly power. Shelby, in response, entered into a long argument to show that he could not interfere with the expedition, and that he doubted his constitutional power to do anything in the matter; his reasons being of the familiar kind usually advanced in such cases, where a government officer, from timidity or any other cause, refuses to do his duty. If his contention as to his own powers and the powers of the General Government had been sound, it would logically have followed that there was no power anywhere to back up the law. Innes, the Federal judge, showed himself equally luke-warm in obeying the Federal authorities.

Blount, the governor of the Southwestern Territory, acted as vigorously and patriotically as St. Clair and Wayne, and his conduct showed in marked contrast to Shelby's. He possessed far too much political good sense not to be disgusted with the conduct of Genet, which he denounced in unmeasured terms. He expressed great pleasure when Washington summarily rebuked the blatant French envoy. He explained to the Tennesseeans that Genet had as his chief backers the disappointed office-hunters and other unsavory characters in New York and in the seacoast cities, but that the people at large were beginning to realize what the truth was, and to show a proper feeling for the President and his government. Some of the Cumberland people, becoming excited by the news of Clark's preparation, prepared to join him, or to undertake a separate filibustering attack on their own account. Blount immediately wrote to Robertson directing him to explain to these "inconsiderate persons" that all they could possibly do was to attempt the conquest of West Florida, and that they would "lay themselves liable to heavy Pains and Penalties, both pecuniary and corporal in case they ever returned to their injured country." He warned Robertson that it was his duty to prevent the attempt, and that the legal officers of the district must proceed against any of the men having French commissions, and must do their best to stop the movement; which, he said, proceeded "from the Machinations no doubt of that Jacobin Incendiary, Genet, which is reason sufficient to make every honest mind revolt at the Idea." Robertson warmly supported him, and notified the Spanish commander at New Madrid of the steps which he was taking; at which the Spaniards expressed great gratification.

However, the whole movement collapsed when Genet was recalled early in 1794, Clark being forced at once to abandon his expedition. Clark found himself out of pocket as the result of what he had done; and as there was no hope of reimbursing himself by Spanish plunder, he sought to obtain from the French Government reimbursement for the expenses, forwarding to the French Assembly, through an agent in France, his bill for the "Expenses of Expedition ordered by Citizen Genet." The agent answered that he would try to secure the payment; and after he got to Paris he first announced himself as hopeful; but later he wrote that he had discovered that the French agents were really engaged in a dangerous conspiracy against the Western country, and he finally had to admit that the claim was disallowed. With this squabble between the French and Americans the history of the abortive expedition ends.

Of course, the action of the American Government in procuring the recall of Genet and putting a stop to Clark's operations lightened for a moment the pressure of the backwoodsmen upon the Spanish dominions; but it was only for a moment. The Westerners were bent on seizing the Spanish territory; and they were certain to persist in their efforts until they were either successful or were definitely beaten in actual war. The acts of aggression were sure to recur; it was only the form that varied. When the chance of armed conquest under the banner of the French Republic vanished, there was an immediate revival of plans for getting possession of some part of the Spanish domain through the instrumentality of the great land companies.

Much the most famous, or, it would be more correct to say, infamous, of these companies were those organized in connection with the Yazoo lands. The country in what is now middle and northern Mississippi and Alabama possessed, from its great fertility, peculiar fascinations in the eyes of the adventurous land speculators. It was unoccupied by settlers, because as a matter of fact it was held in adverse possession by the Indians, under Spanish protection. It was claimed by the Georgians, and its cession was sought by the United States Government, so that there was much uncertainty as to the title, which could in consequence be cheaply secured.

Wilkinson, Brown, Innes, and other Kentuckians had applied to the Spaniards to be allowed to take these lands and hold them, in their own interests, but on behalf of Spain, and against the United States. The application had not been granted, and the next effort was of a directly opposite character, the adventurers this time proposing, as they could not hold the territory as armed subjects of Spain, to wrest it from Spain by armed entry after getting title from Georgia. In other words, they were going to carry on war as a syndicate, the military operations for the occupation of the ceded territory being part of the business for which the company was organized. Their relations with the Union were doubtless to be determined by the course of events.

This company was the South Carolina Yazoo Company. In 1789 several companies were formed to obtain from the Georgia legislature grants of the Western Territory which Georgia asserted to be hers. One, the Virginia Company, had among its incorporators Patrick Henry, and received a grant of nearly twenty thousand square miles, but accomplished nothing. Another, the Tennessee Company, received a grant of what is now most of northern Alabama, and organized a body of men, under the leadership of an adventurer named Zachariah Cox, who drifted down the Tennessee in flatboats to take possession, and repeated the attempt more than once. They were, however, stopped, partly by Blount and partly by the Indians. The South Carolina Yazoo Company made the most serious effort to get possession of the coveted territory. Its grant included about fifteen thousand square miles in what is now middle Mississippi and Alabama; the nominal price being sixty-seven thousand dollars. One of the prime movers in this company was a man named Walsh, who called himself Washington, a person of unsavory character, who, a couple of years later, was hung at Charleston for passing forged paper money in South Carolina. All these companies had hoped to pay the very small prices they were asked for the lands in the depreciated currency of Georgia; but they never did make the full payments or comply with the conditions of the grants, which therefore lapsed.

Before this occurred the South Carolina Yazoo Company had striven to take possession of its purchase by organizing a military expedition to go down the Mississippi from Kentucky. For commander of this expedition choice was made of a Revolutionary soldier named James O'Fallon, who went to Kentucky, where he married Clark's sister. He entered into relations with Wilkinson, who drew him into the tangled web of Spanish intrigue. He raised soldiers and drew up a formal contract, entered into between the South Carolina Yazoo Company and their troops of the Yazoo Battalion—over five hundred men in all, cavalry, artillery, and infantry. Each private was to receive two hundred and fifty acres of "stipendiary" lands and the officers in proportion, up to the lieutenant-colonel, who was to receive six thousand. Commissions were formally issued, and the positions of all the regular officers were filled, so that the invasion was on the point of taking place. However, the Spanish authorities called the matter to the attention of the United States, and the Federal Government put a prompt stop to the movement. O'Fallon was himself threatened with arrest by the Federal officers and had to abandon his project. He afterward re-established his relations with the government and became one of Wayne's correspondents; but he entered heartily into Clark's plans for the expedition under Genet and, like all the other participators in that wretched affair, became involved in broils with Clark and every one else.

In 1795, the land companies, encouraged by the certainty that the United States would speedily take possession of the Yazoo territory, again sprang into life. In that year four—the Georgia, the Georgia-Mississippi, the Tennessee, and the upper Mississippi—companies obtained grants from the Georgia legislature to a territory of over thirty millions of acres, for which they paid but five hundred thousand dollars, or less than two cents an acre. Among the grantees were many men of note—congressmen, senators, even judges. The grants were secured by the grossest corruption, every member of the legislature who voted for them, with one exception, being a stockholder in some one of the companies, while the procuring of the cessions was undertaken by James Gunn, one of the two Georgia senators. The outcry against the transaction was so universal thoroughout the State that at the next session of the legislature, in 1796, the acts were repealed and the grants rescinded. This caused great confusion, as most of the original grantees had hastily sold out to third parties, the purchases being largely made in South Carolina and Massachusetts. Efforts were made by the original South Carolina Yazoo Company to sue Georgia in the Federal courts, which led to the adoption of the Constitutional provision forbidding such action. When, in 1802, Georgia ceded the territory in question, including all of what is now middle and northern Alabama and Mississippi, to the United States for the sum of twelve hundred and fifty thousand dollars, the National Government became heir to these Yazoo difficulties. It was not until 1814 that the matter was settled by a compromise, after interminable litigation and legislation. The land companies were more important to the speculators than to the actual settlers of the Mississippi; nevertheless, they did stimulate settlement in certain regions, and therefore increased by just so much the Western pressure upon Spain.

In such a welter of intrigue, of land speculation, and of more or less piratical aggression, there was imminent danger that the West would relapse into anarchy unless a firm government were established, and unless the boundaries with England and Spain were definitely established. As Washington's administration grew steadily in strength and in the confidence of the people the first condition was met. The necessary fixity of boundary was finally obtained by the treaties negotiated through John Jay with England, and through Thomas Pinckney with Spain.

Jay's treaty aroused a perfect torrent of wrath throughout the country, and nowhere more than in the West. A few of the coolest and most intelligent men approved it, and rugged old Humphrey Marshall, the Federalist senator from Kentucky, voted for its ratification; but the general feeling against it was intense. Even Blount, who by this time was pretty well disgusted with the way he had been treated by the Central Government, denounced it, and expressed his belief that Washington would have hard work to explain his conduct in procuring its ratification.

Yet the Westerners were the very people who had no cause whatever to complain of the treaty. It was not an entirely satisfactory treaty; perhaps a man like Hamilton might have procured rather better terms; but, taken as a whole, it worked an immense improvement upon the condition of things already existing. Washington's position was undoubtedly right. He would have preferred a better treaty, but he regarded the Jay treaty as very much better than none at all. Moreover, the last people who had a right to complain of it were those who were most vociferous in their opposition. The anti-Federalist party was on the whole the party of weakness and disorder, the party that was clamorous and unruly, but ineffective in carrying out a sustained policy, whether of offense or of defense, in foreign affairs. The people who afterward became known as Jeffersonian Republicans numbered in their ranks the extremists who had been active as the founders of

Democratic societies in the French interest, and they were
ferocious in their wordy hostility to Great Britain; but they
were not dangerous foes to any foreign government which did
not fear words. Had they possessed the foresight and intelligence to strengthen the Federal Government the Jay treaty
would not have been necessary. Only a strong, efficient central
government, backed by a good fleet and a well-organized army,
could hope to wring from England what the French party, the
forerunners of the Jeffersonian Democracy, demanded. But
the Jeffersonians were separatists and States'-rights men.
They believed in a government so weak as to be ineffective,
and showed a folly literally astounding in their unwillingness
to provide for the wars which they were ready to provoke.
They resolutely refused to provide an army or a navy, or to
give the Central Government the power necessary for wag-
ing war. They were quite right in their feeling of hostility
to England, and one of the fundamental and fatal weaknesses
of the Federalists was the Federalist willingness to submit to
England's aggressions without retaliation; but the Jeffersonians
had no gift for government, and were singularly deficient in
masterful statesmen of the kind imperatively needed by any
nation which wishes to hold an honorable place among other
nations. They showed their governmental inaptitude clearly
enough later on when they came into power, for they at once
stopped building the fleet which the Federalists had begun,
and allowed the military forces of the nation to fall into utter
disorganization, with, as a consequence, the shameful humili-
ations of the War of 1812. This war was in itself eminently
necessary and proper, and was excellent in its results, but it
was attended by incidents of shame and disgrace to America
for which Jefferson and Madison and their political friends
and supporters among the politicians and the people have never
received a sufficiently severe condemnation.

In dealing with the British the Americans sometimes had
to encounter bad faith, but more often a mere rough disregard
for the rights of others, of which they could themselves
scarcely complain with a good grace, as they showed precisely
the same quality in their own actions. In dealing with the
Spaniards, on the other hand, they had to encounter deliberate
and systematic treachery and intrigue. The open negotiations
between the two governments over the boundary ran side by

side with a current of muddy intrigue between the Spanish Government on the one hand and certain traitorous Americans on the other, the leader of these traitors being, as usual, the arch-scoundrel, Wilkinson.

It was the existence of these Western separatists, nominally the fiercest foes of Spain, that in reality gave Spain the one real hope of staying the Western advance. In 1794, the American agents in Spain were carrying on an interminable correspondence with the Spanish court in the effort to come to some understanding about the boundaries. The Spanish authorities were solemnly corresponding with the American envoys, as if they meant peace; yet at the same time they had authorized Carondelet to do his best to treat directly with the American States of the West so as to bring about their separation from the Union. In 1794, Wilkinson, who was quite incapable of understanding that his infamy was heightened by the fact that he wore the uniform of a brigadier-general of the United States, entered into negotiations for a treaty, the base of which should be the separation of the Western States from the Atlantic States. He had sent two confidential envoys to Carondelet. Carondelet jumped at the chance of once more trying to separate the West from the East; and under Wilkinson's directions he renewed his efforts to try by purchase and pension to attach some of the leading Kentuckians to Spain. As a beginning, he decided to grant Wilkinson's request, and send him twelve thousand dollars for himself. But the effort miscarried. The money was sent by two men, Collins and Owen, each of whom bore cipher letters to Wilkinson, including some that were sewed into the collars of their coats. Collins reached Wilkinson in safety, but Owen was murdered, for the sake of the money he bore, by his boat's crew while on the Ohio River. The murderers were arrested and were brought before the Federal judge, Harry Innes. Owen was a friend of Innes, and had been by him recommended to Wilkinson as a trustworthy man for any secret and perilous service. Nevertheless, although it was his own friend who had been murdered, Innes refused to try the murderers on the ground that they were Spanish subjects—a reason which was simply nonsensical. He forwarded them to Wilkinson at Fort Warren. The latter sent them back to New Madrid. On their way they were stopped by the officer at Fort Massac, a thoroughly loyal man, who had not been engaged in the intrigues of Wilkinson and Innes. He sent to the Spanish commander at New Madrid for an interpreter to interrogate the men. Of course, the Spaniards were as reluctant as Wilkinson and Innes that the facts as to the relations between Carondelet and Wilkinson should be developed, and, like Wilkinson and Innes, they preferred that the murderers should escape rather than that these facts should come to light. Accordingly, the interpreter did not divulge the confession of the villains, all evidence as to their guilt was withheld, and they were finally discharged. The Spaniards were very nervous about the affair, and were even afraid lest travellers might dig up Owen's body and find the despatches hidden in his collar; which, said De Lemos, they might send to the President of the United States, who would of course take measures to find out what the money and the ciphers meant.

Neither Carondelet's energy and devotion to the Spanish Government nor his unscrupulous intrigues were able for long to defer the fate which hung over the Spanish possessions. In 1795, Washington nominated as minister to Spain Thomas Pinckney, a member of a distinguished family of South Carolina statemen, and a man of the utmost energy and intelligence. Pinckney finally wrung from the Spaniards a treaty which was as beneficial to the West as Jay's treaty, and was attended by none of the drawbacks which marred Jay's work. The Spaniards at the outset met his demands by a policy of delay and evasion. Finally, he determined to stand this no longer, and, on October 24, 1795, demanded his passports, in a letter to Godoy, the "Prince of Peace." The demand came at an opportune moment; for Godoy had just heard of Jay's treaty. He misunderstood the way in which this was looked at in the United States, and feared lest, if not counteracted, it might throw the Americans into the arms of Great Britain, with which country Spain was on the verge of war. It is not a little singular that Jay should have thus rendered an involuntary but important additional service to the Westerners who so hated him.

The Spaniards now promptly came to terms. They were in no condition to fight the Americans; they knew that war would be the result if the conflicting claims of the two peoples were not at once definitely settled one way or the other;

and they concluded the treaty forthwith. Its two most important provisions were the settlement of the southern boundary on the lines claimed by the United States and the granting of the right of deposit to the Westerners. The boundary followed the thirty-first degree of latitude from the Mississippi to the Chattahoochee, down it to the Flint, thence to the head of the St. Mary's, and down it to the ocean. The Spanish troops were to be withdrawn from this territory within the space of six months. The Westerners were granted for three years the right of deposit at New Orleans; after three years, either the right was to be continued or another equivalent port of deposit was to be granted somewhere on the banks of the Mississippi. The right of deposit carried with it the right to export goods from the place of deposit free from any but an inconsiderable duty.

The treaty was ratified in 1796, but with astonishing bad faith the Spaniards refused to carry out its provisions. At this time Carondelet was in the midst of his negotiations with Wilkinson for the secession of the West, and had high hopes that he could bring it about. He had chosen as his agent an Englishman, named Thomas Power, who was a naturalized Spanish subject, and very zealous in the service of Spain. Power went to Kentucky, where he communicated with Wilkinson, Sebastian, Innes, and one or two others, and submitted to them a letter from Carondelet. This letter proposed a treaty, of which the first article was that Wilkinson and his associates should exert themselves to bring about a separation of the Western country and its formation into an independent government wholly unconnected with that of the Atlantic States; and Carondelet, in his letter, assured the men to whom he was writing that, because of what had occurred in Europe since Spain had ratified the treaty of October 27th, the treaty would not be executed by his Catholic Majesty. Promises of favor to the Western people were held out, and Wilkinson was given a more substantial bribe, in the shape of ten thousand dollars, by Power. Sebastian, Innes, and their friends were also promised a hundred thousand dollars for their good offices; and Carondelet, who had no more hesitation in betraying red men than white, also offered to help the Westerners subdue their Indian foes—these Indian foes being at the moment the devoted allies of Spain.

The time had gone by, however, when it was possible to hope for success in such an intrigue. The treaty with Spain had caused much satisfaction in the West, and the Kentuckians generally were growing more and more loyal to the Central Government. Innes and his friends, in a written communication, rejected the offer of Carondelet. They declared that they were devoted to the Union and would not consent to break it up; but they betrayed curiously little surprise or indignation at the offer, nor did they in rejecting it use the vigorous language which beseemed men who, while holding the commissions of a government, were proffered a hundred thousand dollars to betray that government. Power, at the close of 1797, reported to his superiors that nothing could be done.

There was one incident, curious rather than important, but characteristic in its way, which marked the close of the transactions of the Western Americans with Spain at this time. During the very years when Carondelet, under the orders of his government, was seeking to delay the execution of the boundary treaty, and to seduce the Westerners from their allegiance to the United States, a senator of the United States, entirely without the knowledge of his government, was engaged in an intrigue for the conquest of a part of the Spanish dominion. This senator was no less a person than William Blount. Enterprising and ambitious, he was even more deeply engaged in land speculations than were the other prominent men of his time. He felt that he had not been well treated by the United States authorities, and, like all other Westerners, he also felt that the misconduct of the Spaniards had been so great that they were not entitled to the slightest consideration. Moreover, he feared lest the territory should be transferred to France, which would be a much more dangerous neighbor than Spain, and he had a strong liking for Great Britain. If he could not see the territory taken by the Americans under the flag of the United States, then he wished to see them enter into possession of it under the standard of the British king.

In 1797, he entered into a scheme which was in part one of land speculation and in part one of armed aggression against Spain. He tried to organize an association with the purpose of seizing the Spanish territory west of the Mississippi, and putting it under the control of Great Britain in the interests of the seizers. The scheme came to nothing. No definite steps were taken, and the British Government refused to take any share in the movement. Finally, the plot was discovered by the President, who brought it to the attention of the Senate, and Blount was properly expelled from the Upper House for entering into a conspiracy to conquer the lands of one neighboring power in the interest of another. The Tennesseeans, however, who cared little for the niceties of international law, and sympathized warmly with any act of territorial aggression against the Spaniards, were not in the least affected by his expulsion. They greeted him with enthusiasm and elected him to high office, and he lived among them the remainder of his days, honored and respected. Nevertheless, his conduct in this instance was indefensible. It was an unfortunate interlude in an otherwise honorable and useful public career.

Chapter XX

The Purchase of Louisiana; and Burr's Conspiracy

A GREAT and growing race may acquire vast stretches of scantily peopled territory in any one of several ways. Often the statesman, no less than the soldier, plays an all-important part in winning the new land; nevertheless, it is usually true that the diplomatists who, by treaty, ratify the acquisition, usurp a prominence in history to which they are in no way entitled by the real worth of their labors.

The territory may be gained by the armed forces of the nation, and retained by treaty. It was in this way that England won the Cape of Good Hope from Holland; it was in this way that the United States won New Mexico. Such a conquest is due, not to the individual action of members of the winning race, but to the nation as a whole, acting through her soldiers and statesmen. It was the English navy which conquered the Cape of Good Hope for England; it was the English diplomats that secured its retention. So it was the American army which added New Mexico to the United States; and its retention was due to the will of the politicians who had set that army in motion. In neither case was there any previous settlement of moment by the conquerors in the conquered territory. In neither case was there much direct pressure by the people of the conquering races upon the soil which was won for them by their soldiers and statesmen. The acquisition of the territory must be set down to the credit of these soldiers and statesmen, representing the nation in its collective capacity; though in the case of New Mexico there would of course ultimately have been a direct pressure of

278

rifle-bearing settlers upon the people of the ranches and the mud-walled towns.

In such cases it is the government itself, rather than any individual or aggregate of individuals, which wins the new land for the race. When it is won without appeal to arms, the credit, which would otherwise be divided between soldiers and statesmen, of course accrues solely to the latter. Alaska, for instance, was acquired by mere diplomacy. No American settlers were thronging into Alaska. The desire to acquire it among the people at large was vague, and was fanned into sluggish activity only by the genius of the far-seeing statesmen who purchased it. The credit of such an acquisition really does belong to the men who secured the adoption of the treaty by which it was acquired. The honor of adding Alaska to the national domain belongs to the statesmen who at the time controlled the Washington government. They were not figureheads in the transaction. They were the vital, moving forces.

Just the contrary is true of cases like that of the conquest of Texas. The government of the United States had nothing to do with winning Texas for the English-speaking people of North America. The American frontiersmen won Texas for themselves, unaided either by the statesmen who controlled the politics of the Republic or by the soldiers who took their orders from Washington.

In yet other cases the action is more mixed. Statesmen and diplomats have some share in shaping the conditions under which a country is finally taken; in the eye of history they often usurp much more than their proper share; but in reality they are able to bring matters to a conclusion only because adventurous settlers, in defiance or disregard of governmental action, have pressed forward into the longed-for land. In such cases the function of the diplomats is one of some importance, because they lay down the conditions under which the land is taken; but the vital question as to whether the land shall be taken at all, upon no matter what terms, is answered not by the diplomats, but by the people themselves.

It was in this way that the Northwest was won from the British, and the boundaries of the Southwest established by treaty with the Spaniards. Adams, Jay, and Pinckney deserve much credit for the way they conducted their several negotiations; but there would have been nothing for them to negotiate about had not the settlers already thronged into the disputed territories or strenuously pressed forward against their boundaries.

So it was with the acquisition of Louisiana. Jefferson, Livingston, and their fellow statesmen and diplomats concluded the treaty which determined the manner in which it came into our possession; but they did not really have much to do with fixing the terms even of this treaty; and the part which they played in the acquisition of Louisiana in no way resembles, even remotely, the part which was played by Seward, for instance, in acquiring Alaska. If it had not been for Seward, and the political leaders who thought as he did, Alaska might never have been acquired at all; but the Americans would have won Louisiana in any event, even if the treaty of Livingston and Monroe had not been signed. The real history of the acquisition must tell of the great westward movement begun in 1769, and not merely of the feeble diplomacy of Jefferson's administration. In 1802 American settlers were already clustered here and there on the eastern fringe of the vast region which then went by the name of Louisiana. All the stalwart freemen who had made their rude clearings, and built their rude towns, on the hither side of the mighty Mississippi, were straining with eager desire against the forces which withheld them from seizing with strong hand the coveted province. They did not themselves know, and far less did the public men of the day realize, the full import and meaning of the conquest upon which they were about to enter. For the moment the navigation of the mouth of the Mississippi seemed to them of the first importance. Even the frontiersmen themselves put second to this the right to people the vast continent which lay between the Pacific and the Mississippi. The statesmen at Washington viewed this last proposition with positive alarm, and cared only to acquire New Orleans. The winning of Louisiana was due to no one man, and least of all to any statesman or set of statesmen. It followed inevitably upon the great westward thrust of the settler-folk—a thrust which was delivered blindly, but which no rival race could parry until it was stopped by the ocean itself.

The Spanish rulers realized fully that they were too weak

effectively to cope with the Americans, and as the pressure upon them grew ever heavier and more menacing, they began to fear not only for Louisiana, but also for Mexico. They clung tenaciously to all their possessions; but they were willing to sacrifice a part, if by so doing they could erect a barrier for the defense of the remainder. Such a chance was now seemingly offered them by France.

At the beginning of the century Napoleon was First Consul; and the France over which he ruled was already the mightiest nation in Europe, and yet had not reached the zenith of her power. It was at this time that the French influence over Spain was most complete. Both the Spanish king and the Spanish people were dazzled and awed by the splendor of Napoleon's victories. Napoleon's magnificent and wayward genius was always striving after more than merely European empire. As throne after throne went down before him he planned conquests which should include the interminable wastes of snowy Russia and the seagirt fields of England; and he always dreamed of yet vaster, more shadowy triumphs, won in the realms lying eastward of the Mediterranean, or among the islands and along the coasts of the Spanish Main. In 1800, his dream of Eastern conquest was over, but his lofty ambition was planning for France the re-establishment in America of that colonial empire which a generation before had been wrested from her by England.

The need of the Spaniards seemed to Napoleon his opportunity. By the bribe of a petty Italian principality he persuaded the Bourbon King of Spain to cede Louisiana to the French, at the treaty of San Ildefonso , concluded in October, 1800. The cession was agreed to by the Spaniards on the express pledge that the territory should not be transferred to any other power; and chiefly for the purpose of erecting a barrier which might stay the American advance, and protect the rest of the Spanish possessions.

Every effort was made to keep the cession from being made public, and owing to various political complications it was not consummated for a couple of years; but meanwhile it was impossible to prevent rumors from going abroad, and the mere hint of such a project was enough to throw the West into a fever of excitement. Moreover, at this moment, before the treaty between France and Spain had been consummated,

Morales, the intendant of New Orleans, deliberately threw down the gage of battle to the Westerners. On October 16, 1802, he proclaimed that the Americans had forfeited their right of deposit in New Orleans. By Pinckney's treaty this right had been granted for three years, with the stipulation that it should then be extended for a longer period, and that if the Spaniards chose to revoke the permit so far as New Orleans was concerned, they should make some other spot on the river a port of free entry. The Americans had taken for granted that the privilege, when once conferred, would never be withdrawn; but Morales, under pretense that the Americans had slept on their rights by failing to discover some other spot as a treaty port, declared that the right of deposit had lapsed, and would not be renewed.

The act was not done with the knowledge of France. Of this, however, the Westerners were ignorant. They felt sure that any alteration in policy so fatal to their interests must be merely a foreshadowing of the course the French intended thereafter to follow. They believed that their worst fears were justified. Kentucky and Tennessee clamored for instant action, and Claiborne offered to raise in the Mississippi Territory alone a force of volunteer riflemen sufficient to seize New Orleans before its transfer into French hands could be effected.

Jefferson was President, and Madison secretary of state. Jefferson was the least warlike of presidents, and he loved the French with a servile devotion. But his party was strongest in precisely those parts of the country where the mouth of the Mississippi was held to be of right the property of the United States; and the pressure of public opinion was too strong for Jefferson to think of resisting it. The South and the West were a unit in demanding that France should not be allowed to establish herself on the lower Mississippi. Jefferson was forced to tell his French friends that if their nation persisted in its purpose, America would be obliged to marry itself to the navy and army of England. Even he could see that for the French to take Louisiana meant war with the United States sooner or later; and as above all things else he wished peace, he made every effort to secure the coveted territory by purchase.

For some time it appeared that Napoleon was bent upon occupying Louisiana in force and using it as a basis for the rebuilding of the French colonial power. But at this very time the French failed to conquer the negro republic which Toussaint L'Ouverture had founded in Hayti. What they thus failed to accomplish in one island, against insurgent negroes, it was folly to think they could accomplish on the American continent, against the power of the American people—[for the Americans would surely have resisted his efforts to occupy Louisiana]. This struggle with the revolutionary slaves in Hayti hindered Napoleon from immediately throwing an army into Louisiana; but it did more, for it helped to teach him the folly of trying to carry out such a plan at all.

A very able and faithful French agent in the meanwhile sent a report to Napoleon, plainly pointing out the impossibility of permanently holding Louisiana against the Americans. He showed that on the Western waters alone it would be possible to gather armies amounting in the aggregate to twenty or thirty thousand men, all of them inflamed with the eager desire to take New Orleans. Some of Napoleon's ministers were equally far-sighted. One of them, Barbé-Marbois, represented to him in the strongest terms the hopelessness of the undertaking on which he proposed to embark. He pointed out that the United States was sure to go to war with France if France took New Orleans, and that in the end such a war could only result in victory for the Americans.

Napoleon could not afford to hamper himself with the difficult defense of a distant province, and to incur the hostility of a new foe, at the very moment when he was entering on another struggle with his old European enemies. Moreover, he needed money in order to carry on the struggle. To be sure, he had promised Spain not to turn over Louisiana to another power; but he was quite as incapable as any Spanish statesman, or as Talleyrand himself, of so much as considering the question of breach of faith or loss of honor if he could gain any advantage by sacrificing either. Chancellor Robert R. Livingston, the American representative at Paris, was astonished to find that Napoleon had suddenly changed front, and that there was every prospect of gaining what for months had seemed impossible. For some time there was haggling over the terms. Napoleon at first demanded an exorbitant sum; but having once made up his mind to part with Louisiana his impatient disposition made him anxious to conclude the bargain. He rapidly abated his demands, and the cession was finally made for fifteen millions of dollars.

The treaty was signed in May, 1803. The definition of the exact boundaries of the ceded territory was purposely left very loose by Napoleon. On the east, the Spanish Government of the Floridas still kept possession of what are now several parishes in the State of Louisiana. In the far West the boundary-lines which divided upper Louisiana from the possessions of Britain on the north and of Spain on the south led through a wilderness where no white man had ever trod, and they were of course unmapped, and only vaguely guessed at. Thus Napoleon forced Livingston and Monroe to become the reluctant purchasers, not merely of New Orleans, but of all the immense territory which stretched vaguely northwestward to the Pacific.*

It was not until December 1, 1803, that the French took final possession of the province. Twenty days afterward they turned it over to the American authorities. Wilkinson, now commander of the American army—the most disgraceful head it has ever had—was intrusted with the governorship of all of upper Louisiana. Claiborne was made governor of lower Louisiana, officially styled the Territory of Orleans. He was an honest man, loyal to the Union, but had no special qualifications for getting on well with the creoles. He could not speak French, and he regarded the people whom he governed with a kindly contempt, which they bitterly resented. The Americans, pushing and masterful, were inclined to look down on their neighbors, and to treat them overbearingly; while the creoles in their turn disliked the Americans as rude and uncultivated barbarians. For some time they felt much discontent with the United States; nor was this discontent allayed when, in 1804, the Territory of Orleans was reorganized with a government much less liberal than that enjoyed by Indiana or Mississippi; nor even when in 1805 an ordinary territorial government was provided. A number of years were to pass before Louisiana

---

*In Henry Adams's "History of the United States," the account of the diplomatic negotiations at this period between France, Spain, and the United States is the most brilliant piece of diplomatic history, so far as the doings of the diplomats themselves are concerned, that can be put to the credit of any American writer.

felt itself, in fact no less than in name, part of the Union.

Naturally, there was a fertile field for seditious agitation in New Orleans, a city of mixed population, where the numerically predominant race felt a puzzled distrust for the nation of which it suddenly found itself an integral part, and from past experience firmly believed in the evanescent nature of any political connection it might have whether with Spain, France, or the United States.

Under such conditions, New Orleans, even more than the rest of the West, seemed to offer an inviting field for adventurers whose aim was both revolutionary and piratical. A particularly spectacular adventurer of this type now appeared in the person of Aaron Burr. Burr's conspiracy attracted an amount of attention, both at home and in the pages of history, altogether disproportioned to its real consequence. His career had been striking. He had been Vice-President of the United States. He had lacked but one vote of being made President, when the election of 1800 was thrown into the House of Representatives. As friend or as enemy he had been thrown intimately and on equal terms with the greatest political leaders of the day. He had supplied almost the only feeling which Jefferson, the chief of the Democratic party, and Hamilton, the greatest Federalist, ever possessed in common; for bitterly though Hamilton and Jefferson had hated each other, there was one man whom each of them had hated more, and that was Aaron Burr. There was not a man in the country who did not know about the brilliant and unscrupulous party leader who had killed Hamilton in the most famous duel that ever took place on American soil, and who, by a nearly successful intrigue, had come within one vote of supplanting Jefferson in the presidency.

Burr began his treasonable scheming before he ceased to be Vice-President. He was an old friend and crony of Wilkinson; and he knew much about the disloyal agitations which had convulsed the West during the previous two decades. These agitations always took one or the other of two forms that at first sight would seem diametrically opposed. Their end was always either to bring about a secession of the West from the East by the aid of Spain or some other foreign power; or else a conquest of the Spanish dominions by the West, in defiance of the wishes of the East and of the Central Government. Burr proposed to carry out both of these plans.

The exact shape which his proposals took would be difficult to tell. Seemingly, they remained nebulous even in his own mind. They certainly so remained in the minds of those to whom he confided them. At any rate his schemes, though in reality less dangerous than those of his predecessors in Western treason, were in theory much more comprehensive. He planned the seizure of Washington, the kidnapping of the President, and the corruption of the United States navy. He also endeavored to enlist foreign powers on his side. His first advances were made to the British. He proposed to put the new empire, no matter what shape it might assume, under British protection in return for the assistance of the British fleet in taking New Orleans. He gave to the British ministers full—and false—accounts of the intended uprising, and besought the aid of the British Government on the ground that the secession of the West would so cripple the Union as to make it no longer a formidable enemy of Great Britain. Burr's audacity and plausibility were such that he quite dazzled the British minister, who detailed the plans at length to his home government, putting them in as favorable a light as he could. The statesmen at London, however, although at this time almost inconceivably stupid in their dealings with America, were not sunk in such abject folly as to think Burr's schemes practicable, and they refused to have anything to do with them.

In April, 1805, Burr started on his tour to the West. One of his first stoppages was at an island on the Ohio, near Parkersburg, where an Irish gentleman named Blennerhassett had built what was, for the West, an unusually fine house. Only Mrs. Blennerhassett was at home at the time; but Blennerhassett later became a mainstay of the "conspiracy." He was a warmhearted man, with no judgment and a natural tendency toward sedition, who speedily fell under Burr's influence, and entered into his plans with eager zeal. With him Burr did not have to be on his guard, and to him he confided freely of his plans; but elsewhere, and in dealing with less emotional people, he had to be more guarded.

It is, therefore, impossible to say exactly how far the Westerners with whom Burr was intimate were privy to his plans. It is certain that the great mass of the Westerners never seriously considered entering into any seditious movement under him. It is equally certain that a number of their leaders were more or less compromised by their associations with him. It seems probable that to each of these leaders he revealed what he thought would most attract him in the scheme; but that to very few did he reveal an outright proposition to break up the Union. Many of them were very willing to hear the distinguished Easterner make vague proposals for increasing the power of the West by means which were hinted at with sinister elusiveness; and many others were delighted to go into any movement which promised an attack upon the Spanish territory; but it seems likely that there were only a few men— Wilkinson, for instance, and Adair of Kentucky—who were willing to discuss a proposition to commit downright treason.

Burr stopped at Cincinnati, in Ohio, and at one or two places in Kentucky. In both States many prominent politicians, even United States senators, received him with enthusiasm. He then visited Nashville, where he became the guest of Andrew Jackson. Jackson was now major-general of the Tennessee militia; and the possibility of war, especially of war with the Spaniards, roused his hot nature to uncontrollable eagerness. Burr probably saw through Jackson's character at once, and realized that with him it was important to dwell solely upon that part of the plan which contemplated an attack upon the Spaniards.

From Nashville, Burr drifted down the Cumberland, and at Fort Massac, on the Ohio, he met Wilkinson, a kindred spirit, who possessed neither honor nor conscience, and could not be shocked by any proposal. Moreover, Wilkinson much enjoyed the early stages of a seditious agitation, when the risk to himself seemed slight; and as he was at this time both the highest military officer of the United States, and also secretly in the pay of Spain, the chance to commit a double treachery gave an added zest to his action. He entered cordially into Burr's plans, and as soon as he returned to his headquarters, at St. Louis, he set about trying to corrupt his subordinates, and seduce them from their allegiance.

Meanwhile, Burr passed down the Mississippi to New Orleans, where he found himself in the society of persons who seemed more willing than any others he had encountered to fall in with his plans. Even here he did not clearly specify his purposes, but he did say enough to show that they bordered on the treasonable; and he was much gratified at the acquiescence of his listeners. His gratification, however, was overhasty. The creoles, and some of the Americans, were delighted to talk of their wrongs and to threaten any course of action which they thought might yield vengeance, but they had little intention of proceeding from words to deeds. Claiborne, a straightforward and honest man, set his face like a flint against all of Burr's doings.

From New Orleans Burr retraced his steps and visited Wilkinson at St. Louis. But Wilkinson was no longer in the same frame of mind as at Fort Massac. He had tested his officers, to see if they could be drawn into any disloyal movement, and had found that they were honorable men, firm in their attachment to the Union; and he was beginning to perceive that the people generally were quite unmoved by Burr's intrigues. Accordingly, when Burr reached him he threw cold water on his plans, and though he did not denounce or oppose them, he refrained from taking further active part in the seditious propaganda.

After visiting Harrison, the governor of the Indiana Territory, Burr returned to Washington. If he had possessed the type of character which would have made him really dangerous as a revolutionist, he would have seen how slight was his hope of stirring up revolt in the West; but he would not face facts, and he still believed he could bring about an uprising against the Union in the Mississippi valley. His immediate need was money. This he hoped to obtain from some foreign government. He found that nothing could be done with Great Britain; and then, incredible though it may seem, he turned to Spain, and sought to obtain from the Spaniards themselves the funds with which to conquer their own territories.

This was the last touch necessary to complete the grotesque fantasy which his brain had evolved. He approached the Spanish minister first through one of his fellow conspirators, and then in his own person. At one time he made his request on the pretense that he wished to desert the other filibusters, and save Spain by committing a double treachery, and betraying the treasonable movement into which he had entered; and again he asked funds on the ground that all he wished to do was to establish a separate government in the West, and thus destroy the power of the United States to molest Spain. However, his efforts came to naught, and he was obliged to try what he could do unaided in the West.

In August, 1806, he again crossed the Alleghanies. His first stop of importance was at Blennerhassett's. Blennerhassett was the one person of any importance who took his schemes so seriously as to be willing to stake his fortune on their succeess. Burr took with him to Blennerhassett's his daughter, Theodosia, a charming woman, the wife of a South Carolinian, Allston. The attractions of the daughter, and Burr's own address and magnetism, completely overcame both Blennerhassett and his wife. They gave the adventurer all the money they could raise, with the understanding that they would receive it back a hundredfold as the result of a land speculation which was to go hand in hand with the expected revolution. Then Blennerhassett began, in a very noisy and ineffective way, to make what preparations were possible in the way of rousing the Ohio settlers, and of gathering a body of armed men to serve under Burr when the time came. It was all done in a way that savored of farce rather than of treason.

There was much less comedy, however, in what went on in Kentucky and Tennessee, where Burr next went. At Nashville he was received with open arms by Jackson and Jackson's friends. This was not much to Jackson's credit; for by this time he should have known Burr's character; but the temptation of an attack on the Spaniards proved irresistible. As major-general, he called out the militia of West Tennessee, and began to make ready in good earnest to invade Florida or Mexico. At public dinners he and his friends and Burr made speeches in which they threatened immediate war against Spain, with which country the United States was at peace; but they did not threaten any attack on the Union, and indeed Jackson exacted from Burr a guarantee of his loyalty to the Union.

From Nashville the restless conspirator returned to Kentucky to see if he could persuade the most powerful of the Western States to take some decided step in his favor. Senator John Adair, former companion-in-arms of Wilkinson in the wars against the northwestern Indians, enlisted in support of Burr with heart and soul. Kentucky society generally received him with enthusiasm. But there was in the State a remnant of the old Federalist party, which, although not formidable in numbers, possessed weight because of the vigor and ability of its leaders. The chief among them were Humphrey Marshall, former United States senator, and Joseph H. Daveiss, who was still district attorney, not having, as yet, been turned out by Jefferson. These men saw—what Eastern politicians could not see—the connection between Burr's conspiracy and the former Spanish intrigues of men like Wilkinson, Sebastian, and Innes. They were loyal to the Union; and they felt a bitter factional hatred for their victorious foes, in whose ranks were to be found all the old-time offenders; so they attacked the new conspiracy with a double zest. They not only began a violent newspaper war upon Burr and all the former conspirators, but also proceeded to invoke the aid of the courts and the legislature against them. Their exposure of the former Spanish intrigues, as well as of Burr's plots, attracted wide-spread attention in the West, even at New Orleans; but the Kentuckians, though angry and ashamed, were at first reluctant to be convinced. Twice Daveiss presented Burr for treason before the grand jury; twice the grand jury declared in his favor; and the leaders of the Kentucky Democracy gave him their countenance, while Henry Clay acted as his counsel. Daveiss, by a constant succession of letters, kept Jefferson fully informed of all that was done. Though his attacks on Burr for the moment seemed failures, they really accomplished their object. They created such uneasiness that the prominent Kentuckians made haste to clear themselves of all possible connection with any treasonable scheme. Henry Clay demanded and received from Burr a formal pledge that his plans were in nowise hostile to the Union; and the other people upon whom Burr counted most, both in Ohio and Kentucky, hastily followed this example. This immediate defection showed how hopeless Burr's plans were. The moment he attempted to put them into execution, their utter futility was certain to be exposed.

When Burr found that he could do nothing in Kentucky and Tennessee, he prepared to go to New Orleans. The few boats that Blennerhassett had been able to gather were sent hurriedly downstream lest they should be interfered with by the Ohio authorities. Burr had made another visit to Nashville. Slipping down the Cumberland, he joined his little flotilla, passed Fort Massac, and began the descent of the Mississippi.

The plot was probably most dangerous at New Orleans, if it could be said to be dangerous anywhere. Claiborne grew very much alarmed about it, chiefly because of the elusive mystery in which it was shrouded. But when the pinch came it proved as unsubstantial there as elsewhere. The leaders who had talked most loosely about revolutionary proceedings grew alarmed, as the crisis approached, lest they might be called on to make good their words; and they hastened to repudiate all connection with Burr, and to avow themselves loyal to the Union. Even the creole militia—a body which Claiborne regarded with just suspicion—volunteered to come to the defense of the government when it was thought that Burr might actually attack the city.

But Burr's career was already ruined. Jefferson, goaded into action, had issued a proclamation for his arrest; and even before this proclamation was issued, the fabric of the conspiracy had crumbled into shifting dust. The Ohio legislature had passed resolutions, demanding prompt action against the conspirators; and the other Western communities followed suit. There was no real support for Burr anywhere. All his plot had been but a dream; at the last he could not do anything which justified, in even the smallest degree, the alarm and curiosity he had excited. The men of keenest insight and best judgment feared his unmasked efforts less than they feared Wilkinson's dark and tortuous treachery. As he drifted down the Mississippi with his little flotilla, he was overtaken by Jefferson's proclamation, which was sent from one to another of the small Federal garrisons. Near Natchez, in January, 1807, he surrendered his flotilla, without resistance, to the acting governor of Mississippi Territory. He himself escaped into the land of the Choctaws and Creeks, disguised as a Mississippi boatman; but a month later he was arrested near the Spanish border, and sent back to Washington. There he was put on trial for high treason with Wilkinson as State's evidence. Jefferson made himself the especial champion of Wilkinson. Nevertheless, the general cut a contemptible figure at the trial, for no explanation could make his course square with honorable dealing. Burr was acquitted on a technicality. Wilkinson, the double traitor, the bribe-taker, the corrupt servant of a foreign government, remained at the head of the American army.

Chapter XXI

The Men of the Western Waters

THERE was as yet no hard-and-fast line drawn between North and South among the men of the Western waters.

Their sense of political cohesion was not fully developed, and the same qualities that at times made them lose their ideas of allegiance to the Union at times also presented a vivid realization on their part of their own political and social solidarity; but they were always more or less conscious of this solidarity, and, as a rule, they acted together.

Most important of all, the slavery question, which afterward rived in sunder the men west of the Alleghanies as it rived in sunder those east of them, was of small importance in the early years. West of the Alleghanies slaves were still to be found almost everywhere, while almost everywhere there were also frequent and open expressions of hostility to slavery. The Southerners still rather disliked slavery, while the Northerners did not as yet feel any very violent antagonism to it. In the Indiana Territory there were hundreds of slaves, the property of the old French inhabitants and of the American settlers who had come there prior to 1787; and the majority of the population of this Territory actually wished to reintroduce slavery, and repeatedly petitioned Congress to be allowed the reintroduction. Congress, with equal patriotism and wisdom, always refused the petition; but it was not until the new century was well under way that the antislavery element obtained control in Indiana and Illinois. Even in Ohio there was a considerable party which favored the introduction of slavery, and though the majority was against this, the people had small sympathy with the negroes, and passed very severe laws against the introduction of free blacks into the States; and even against those already in residence therein. On the

293

other hand, when Kentucky's first constitutional convention sat, a resolute effort was made to abolish slavery within the State, and this effort was only defeated after a hard struggle and a close vote. To their honor be it said that all of the clergymen—three Baptists, one Methodist, one Dutch Reformed, and one Presbyterian—who were members of the constitutional convention, voted in favor of the abolition of slavery. In Tennessee no such effort was made, but the leaders of thought did not hesitate to express their horror of slavery and their desire that it might be abolished. There was no sharp difference between the attitudes of the northwestern and the southwestern States toward slavery.

North and South alike, the ways of life were substantially the same; though there were differences, of course, and these differences, tended to become accentuated. Thus, in the Mississippi Territory the planters, in the closing years of the century, began to turn their attention to cotton instead of devoting themselves to the crops of their brethren farther north; and cotton soon became their staple product. But as yet the typical settler everywhere was the man of the axe and rifle, the small pioneer farmer who lived by himself, with his wife and his swarming children, on a big tract of wooded land, perhaps three or four hundred acres in extent. Of these three or four hundred acres he rarely cleared more than eight or ten; and these were cleared imperfectly. On this clearing he tilled the soil, and there he lived in his rough log house with but one room, or at most two and a loft.

The man of the Western waters was essentially a man who dwelt alone in the midst of the forest on his rude little farm, and who eked out his living by hunting. Game still abounded everywhere, save in the immediate neighborhood of the towns; so that many of the inhabitants lived almost exclusively by hunting and fishing, and, with their return to the pursuits of savagery, adopted not a little of the savage idleness and thriftlessness. Bear, deer, and turkey were staple foods. Elk had ceased to be common, though they hung on here and there in out-of-the-way localities for many years; and by the close of the century the herds of bison had been driven west of the Mississippi. Smaller forms of wild life swarmed. Gray squirrels existed in such incredible numbers that they caused very serious damage to the crops, and at one time the Kentucky legislature passed a law imposing upon every male over sixteen years of age the duty of killing a certain number of squirrels and crows every year. The settlers possessed horses and horned cattle, but only a few sheep, which were not fitted to fight for their own existence in the woods, as the stock had to. On the other hand, slab-sided, long-legged hogs were the most plentiful of domestic animals, ranging in great, half-wild droves through the forest.

All observers were struck by the intense fondness of the frontiersmen for the woods and for a restless, lonely life. They pushed independence to an extreme; they did not wish to work for others or to rent land from others. Each was himself a small landed proprietor, who cleared only the ground that he could himself cultivate. Workmen were scarce and labor dear. It was almost impossible to get men fit to work as mill-hands, or to do high-class labor in forges even by importing them from Pennsylvania or Maryland. Even in the few towns the inhabitants preferred that their children should follow agriculture rather than become handicraftsmen; and skilled workmen, such as carpenters and smiths, made a great deal of money, so much so that they could live a week on one day's wage.

In addition to farming there was a big trade along the river. Land transportation was very difficult indeed, and the frontiersman's whole life was one long struggle with the forest and with poor roads. The waterways were consequently of very great importance, and the flat-boatmen on the Mississippi and Ohio became a numerous and noteworthy class. The rivers were covered with their craft. There was a driving trade between Pittsburgh and New Orleans, the goods being drawn to Pittsburgh from the seacoast cities by great four-horse wagons, and being exported in ships from New Orleans to all parts of the earth. Not only did the Westerners build river-craft, but they even went into ship-building; and on the upper Ohio, at Pittsburgh, and near Marietta, at the beginning of the present century, seagoing ships were built and launched to go down the Ohio and Mississippi, and thence across the ocean to any foreign port. There was, however, much risk in this trade; for the demand for commodities at Natchez and New Orleans was uncertain, while the waters of the Gulf swarmed with British and French cruisers, always ready to pounce like pirates on the ships of neutral powers.

Yet the river trade was but the handmaid of frontier agriculture. The Westerners were a farmer folk who lived on the clearings their own hands had made in the great woods, and who owned the land they tilled. Towns were few and small. At the end of the century there were some four hundred thousand people in the West; yet the largest town was Lexington, which contained less than three thousand people. Lexington was a neatly built little burg, with fine houses and good stores. The leading people lived well and possessed much cultivation. Louisville and Nashville were each about half its size. In Nashville, of the one hundred and twenty houses, but eight were of brick, and most of them were mere log huts. Cincinnati was a poor little village. Cleveland consisted of but two or three log cabins, at a time when there were already a thousand settlers in its neighborhood on the Connecticut Reserve, scattered out on their farms. Natchez was a very important town, nearly as large as Lexington. It derived its importance from the river traffic on the Mississippi. All the boatmen stopped there, and sometimes as many as one hundred and fifty craft were moored to the bank at the same time. The men who did this laborious river work were rude, powerful, and lawless, and when they halted for a rest their idea of enjoyment was the coarsest and most savage dissipation. At Natchez there speedily gathered every species of purveyor to their vicious pleasures, and the part of the town known as "Natchez under the Hill" became a byword for crime and debauchery.

Kentucky had grown so in population, possessing over two hundred thousand inhabitants, that she had begun to resemble an Eastern State. When, in 1796, Benjamin Logan, the representative of the old wood-choppers and Indian fighters, ran for governor and was beaten, it was evident that Kentucky had passed out of the mere pioneer days. It was more than a mere coincidence that in the following year Henry Clay should have taken up his residence in Lexington. It showed that the State was already attracting to live within her borders men like those who were fitted for social and political leadership in Virginia.

In the strongly marked frontier character no traits were more pronounced than the dislike of crowding and the tendency to roam to and fro, hither and thither, always with a westward trend. Boone, the typical frontiersman, embodied in his own person the spirit of loneliness and restlessness which marked the first venturers into the wilderness. He had wandered in his youth from Pennsylvania to Carolina, and, in the prime of his strength, from North Carolina to Kentucky. When Kentucky became well settled in the closing years of the century, he crossed into Missouri, that he might once more take up his life where he could see the game come out of the woods at nightfall, and could wander among trees untouched by the axe of the pioneer. An English traveler of note who happened to encounter him about this time has left an interesting account of the meeting. It was on the Ohio, and Boone was in a canoe, alone with his dog and gun, setting forth on a solitary trip into the wilderness to trap beaver. He would not even join himself to the other travellers for a night, preferring to plunge at once into the wild, lonely life he so loved. His strong character and keen mind struck the Englishman, who yet saw that the old hunter belonged to the class of pioneers who could never themselves civilize the land, because they ever fled from the face of the very civilization for which they had made ready the land. In Boone's soul the fierce impatience of all restraint burned like a fire. He told the Englishman that he no longer cared for Kentucky, because its people had grown too easy of life; and that he wished to move to some place where men still lived untrammelled and unshackled, and enjoyed uncontrolled the free blessings of nature. The isolation of his life and the frequency with which he changed his abode brought out the frontiersman's wonderful capacity to shift for himself, but it hindered the development of his power of acting in combination with others of his kind. The first comers to the new country were so restless and so intolerant of the presence of their kind, that as neighbors came in they moved ever westward. They could not act with their fellows.

Of course, in the men who succeeded the first pioneers, and who were the first permanent settlers, the restlessness and the desire for a lonely life were much less developed. These men wandered only until they found a good piece of land, and took up claims on this land not because the country was lonely but because it was fertile. They hailed with joy the advent of new settlers and the upbuilding of a little market town in the neighborhood. They joined together eagerly in the effort to obtain schools for their children. As yet, there were no public schools supported by government in any part of the West, but all the settlers with any pretension to respectability were anxious to give their children a decent education. Even the poorer people, who were still engaged in the hardest and roughest struggle for a livelihood, showed appreciation of the need of schooling for their children; and wherever the clearings of the settlers were within reasonable distance of one another, a log schoolhouse was sure to spring up. The school-teacher boarded around among the different families, and was quite as apt to be paid in produce as in cash. Sometimes he was a teacher by profession; more often he took up teaching simply as an interlude to some of his other occupations. Schoolbooks were more common than any others in the scanty libraries of the pioneers.

The fact that the government did so little for the individual and left so much to be done by him, rendered it necessary for the individuals voluntarily to combine. Huskings and house-raisings were times when all joined freely to work for the man whose corn was to be shucked or whose log cabin was to be built, and turned their labor into a frolic and merry-making, where the men drank much whiskey and the young people danced vigorously to the sound of the fiddle. Such merry-makings were attended from far and near, offering a most welcome break to the dreariness of life on the lonely clearings in the midst of the forest. Ordinarily, the frontiersman at his home drank milk or water; but at the taverns and social gatherings there was much drunkenness, for the men craved whiskey, drinking the fiery liquor in huge draughts. Often the orgies ended with brutal brawls. To the outsiders the craving of the backwoodsman for whiskey was one of his least attractive traits. It must always be remembered, however, that even the most friendly outsider is apt to apply to others his own standards in matters of judgment. The average traveller overstated the drunkenness of the backwoodsman, exactly as he overstated his misery.

The frontiersman was very poor. He worked hard and lived roughly, and he and his family had little beyond coarse food, coarse clothing, and a rude shelter. In the severe winters they suffered both from cold and hunger. In the summers there was sickness everywhere, fevers of various kinds scourging all the new settlements. The difficulty of communication was so great that it took three months for the emigrants to travel from Connecticut to the Western Reserve, near Cleveland, and a journey from a clearing, over the forest roads, to a little town not fifty miles off was an affair of moment, to be undertaken but once a year. Yet, to the frontiersmen themselves, the life was far from unattractive. It gratified their intense love of independence; the lack of refinement did not grate on their rough, bold natures; and they prized the entire equality of a life where there were no social distinctions, and few social restraints. Game was still a staple, being sought after for the flesh and the hide, and of course all the men and boys were enthralled by the delights of the chase. The life was as free as it was rude, and it possessed great fascinations, not only for the wilder spirits, but even for many men who, when they had the chance, showed that they possessed ability to acquire cultivation.

One old pioneer has left a pleasant account of the beginning of an ordinary day's work in a log cabin. "I know of no scene in civilized life more primitive than such a cabin hearth as that of my mother. In the morning, a buckeye back-log, a hickory forestick, resting on stone and irons, with a johnnycake, on a clean ash-board, set before the fire to bake; a frying-pan, with its long handle resting on a split-bottom turner's chair, sending out its peculiar music, and the teakettle swung from a wooden lug pole, with myself setting the table or turning the meat, or watching the johnny-cake, while she sat nursing the baby in the corner and telling the little ones to hold still and let their sister Lizzie dress them. Then came blowing the conch-shell for father in the field, the howling of old Lion, the gathering round the table, the blessing, the dull clatter of pewter spoons and pewter basins, the talk about the crop and stock, the inquiry whether Dan'l [the boy] could be spared from the house, and the general arrangements for the day. Breakfast over, my function was to provide the sauce for dinner; in winter, to open the potato or turnip hole, and wash what I took out; in spring, to go into the field and collect the greens; in summer and fall, to explore the truck patch, our little garden. If I afterward went to the field my household labors ceased until night; if not, they continued through the day. As often as possible mother would engage in making pumpkin pies, in which I generally bore a part, and one of these more commonly graced the supper than the dinner table. My pride was in the labors of the field. Mother did the spinning. The standing dye-stuff was the inner bark of the white walnut, from which we obtained that peculiar and permanent shade of dull yellow, the butternut [so common and typical in the clothing of the backwoods farmer]. Oak bark, with copperas as a mordant, when father had money to purchase it, supplied the ink with which I learned to write. I drove the horses to and from the range, and salted them. I tended the sheep, and hunted up the cattle in the woods." This was the life of the thrifty pioneers, whose children more than held their own in the world. The shiftless men, without ambition and without thrift, lived in laziness and filth; their eating and sleeping arrangements were as unattractive as those of an Indian wigwam.

The pioneer, in his constant struggle with poverty, was prone to look with puzzled anger at those who made more money than he did, and whose lives were easier. The backwoods farmer or planter of that day looked upon the merchant with much the same suspicion and hostility now felt by his successor for the banker or the railroad magnate. He did not quite understand how it was that the merchant, who seemed to work less hard than he did, should make more money; and, being ignorant and suspicious, he usually followed some hopelessly wrong-headed course when he tried to remedy his wrongs. Sometimes these efforts to obtain relief took the form of resolutions not to purchase from merchants or traders such articles as woollens, linens, cottons, hats, or shoes, unless the same could be paid for in articles grown or manufactured by the farmers themselves. This particular move was taken because of the alarming scarcity of money, and was aimed particularly at the inhabitants of the Atlantic States. It was, of course, utterly ineffective. A much less wise and less honest course was that sometimes followed of refusing to pay debts when the latter became inconvenient and pressing.

The frontier virtue of independence and of impatience of outside direction found a particularly vicious expression in the frontier abhorrence of regular troops, and advocacy of a hopelessly feeble militia system. The people were foolishly convinced of the efficacy of their militia system, which they loudly proclaimed to be the only proper mode of national defense. While in the actual presence of the Indians the stern necessities of border warfare forced the frontiersmen into a certain semblance of discipline. As soon as the immediate pressure was relieved, however, the whole militia system sank into a mere farce. At certain stated occasions there were musters for company or regimental drill. These training days were treated as occasions for frolic and merrymaking. There were pony races and wrestling matches, with unlimited fighting, drunkenness, and general uproar. Such musters were often called, in derision, cornstalk drills, because many of the men, either having no guns or neglecting to bring them, drilled with cornstalks instead. The officers were elected by the men, and when there was no immediate danger of war they were chosen purely for their social qualities. For a few years after the close of the long Indian struggle there were here and there officers who had seen actual service and who knew the rudiments of drill; but in the days of peace the men who had taken part in Indian fighting cared but little to attend the musters, and left them more and more to be turned into mere scenes of horse-play.

The frontier people of the second generation in the West thus had no military training whatever, and though they possessed a skeleton militia organization, they derived no benefit from it, because their officers were worthless, and the men had no idea of practicing self-restraint or of obeying orders longer than they saw fit. The frontiersmen were personally brave, but their courage was entirely untrained, and being unsupported by discipline, they were sure to be disheartened at a repulse, to be distrustful of themselves and their leaders, and to be unwilling to persevere in the face of danger and discouragement. They were hardy, and physically strong, and they were good marksmen; but here the list of their soldierly qualities was exhausted. They had to be put through a severe course of training by some man like Jackson before they became fit to contend on equal terms with regulars in the open or with Indians in the woods. Their utter lack of discipline was decisive against them at first in any contest with regulars. In warfare with the Indians there were a very few of their number, men of exceptional qualities as woodsmen, who could hold their own; but the average frontiersman, though he did a good deal of hunting and possessed much knowledge of woodcraft, was primarily a tiller of the soil and a feller of trees, and he was necessarily at a disadvantage when pitted against an antagonist whose entire life was passed in woodland chase and woodland warfare. These facts must all be remembered if we wish to get an intelligent explanation of the utter failure of the frontiersmen when, in 1812, they were pitted against the British and the forest tribes. They must also be taken into account when we seek to explain why it was possible but a little later to develop out of the frontiersmen fighting armies which, under competent generals, could overmatch the redcoat and the Indian alike.

The extreme individualism of the frontier, which found expression for good and for evil both in its governmental system in time of peace and in its military system in time of war, was also shown in religious matters. In 1799 and 1800 a great revival of religion swept over the West. Up to that time the Presbyterian had been the leading creed beyond the mountains. There were a few Episcopalians here and there, and there were Lutherans, Catholics, and adherents of the Reformed Dutch and German churches; but, aside from the Presbyterians, the Methodists and Baptists were the only sects powerfully represented. The great revival of 1799 was mainly carried on by Methodists and Baptists, and under their guidance the Methodist and Baptist churches at once sprang to the front and became the most important religious forces in the frontier communities. The Presbyterian Church remained the most prominent as regards the wealth and social standing of its adherents, but the typical frontiersman who professed religion at all became either a Methodist or a Baptist, adopting a creed which was intensely democratic and individualistic, which made nothing of social distinctions, which distrusted educated preachers, and worked under a republican form of ecclesiastical government.

The great revival was accomplished by scenes of intense excitement. Under the conditions of a vast wooded wilderness and a scanty population the camping-meeting was evolved as the typical religious festival. To the great camp-meetings the frontiersmen flocked from far and near, on foot, on horseback, and in wagons. Every morning at daylight the multitude was summoned to prayer by sound of trumpet. No preacher or exhorter was suffered to speak unless he had the power of stirring the souls of his hearers. The preaching, the praying, and the singing went on without intermission, and under the tremendous emotional stress whole communities became fervent professors of religion. Many of the scenes at these camp-meetings were very distasteful to men whose religion was not emotional and who shrank from the fury of excitement into which the great masses were thrown, for under the strain many individuals literally became like men possessed, whether of good or of evil spirits, falling into ecstasies of joy or agony, dancing, shouting, jumping, fainting, while there were wide-spread and curious manifestations of a hysterical character, both among the believers and among the scoffers; but though this might seem distasteful to an observer of education and self-restraint, it thrilled the heart of the rude and simple backwoodsman, and reached him as he could not possibly have been reached in any other manner. Often the preachers of the different denominations worked in hearty unison; but often they were sundered by bitter jealousy and distrust. The fiery zeal of the Methodists made them the leaders; and in their war on the forces of evil they at times showed a tendency to include all non-Methodists—whether Baptists, Lutherans, Catholics, or infidels—in a common damnation. Of course, as always in such a movement, many even of the earnest leaders at times confounded the essential and the non-essential, and railed as bitterly against dancing as against drunkenness and lewdness, or anathematized the wearing of jewelry as fiercely as the commission of crime. More than one hearty, rugged old preacher who did stalwart service for decency and morality, hated Calvinism as heartily as Catholicism, and yet yielded to no Puritan in his austere condemnation of amusement and luxury.

Often men backslid, and to a period of intense emotional religion succeeded one of utter unbelief and of reversion to the worst practices which had been given up. Nevertheless, on the whole, there was an immense gain for good. The people received a new light, and were given a sense of moral responsibility such as they had not previously possessed. Much of the work was done badly or was afterward undone, but very much was really accomplished. The whole West owes an immense debt to the hard-working frontier preachers, sometimes Presbyterian, generally Methodist or Baptist, who so gladly gave their lives to their labors and who struggled with such fiery zeal for the moral well-being of the communities to which they penetrated. Wherever there was a group of log cabins, thither some Methodist circuit-rider made his way, or there some Baptist preacher took up his abode. Their prejudices and narrow dislikes, their raw vanity and sullen distrust of all who were better schooled than they, count for little when weighed against their intense earnestness and heroic self-sacrifice. They proved their truth by their endeavor. They yielded scores of martyrs, nameless and unknown men who perished at the hands of the savages or by sickness or in flood or storm. They had to face no little danger from the white inhabitants themselves. In some of the communities most of the men might heartily support them, but in others, where the vicious and lawless elements were in control, they were in constant danger from mobs. The Godless and lawless people hated the religious with a bitter hatred, and gathered in great crowds to break up their meetings. On the other hand, those who had experienced religion were no believers in the doctrine of non-resistance. At the core, they were thoroughly healthy men, and they fought as valiantly against the powers of evil in matters physical as in matters moral. Some of the successful frontier preachers were men of weak frame, whose intensity of conviction and fervor of religious belief supplied the lack of bodily powers; but as a rule the preacher who did most was a stalwart man, as strong in body as in faith. One of the continually recurring incidents in the biographies of the famous frontier preachers is that of some particularly hardened sinner who was never converted until, tempted to assault the preacher of the Word, he was soundly thrashed by the latter, and his eyes thereby rudely opened through his sense of physical shortcoming to an appreciation of his moral iniquity.

In sum, the Western frontier folk, at the beginning of the nineteenth century, possessed in common marked and peculiar characteristics, which the people of the rest of the country shared to a much less extent. They were backwoods farmers, each man preferring to live alone on his own freehold, which he himself tilled and from which he himself had cleared the timber. The towns were few and small; the people were poor, and often ignorant, but hardy in body and in temper. They joined hospitality to strangers with suspicion of them. They were essentially warlike in spirit, and yet utterly unmilitary in all their training and habits of thought. They prized beyond measure their individual liberty and their collective freedom, and were so jealous of governmental control that they often, to their own great harm, fatally weakened the very authorities whom they chose to act over them. The peculiar circumstances of their lives forced them often to act in advance of action by the law, and this bred a lawlessness in certain matters which their children inherited for generations; yet they knew and appreciated the need of obedience to the law, and they thoroughly respected the law.

The separatist agitations had largely died out. In 1798 and 1799 Kentucky divided with Virginia the leadership of the attack on the Alien and Sedition laws; but her extreme feelings were not shared by the other Westerners, and she acted not as a representative of the West, but on a footing of equality with Virginia. Tennessee sympathized as little with the nullification movement of these two States at this time as she sympathized with South Carolina in her nullification movement a generation later. With the election of Jefferson, the dominant political party in the West became in sympathy with the party in control of the nation, and the West became stoutly loyal to the National Government.

The West had thus achieved a greater degree of political solidarity, both as within itself and with the nation as a whole, than ever before. Its wishes were more powerful with the East. The pioneers stood for an extreme Americanism, in social, political, and religious matters alike. The trend of American thought was toward them, not away from them. More than ever before, the Westerners were able to make their demands felt at home, and to make their force felt in the event of a struggle with a foreign power.

The Settlement of the Northwest as Compared to that of the Southwest

THE frontiersmen who chopped the first trails across the Alleghanies, who earliest wandered through the lonely Western lands, and who first built stockaded hamlets on the banks of the Watauga, the Kentucky, and the Cumberland, acted each in consequence of his own restless eagerness for adventure and possible gain. The nation neither encouraged them to undertake the enterprises on which they embarked, nor protected them for the first few years of uncertain foothold in the new-won country. Only the backwoodsmen themselves felt the thirst for exploration of the unknown, the desire to try the untried, which drove them hither and thither through the dim wilderness. The men who controlled the immediate destinies of the confederated commonwealths knew little of what lay in the forest-shrouded country beyond the mountains, until the backwoods explorers of their own motion penetrated its hidden and inmost fastnesses. Singly, or in groups, the daring hunters roved through the vast reaches of sombre woodland and pitched their camps on the banks of rushing rivers, nameless and unknown. In bands of varying size the hunter-settlers followed close behind, and built their cabins and blockhouses here and there in the great forest land. They elected their own military leaders, and waged war on their own account against their Indian foes. They constructed their own governmental systems, on their own motion, without assistance or interference from the parent States,

306

until the settlements were firmly established and the work of civic organizaion well under way.

Of course, some help was ultimately given by the parent States; and the indirect assistance rendered by the nation had been great. The West could neither have been won nor held by the frontiersmen save for the backing given by the Thirteen States. England and Spain would have made short work of the men whose advance into the lands of their Indian allies they viewed with such jealous hatred, had they not also been forced to deal with the generals and soldiers of the Continental army and the statesmen and diplomats of the Continental Congress. But the real work was done by the settlers themselves. The distinguishing feature in the exploration, settlement, and upbuilding of Kentucky and Tennessee was the individual initiative of the backwoodsmen.

The direct reverse of this was true of the settlement of the country northwest of the Ohio. Here, also, the enterprise, daring, and energy of the individual settlers were of the utmost consequence; the land could never have been won had not the incomers possessed these qualities in a very high degree. But the settlements sprang directly from the action of the Federal Government, and the first and most important of them would not have been undertaken save for that action. The settlers were not the first comers in the wilderness they cleared and tilled. They did not themselves form the armies which met and overthrew the Indians. The regular forces led the way in the country north of the Ohio. The Federal forts were built first; it was only afterward that the small towns sprang up in their shadow. The Federal troops formed the vanguard of the white advance. They were the mainstay of the force behind which, as behind a shield, the founders of the commonwealths did their work.

Unquestionably many of the settlers did their full share in the fighting; and they and their decendants, on many a stricken field, and through many a long campaign, proved that no people stood above them in hardihood and courage; but the land on which they settled was won less by themselves than by the statesmen who met in the national capital, and the scarred soldiers who on the frontier upbore the national colors. Moreover, instead of being absolutely free to choose their own form of government and shape their own laws and social conditions untrammelled by restrictions, the northwesterners were allowed to take the land only upon certain definite conditions. The National Government ceded to settlers part of its own domain, and provided the terms upon which States of the Union should afterward be made out of this domain; and with a wisdom and love of righteousness which have been of incalculable consequence to the whole nation, it stipulated that slavery should never exist in the States thus formed. This condition alone profoundly affected the whole development of the Northwest, and sundered it by a sharp line from those portions of the new country which, for their own ill fortune, were left free from all restriction of the kind. The Northwest owes its life and owes its abounding strength and vigorous growth to the action of the nation as a whole. It was founded not by individual Americans, but by the United States of America. The mighty and populous commonwealths that lie north of the Ohio and in the valley of the upper Mississippi are in a peculiar sense the children of the National Government, and it is no mere accident that has made them in return the especial guardians and protectors of that government; for they form the heart of the nation.

In the Northwest it was the nation which acted. In the Southwest the determining factor was the individual initiative of the pioneers. The most striking feature in the settlement of the Southwest was the free play given to the workings of extreme individualism. The settlement of the Northwest represented the triumph of an intelligent collectivism, which yet allowed to each man a full measure of personal liberty.

Another difference of note was the difference in stock of the settlers. The Southwest was settled by the true backwoodsmen, the men who lived on their small clearings among the mountains of western Pennsylvania, Virginia, and North Carolina. The first settlement in Ohio, the settlement which had most effect upon the history of the Northwest and which largely gave it its peculiar trend, was the work of New Englanders. [The founding of Marietta was attended by great hardships; like all such ventures, it required great courage and daring on the part of the settlers.] Yet it must not be forgotten that the daring needed for the performance of this particular deed can in no way be compared with that shown by the real pioneers—the early explorers and Indian fighters. The very fact that the settlement around Marietta was national in its character, that it was the outcome of national legislation, and was undertaken under national protection, made the work of the individual settler count for less in the scale. The founders and managers of the Ohio Company and the statesmen of the Federal Congress deserve much of the praise that in the Southwest would have fallen to the individual settlers only. The credit to be given to the nation in its collective capacity was greatly increased, and that due to the individual was correspondingly diminished.

Rufus Putnam and his fellow New Englanders built their new town under the guns of a Federal fort, only just beyond the existing boundary of settlement, and on land guaranteed them by the Federal Government. The dangers they ran and the hardships they suffered in nowise approached those undergone and overcome by the iron-willed, iron-limbed hunters who first built their lonely cabins on the Cumberland and Kentucky. The founders of Marietta trusted largely to the Federal troops for protection and were within easy reach of the settled country; but the wild wood-wanderers who first roamed through the fair lands south of the Ohio built their little towns in the heart of the wilderness, many scores of leagues from all assistance, and trusted solely to their own long rifles in time of trouble. The settler of 1788 journeyed at ease over paths worn smooth by the feet of many thousands of predecessors; but the early pioneers cut their own trails in the untrodden wilderness, and warred single-handed against wild nature and wild man.

In the summer of 1788, Doctor Manasseh Cutler visited the colony he had helped to found and kept a diary of his journey. His trip through Pennsylvania was marked merely by such incidents as were common at that time on every journey in the United States away from the larger towns. He travelled with various companions, stopping at taverns and private houses; and both guests and hosts were fond of trying their skill with the rifle, either at a mark or at squirrels. In mid-August he reached Coxe's fort, on the Ohio, and came for the first time to the frontier proper. Here he embarked on a big flatboat, with on board forty-eight souls all told, besides cattle. They drifted and paddled downstream, and on the evening of the second day reached the Muskingum. Here and there along the Virginian shore the boat passed settlements, with grain-fields and orchards; the houses were sometimes squalid cabins, and sometimes roomy, comfortable buildings. When he reached the newly built town, he was greeted by General Putnam, who invited Cutler to share the marquee in which he lived; and that afternoon he drank tea with another New England general, one of the original founders.

Such a trip was a mere holiday picnic. It offers as striking a contrast as well could be offered to the wild and lonely journeyings of the stark wilderness hunters and Indian fighters who first went west of the mountains. General Rufus Putnam and his associates did a deed, the consequences of which were of vital importance. They showed that they possessed the highest attributes of good citizenship—resolution and sagacity, stern morality, and the capacity to govern others as well as themselves. But they performed no pioneer feat of any note as such, and they were not called upon to display a tithe of the reckless daring and iron endurance of hardship which characterized the conquerors of the Illinois and the founders of Kentucky and Tennessee. This is in no sense a reflection upon them. They did not need to give proof of a courage they had shown time and again in bloody battles against the best troops of Europe. In this particular enterprise, in which they showed so many admirable qualities, they had little chance to show the quality of adventurous bravery. They drifted comfortably downstream, from the log fort whence they started, past many settlers' houses, until they came to the post of a small Federal garrison, where they built their town. Such a trip is not to be mentioned in the same breath with the long wanderings of Clark and Boone and Robertson, when they went forth unassisted to subdue the savage and make tame the shaggy wilderness.

THE END

Index

Index

A